AMERICAN PACIFIC OCEAN TRADE

AMERICAN PACIFIC OCEAN TRADE

*Its Impact on Foreign Policy
and Continental Expansion, 1784-1860*

J. WADE CARUTHERS

382.0973
C 329a

An Exposition-University Book

Exposition Press   New York

TO

ERLING M. HUNT,

whose guidance and stimulation

were responsible

for the beginnings of this work

Chapter I was previously published in *American Neptune,* July 1969, Vol. XXIX, No. 3, pp. 199-210.
Chapter II was previously published in *Journal of the West,* April 1971, Vol. X, No. 2, pp. 211-252.
Chapter IV was previously published in *American Neptune,* April 1969, Vol. XXIX, No. 2, pp. 81-101.

FIRST EDITION

© 1973 by J. Wade Caruthers

All rights reserved, including the right of reproduction in whole or in part, in any form or by any means, electronic or mechanical, including photocopying, recording, or by any information storage and retrieval system, without permission in writing from the Publisher. Inquiries should be addressed to Exposition Press, Inc., 50 Jericho Turnpike, Jericho, N. Y. 11753

LIBRARY OF CONGRESS CATALOG CARD NUMBER: 73-77583

SBN 0-682-47711-7

Manufactured in the United States of America

Published simultaneously in Canada by Transcanada Books

Contents

LIST OF TABLES   viii

PREFACE   1

I. SEA TRADE IN EARLY AMERICAN DEVELOPMENT, 1750-1830   3
   Contribution to Early Nationality, 3: British Regulation of Colonial Trade, 4; Merchants and the American Revolution, 5. *Merchants in the New Nation*, 7: Merchants and New England Federalism, 8; Emergence of Economic Nationalism, 10; Capital for New Industry, 10. *Trade in the Background of the Monroe Doctrine*, 12. *Far Eastern Influence on American Culture*, 15.

II. THE SEABORNE FRONTIER ON THE NORTHWEST COAST, 1778-1850   18
    Maritime Trade, 1778-1825, 18: British-American Rivalry in the Northwest, 19; Discovery and Exploration, 21; Economic Returns and Decline, 24; Attempts at Permanent Settlement, 26. *John Ledyard and Thomas Jefferson*, 29: Jefferson's Early Interest, 29; Influence of Ledyard, 30. *Maritime Influences on the Lewis and Clark Expedition*, 34: Jefferson's Pacific Ocean Policy, 34; Instructions to Lewis and Clark, 35. *Early Treaty Negotiations*, 36: Elimination of Spanish and Russian Claims, 37; Beginning of Joint Occupation, 39. *Northwest Boundary Negotiations and Congressional Action*, 41: Interest of a Congressional Group, 41; British-American Negotiations, 43; Continued Action in Congress, 44; Agitation of Jackson Hall Kelley, 45; Growth of

Popular Interest, 47; The Linn Report, 49; The Cushing Report, 51; The Pendleton Report, 52; Appraisal of Congressional Action, 54; Settlement of the Boundary Dispute, 56. *Russian-American Contacts,* 59: Basis of the Non-Colonization Principle, 60; Background of the Alaskan Purchase, 62. *Rails to the Pacific,* 64: Early Interest of Asa Whitney, 64; Pressure on Congress, 65; Publicity Campaign, 67; Congressional Reaction, 69.

III. AMERICAN POLICY TOWARD CHINA — 71

Scope and Structure of the Early China Trade, 71: Early Routes, 72; Cargoes, 75; First Chinese Contacts, 75; Trade of Salem, 78; Trade of Boston, 80. *Trends After 1812,* 83: Changed Routes and Cargoes, 84; Rise of New York, 85; Opium Trade, 86; Statistical View, 88. *Beginnings of Official Policy, 1831,* 92: Obstacles to Trade, 93; First Official Interest, 94; Emergence of China Policy, 96. *Background of the Cushing Mission, 1834-1844,* 97: Disturbances in Canton, 98; Pressure on Congress, 99; Work of Commodore Kearny, 100; Agitation for a China Mission, 103. *The Cushing Mission, 1844,* 108: Cushing's Interest in the China Trade, 108; Cushing's Instructions, 109; Treaty of Wanghai, 111; Significance of Wanghai, 112. *The Wanghai Policy to 1898,* 115: Developments in China after Wanghai, 115; Work of Humphrey Marshall, 116; McLane and Chinese Customs Collections, 118; The Parker Interlude, 120; Treaty of Tientsin, 121; The Burlingame Mission, 123. *Continuation of Open-Door Policy, 1898-1941,* 124: Threats to China, 124; The Open Door and Philippine Annexation, 124; Hay's Open Door Statement, 125.

IV. SEABORNE FRONTIER IN CALIFORNIA, 1796-1850 — 128

Early Sea Trade with California, 128: Obstacles to Trade, 129; California-Alaskan Contracts, 130; Trade During Spanish and Early Mexican Rule, 131. *Ameri-*

can *Trade During the Mexican Era,* 134: Hide and Tallow Trade, 135. *Early Seaward Migration of Americans,* 137: Early American Settlers, 138; Economic and Social Activities, 140; Work of T. O. Larkin, 141; Gold Rush Migrations, 143. *Antecedents of Annexation Policy,* 149: Fear of Foreign Aggression, 149; Publications About California, 151; President Jackson's Interest in California, 151; President Tyler's Pacific Coast Policy, 153. *Policy of President Polk,* 154: Instructions to Sloat and Larkin, 155; Larkin's Instructions and Efforts, 156; Slidell's Mission, 157; War Aims, 158; Statehood, 160.

V. THE AMERICANIZATION OF HAWAII 161

Early Trade to 1820, 161: Foreign Competition, 162; The Sandalwood Trade, 162. *Commercial Trends After 1820,* 165: Hawaiian Islands as a Whaling Center, 166; American Establishments Ashore, 167. *Foreign Impact,* 169: Foreigners in the Islands, 170; Influence of American Civilization, 171. *United States Policy, 1842-1867,* 174: Whaling Deserters and Sandalwood Debts, 174; The Tyler Doctrine, 176; Maintaining Hawaiian Independence, 178; Pierce's Interest in Annexation, 180; President Johnson's Policy, 182.

VI. EXPANSION TO JAPAN 185

Early Sea Contacts, 185: Porter's Pacific Cruise, 186; American Whalers in the Pacific, 188; Geographic Scope and Extent, 189. *Systematic Exploration,* 190: Reynolds's Report, 190; Fanning's Agitation for an Expedition, 191; Wilkes's Expedition, 192. *Backgrounds of the Perry Missions,* 193: Pressure from Merchants, 195; Grievances of Whalemen, 196; Plans and Instructions, 197; Development of Perry's Mission, 198. *The Expeditions to Japan, 1853-1855,* 200: Perry's Purpose, 200; Surveying Expedition, 203; Results of Perry's Mission, 205.

EPILOGUE	208
BIBLIOGRAPHY	210
INDEX	221

List of Tables

1.	Comparative Numbers of British and American Ships in Northwest Trade, 1775-1814	20
2.	Characteristic Profits of Northwest Coast Voyages, 1791-1810	25
3.	Comparative Value of American World Trade and American China Trade	90
4.	Amount of Shipping Engaged in the China Trade for Selected Years	91
5.	Growth of Domestic Produce as Exports to Canton	91
6.	Rank of Chinese-American Trade in World Commerce	92
7.	Statistical View of Japanese Commerce Following the Perry Mission	206

Preface

Historians have explored and reinterpreted many aspects of American nationalism, economic development, westward and overseas expansion, and foreign relations during the twentieth century. Yet the role of the sea and maritime trade in our history has been largely neglected, partly, perhaps, because of our long continuing period of apparent continental isolationism and partly because of our relative inactivity on the sea after 1860. Our maritime history in the Pacific Ocean particularly has been thrust into the background of what many scholars consider the body of the living traditions of present-day America. The recent wars, resulting in American dominance and responsibilities in the Pacific Ocean, recall a long period of earlier expansion and interest in the area. The necessity of a struggle with Japan revealed the obvious fact that America was, and had long been, more deeply committed in the Pacific than in many other more familiar areas of the world.

Changed conditions in American world relations since 1941 make an understanding of the basis of America's position in the Pacific an urgent matter. In this study it is emphasized that the important antecedents of American westward expansion and foreign policy in the Pacific are found in the period prior to 1860. Both developments were parts of the same process. Annexation, imperialism, and war were not unheralded developments, but rather a culmination of events based solidly on the American Pacific development earlier in the nineteenth century.

It is the central aim of this work to bring together evidence bearing upon Pacific Ocean influences on American westward expansion, foreign policy, and later overseas expansion and to present it in a synthesized, unified manner.

In the collection of information from a wide variety of sources, well-recognized monographs and specialized works were depended upon to fill in much of the framework. Original sources were used from time to time in the maritime aspects of the study to highlight and underline the important points in the basic story. Government documents were used extensively to trace the development of foreign policy prior to 1860. Records compiled by the naval commanders in the Pacific and maintained by the Navy Department were consulted when they were used to reinforce the documents of Congress.

This study was consciously planned and written to be broad and comprehensive rather than narrow and detailed. Due to the geographic and chronological scope of this work, it was not practical to treat fully all of the aspects of international relations, such as European influence on American policy or Oriental reactions to American contacts, important as they are. This study treats mainly with the American problems in a complex area of relationships. It is hoped that this book will be of particular value as a body of subject matter since it is the first single study that has been assembled to summarize and interpret the main Pacific Ocean influences upon American development.

Chapter I

Sea Trade in Early American Development, 1750-1830

There has never been any real isolation for people on the North American continent. In colonial times this was probably more true than during certain brief periods after independence. From the first, commercial dependence upon England involved the colonies in British problems and European wars. Civil war in England in 1641 cut off colonial supplies, causing such economic straits in America that the colonists around Massachusetts Bay were obliged to put to sea for fish and for trade with the West Indies.¹ This was the beginning of the American maritime activity that was to keep the American colonies involved periodically in European wars until 1763.²

CONTRIBUTION TO EARLY NATIONALITY

Meanwhile the economic returns from a lucrative trade built a new mercantile class in America that soon rose to a position of power and influence in the colonial system. Although land was the main source of wealth until after the Revolution,³ the welfare of the colonists depended upon commerce to a degree never again equaled.⁴ The standard of living was virtually dependent

---

¹Morison, *Maritime History of Massachusetts* (Boston, 1923), p. 12.
²Hart, *Foundations of American Foreign Policy* (New York, 1901), pp. 9-11.
³Myers, *History of Great American Fortunes* (New York, 1936), pp. 48-49.
⁴Kirkland, *A History of American Economic Life* (New York, 1934), p. 98.

upon it. As early as 1700 Boston merchants formed the wealthiest single group in the colonies.[5] Their gains came chiefly from the off-shore fisheries in the North Atlantic as well as from the carrying of whale products to England and salt fish to the Catholic countries of Europe.

British Regulation of Colonial Trade. It was the fishing industry—and particularly whaling—that entangled the northern colonies in early commercial conflict with England. Fisheries were important from the first days of colonization in America. Along with religious freedom, they were the primary incentives for settlement. Provision for the use of the fisheries without restrictions was a prominent part of the royal charter for the New England colonies.[6]

By the middle of the eighteenth century American whaling had expanded to the point where England began to feel the pressure of economic competition. After 1641, when colonial whalers first started cruising the waters of Belle Isle Strait and the Gulf of St. Lawrence, the British Parliament felt it necessary to impose a duty on colonial whale products imported to the British Isles. At the same time, American shipments of whale products to European countries were restricted.[7] Expansion of the colonial fisheries was one part of the process whereby the American colonies began to outgrow the English mercantile system.[8] It was one step toward revolution. Whaling rights and the free use of the fishing grounds were questions that held a prominent place in the peace negotiations after the war.[9] The final settlement of this problem was one of the few diplomatic triumphs enjoyed by the new nation in its early existence.

The English commercial system worked for a time to the

---

[5]Myers, *op. cit.*, p. 55.

[6]Tower, *A History of the American Whale Fishery* (Philadelphia, 1907), p. 20.

[7]*Ibid.*, pp. 34-35.

[8]Hohman, *The American Whaleman* (New York, 1928), p. 33. Edmund Burke's tribute to the American whale fisheries in his speech of conciliation in 1774 is an indication of the extent to which American enterprise was crowding the English whaling industry.

[9]Tower, *op. cit.*, pp. 39-40.

Sea Trade in Early American Development

mutual advantage of the colonies and the mother country[10] Colonial trade in domestic products or West Indian rum enjoyed protected markets within the British Empire. Increasingly after 1750, as England began manufacturing a surplus, the system began to operate to the disadvantage of colonial merchants.[11] The surplus of manufactured goods was shipped to the colonies for sale and, at the same time, heavy duties were laid on manufactured goods brought to America from other countries. Export duties were also levied on colonial products shipped outside of the British Empire and colonial manufacturers were limited to the British market.[12] The result was a balance of trade that swung heavily against the colonial merchants. The colonies lacked the ready cash and exportable surplus to pay for British articles. Inevitably illegal maritime activity grew in answer to the British system.[13] As the year 1776 approached, a wealthy and powerful merchant class had formed in the principal seaport towns of Philadelphia, New York, Salem, Providence, Newburyport, and Boston.

After 1763 the British government thought it necessary to increase commercial restrictions. A series of Parliamentary acts came in quick succession that were intended (1) to limit imperial shipping to English and colonial vessels; (2) to reap a revenue on the most profitable branch of colonial trade—the West Indian; and (3) to restrict further the purchase and sale of manufactured goods outside the imperial structure. As debts of colonial merchants and planters accumulated, the imperial bonds cut more deeply. As a result the merchant class, now dominant in colonial life, became arrayed against the commercial interests of the mother country.

Merchants and the American Revolution. At first, the merchants, who had a real stake in the Empire, sought not rebel-

---

[10]Schlesinger, *The Colonial Merchants and the American Revolution* (New York, 1939), pp. 30-31.
[11]Kirkland, *op. cit.*, pp. 127-128; Schlesinger, *op. cit.*, p. 39; Adams, *Revolutionary New England* (Boston, 1923), pp. 207-208.
[12]Myers, *op. cit.*, p. 57; Adams, *op. cit.*, p. 208. Bar iron was the chief product.
[13]Schlesinger, *op. cit.*, p. 41

lion but reform.¹⁴ The first step was taken in the maritime colonies when merchants asked colonial assemblies to petition Parliament to repeal the tax on West Indian molasses. The Stamp Act followed close on the heels of this, unifying anti-British opinion among all classes to a greater degree than had the earlier commercial acts of Parliament. Merchants led in the agitation for a boycott of all English goods. Gradually after 1767, a series of overt acts showed that the agitation started by merchants had taken a violent turn.¹⁵ Nonimportation agreements were made in all but one of the colonies in the fall of 1769. Although the merchants lost control of a movement that they had initiated, the colonists struck back at British commercial restrictions with the only weapon then available—the maritime power of the colonies.

The Continental Association, which assembled in the fall of 1774, attempted to restore the conditions of trade existing in the British Empire before 1763. This meeting was not controlled by the merchants, but the document drawn up by the delegates was an attempt to reform the English mercantile system by asking for repeal of the navigation and trade acts.¹⁶ The first overt act of war in April, 1775, changed the character of the Continental Association. It became an instrument of war rather than of peaceful reform. As the merchant group lost control of the movement, it split—some joining the revolutionary movement, others becoming loyalists, still others remaining passive spectators until the issue was decided.

It is significant both that injured maritime interests loosed the forces of colonial discontent, and that the merchants, though disunited during the violent phase of the Revolution, sprang into the first rank after the hostilities to again dominate American affairs.¹⁷

---

¹⁴*Ibid.*, p. 32.

¹⁵*Ibid.*, pp. 100-101. British troops arrived in Boston in 1768 to quell rioting resulting from the seizure of a vessel owned by John Hancock. In 1769 a customs official was assaulted in Providence, Rhode Island. A royal revenue cutter was destroyed in the same year.

¹⁶*Ibid.*, pp. 424-425.

¹⁷Myers, *op. cit.*, pp. 48-49.

MERCHANTS IN THE NEW NATION

The Revolutionary War was but one phase of the American struggle for nationality. From the end of the hostilities to approximately 1830, the United States was continually struggling against the colonialism of England, France, and Spain to establish herself as a respected and self-supporting nation in the world community.

Grievances and restrictions encountered by the new nation were aggravated, particularly in the maritime realm, by European wars and rivalries. After 1783 British acts of hostility were, in part, prompted by the jealousy and fear aroused by the potentialities of American growth. The United States was therefore kept out of the West Indies trade after the Revolution.[18] The long Napoleonic wars, bringing seizures and impressment at sea, sharpened anglophobia and limited American effectiveness as an independent country.[19] The area to the west and south of the Caribbean was held in the rigid mercantile system of Spain, which also controlled the southern border of the United States.

Surrounded thus by potential enemies, there was a serious need for increased national prestige[20] and for independence in cultural patterns. Shipping profits gained during the first forty-five years of independence built much of the economic base for an American nationality.[21] Along with increased wealth, new articles of material culture and new ideas were brought into the country. These contributed to a new feeling of respectability and nationalism. For example, in small New England towns,

---

[18]Kimble, *The East Indies Trade of Providence, 1787-1867* (Brown University, 1898), p. 34.

[19]Fox and Krout, *The Completion of Independence* (New York, 1944), pp. 196-197.

[20]Sparks, *Life of John Ledyard* (Boston, 1855), p. 144. Ledyard in Cadiz in 1784 observed that foreign opinion of America in that quarter was low because she did not have sufficient prestige or power to deal with the piratical Hamet, Emperor of Morocco. Later events were to change this opinion.

[21]Fox and Krout, *op. cit.*, p. 73; Pitkin, *A Statistical View of Commerce* (New York, 1817), p. 351; *ibid.* (New Haven, 1835), p. 307.

which experienced an era of commercial prosperity after the Revolution, the increased wealth made possible a revolution in architecture. Bulfinch rebuilt much of Boston during this period in what came to be known as the Federal style. More characteristically American were some of the New England houses—square, three-storied, and topped by a captain's walk,[22] built originally for utilitarian purposes but later became a decorative feature of American architecture. These examples seem trivial indeed, but they are signs that the sea was furnishing the means and inspiration for some degree of cultural independence from the Old World.

In a slightly later period, a crude form of nationalism was expressed by naval officers. It was suggested that Capitol Hill in Washington be named Meridian Hill and that longitude be measured from Washington.[23] This was intended to be an expression of America's maturity and dominance on the sea. Congress actually passed an act in 1810 to effect the change, but the Ways and Means Committee withheld the necessary funds.[24]

Merchants and New England Federalism. In New England, merchants were among the leaders in port towns and in their states. They were also influential in national politics through John Adams' administration and until after the second war with England. At times their influence was negative. To some of them, the ports of New England were merely resting places between voyages. Many were more familiar with a dozen Pacific islands than with neighboring New England towns. Some Nantucket whale captains never set foot on the American continent. They viewed American nationality dimly. To the small powerful group whose way of life depended upon the returns from the sea, it was not unthinkable that New England should develop into an "American Denmark."[25] Signs of this sectional-

---

[22] Fish, *The Rise of the Common Man* (New York, 1927), p. 14.
[23] Cole, ed., "Documents," *Pacific Historical Review*, vol. 9 (1940), p. 65.
[24] Fox and Krout, *op. cit.*, p. 328.
[25] Morison, *op. cit.*, p. 211.

Sea Trade in Early American Development 9

ism are seen in their opposition to the Louisiana Purchase and the calling of the Hartford convention.[26]

The Federalist control of American policy after the Revolution was, in part, a triumph for the merchants, who had temporarily lost control in 1775. Personifying this development were well-known merchants in positions of political and judicial power. Characterizing the group were Fisher Ames, spokesman for the northern shipping interests; Timothy Pickering, secretary of state under John Adams; George Cabot, presiding officer at the Hartford convention; Tristam Dalton, United States senator from Massachusetts; Theophilus Parsons, chief justice of the Massachusetts Supreme Court; and Stephen Hooper, Jonathan Jackson, Judge John Lowell, Thomas H. Perkins, Israel Thorndike and William Sturgis—all wealthy and influential men dedicated to the interests of the merchant and shipper in overseas trade.[27] These were the men who fought against the rising tide of republicanism, with a degree of influence out of proportion to their numbers.

Allied in New England with the Congregational clergy, and throughout the nation with the landed aristocracy, they led in the conservative reaction against universal suffrage, political equality for the West, and land reforms.[28] The Federal Constitution for them was an instrument for the protection of private property. Their opposition to the abolition of debtor prisons and the passage of lien laws was in keeping with their political creed. The "Essex Junto," as they have been called, believed in the doctrine of rule by the wisest and best. Their theories arrayed them on the side that favored a strong central government. Their section of the country became the rallying point of federalism. As new forces arose in the South and West, New England be-

---

[26]Beard and Beard, *The Rise of American Civilization* (New York, 1935), vol. 1, pp. 401, 427.

[27]Fox and Krout, *op. cit.*, p. 191; Fuess, *Life of Caleb Cushing* (New York, 1923), vol. 1, pp. 11-12, 16-17; Morison, *op. cit.*, p. 167.

[28]Thorp, Curti, Baker, *American Issues* (Philadelphia, 1941), vol. 1, p. 188; Myers, *op. cit.*, pp. 66-67; Fox and Krout, *op. cit.*, p. 162; Greene, *The Foundations of American Nationality* (New York, 1922), p. 538.

came the last stronghold. Before the mercantile class became absorbed in a larger economy, however, it made its permanent contribution to American development.

Emergence of Economic Nationalism. During the first ten years of independence, while Alexander Hamilton wielded tremendous power in President Washington's cabinet, he had as his "privy council" a group of Massachusetts merchants and lawyers.[29] The early acts that Congress passed to protect and encourage the overseas trade indicate the influence of the mercantile class[30] and the importance of sea trade in the early national economy.

Congress, in July, 1789, passed a bill to protect the growth of the American merchant marine by providing for a 10 percent discount on cargoes imported in American ships. Foreign vessels, in turn, were assigned an additional 10 percent of the cargo value. In the same year another act was passed that discriminated against foreign trade in the payment of tonnage duties. American-built and American-owned ships were charged only six cents per ton, while fifty cents per ton was charged foreign-owned and foreign-built ships plying the coastwise trade. Bounties on fish imported by American vessels were provided to maintain this important industry. A bonded warehouse system for teas, suggested by the prominent Salem skipper, E. H. Derby, was successfully recommended by Alexander Hamilton to Congress in 1791.[31] Oriental tea brought in on foreign ships was virtually excluded by a 50 percent duty. In 1794 Congress increased the tariffs on imports carried in foreign vessels by an additional 10 percent. In 1817 all foreign vessels were excluded from the coastwise trade.

Capital for New Industry. This policy of maritime protection was a form of economic nationalism that encouraged maritime expansion at a time when the young nation needed revenue. At the same time it provided an opportunity for a small group of men to amass wealth beyond their immediate needs.

---

[29] Morison, *op. cit.*, p. 167.

[30] Marvin, *The American Merchant Marine* (New York, 1900), pp. 37-42.

[31] Morison, *op. cit.*, p. 166.

Sea Trade in Early American Development

It was this surplus that became the economic base for further national development, such as the building of canals, turnpikes, bridges, and factories. Capital for these enterprises came largely from the merchant-shippers of Philadelphia, New York, and New England ports.[32]

This process started early in the national period.[33] Samuel Slater, who arrived in New York in 1789, contacted a wealthy shipper, Moses Brown, of Providence, who had experimented unsuccessfully with a weaving machine the year before. Brown was eager to finance and encourage Slater in his plans for a textile industry. By a happy combination of money and technical skill, they were able to set up a factory in Pawtucket in 1791. Soon other mills were established near Providence. In a few years Brown's employees and disciples founded similar enterprises in Cohoes, New York. Another example in a later period was Francis Cabot Lowell, a retired importer, who combined resources with a mechanic named Paul Moody to perfect a power loom in 1814. A site was bought on the Charles River at Waltham. Cabot later became an investor in the Boston Manufacturing Company.[34]

The most notable transfer of funds from navigation to industry occurred during and following the War of 1812. The merchants of Boston, Salem, and Providence participated in this development, financing new enterprises in meatpacking, shoemaking, and cotton weaving. Illustrative of the postwar rise in manufacturing was the action of a town meeting held in Salem in the spring of 1826.[35] A committee was appointed to investigate the

---

[32]Phillips, *Salem and the Indies* (Boston, 1947), p. 281; Morison, *op. cit.*, p. 215. The names of the stockholders in early companies would correspond closely to the list of merchants. Fox and Krout, *op. cit.*, p. 371: "Merchants and landlords turned from wharf and farm to calculate the possibilities of factory and forge—and were convinced." Hacker, ed., *op. cit.*, p. 334: "It may be said that American ships and trading voyages really built the canals, railways, and early factories of the United States."

[33]Kirkland, *op. cit.*, pp. 329-330; Shannon, *American Economic Growth* (New York, 1940), p. 217.

[34]Kirkland, *op. cit.*, p. 332.

[35]*Report of the Committee Appointed to Inquire into the Practicability and Expediency of Establishing Manufactures in Salem*, pamphlet (Salem Massachusetts, 1826), pp. 1-31.

advisability of building a dam across North River to provide a source of water power. The report was made, adopted, and the Salem Mill-Dam Corporation was established. Prominent among the names of the original committee and on the list of subscribers were those of merchants and former sea captains.[36] The general trend of wealth from commerce to industry is seen in the final report of the committee. It made reference to the rapid rise of Lowell, Massachusetts, and decided that Salem, too, should look to its future.

> We have, within a few years past, seen extensive manufacturing establishments growing up with unexampled rapidity, sometimes almost in the midst of a commercial community in our seaports, and sometimes in the interior, under the patronage and management of men who have heretofore been exclusively engaged in mercantile pursuits.[37]

TRADE IN THE BACKGROUND OF THE MONROE DOCTRINE

More important in the development of American nationality was the condition existing in the maritime trade of the West Indies and South America. The importance of this commerce contributed strongly to the eventual breaking of the last vestiges of mercantilism and foreign dominance over the Western Hemisphere. The first step was the opening of the British West Indies trade to American commerce in 1830. This achievement ended a fifty-year diplomatic and commercial struggle with England, beginning with the very dawn of independence in 1783. During colonial times, the Caribbean colonies had been the chief source of raw materials. The closing of this trade area to Americans after independence was a serious blow.[38] American merchants began petitioning the government to negotiate with Britain for its reopening. The chief pressure on Britain occurred after the return

---

[36]*Ibid.*, pp. 2, 19.

[37]*Ibid.*, pp. 18-19.

[38]Benns, *The Struggle for the British West Indies Carrying Trade* (Indianapolis, 1923), p. 7. Colonial exports to the British West Indies amounted to 3½ million dollars just before the Revolution.

of peace in 1815. Negotiations went on for the next fifteen years and were finally pushed through successfully early in the administration of Andrew Jackson. The settlement resulted in almost complete reciprocity.[39] This was an important step in opening the last closed colonial area in the Western Hemisphere.

While the controversy over the West Indian trade was going on, American trade was growing in other Caribbean islands and with the continent of South America. As Spain became involved in European wars after 1793, she became less able to maintain her colonial commerce with Vera Cruz, Havana, Caracas, Cartegena, Lima, and Buenos Aires. American merchants in Boston, Providence, New York, Philadelphia, and Baltimore were quick to step into the vacuum.[40] Shortly after independence, American vessels were freighting American dried fish, lumber, and small manufactured articles to these Latin-American ports. The first consular agent was appointed by President Adams in 1797 to reside in Havana.[41]

European wars played into American hands during the 1790's, allowing a swift expansion in trade. After 1800 American commerce with Latin America was extended from the Caribbean ports southward to the mainland. American ships were soon touching at Santa Marta, Rio de Janeiro, Montevideo, La Guaira, and Valparaiso on the Pacific coast. Montevideo, as the main entrepôt for the Rio de la Plata region, received forty-three vessels in 1801 and 1802. They carried away chiefly cattle products and Peruvian wood.[42] The port of New York dominated the trade with the southern countries. Between 1790 and 1810 there were 341 New York merchants in the Caribbean and South American trade.[43]

---

[39]*Ibid.*, p. 187. American ships were allowed to carry products from British West Indies to any point in the world. Nearly all American products were allowed to be brought in. British ships, in turn, were allowed to carry American products to their West Indian islands.

[40]Bernstein, *Origins of Inter-American Interest* (Philadelphia, 1945), pp. 30-31.

[41]*Ibid.*, p. 38.

[42]Morison, *op. cit.*, p. 369; Bernstein, *op. cit.*, p. 47.

[43]Bernstein, *op. cit.*, p. 47.

American commerce stepped in at a time when there was some revolutionary ferment in South America. Revolutionary doctrine was bound to seep in from North America by way of the numerous commercial contacts. It was a common occurrence for American sailors to be incarcerated in South American jails for spreading subversive republican propaganda in the ports. It cannot be said that American commerce led directly to the revolutions in South America, but inter-American contacts accompanied and reinforced the desire for freedom in the southern countries.

Cultural contacts resulting from commercial connections were of some significance, too. Even before 1800 there was some cultural interplay. Philosophical societies in America exchanged books with similar groups to the south and elected Spanish and Spanish-American intellectuals as corresponding members of their organizations. Popular interest in Latin and South America, of course, was more intense in the seaports, in which local periodicals often carried articles on such practical subjects as trade and diplomatic affairs with the southern countries.[44]

Inter-American trade and cultural ties did not stir up popular enthusiasm in America for Latin-American freedom to any appreciable extent. It is of some significance, however, that a few Americans, mostly New Englanders, actively participated in some of the revolutionary movements.[45]

Diplomatic ties and political recognition lagged behind cultural and commercial interests.[46] It was not until 1810 that an "agent for seamen" was assigned to Buenos Aires. His job was to

---

[44]*Ibid.*, p. 60.

[45]Morison, *op. cit.*, p. 182. Examples of fanatical Americans are: Benjamin F. Seaver, whose statue stands in Buenos Aires, who was killed while commanding the Argentine fleet in action against Spain; William P. White, who established a mercantile house at Buenos Aires in 1804 and aided in supplying and fitting out the Argentine fleet; Paul Delano, who commanded a Chilean frigate in the fight for independence; and his kinsman, William Delano, who served on the staff of San Martin.

[46]Bemis, *A Diplomatic History of the United States* (New York, 1942), p. 200. American hands were pretty well tied in the recognition of new Latin republics due to the pending Florida boundary dispute. After 1819 the United States was free to recognize the new republics.

encourage the revolutionists, aid commerce, and obtain information.[47] After 1811 consular agents were maintained in the principal South American and Latin ports. Although it is not safe to say that the commercial ties with Latin America were the direct antecedents of the Monroe Doctrine,[48] the noncolonization principle, which is an essential part of the doctrine, was in keeping with American trade interests. Trade contacts, resulting in cultural and diplomatic interests, accompanied the Latin American movement for independence.[49] This was the first step in the direction of the establishment of the Monroe Doctrine principle, which extended American political protection over most of the Western Hemisphere.

FAR EASTERN INFLUENCE ON AMERICAN CULTURE

The widened geographic scope of American sea trade after the Revolution brought in strange and exotic goods from many lands. In addition to a few glimpses of Latin American culture noticeable in the eastern ports, American ships, after ranging the Mediterranean Sea, Indian Ocean, and Pacific Ocean, brought back ideas and articles of material culture. China was the most familiar source. In the early years Salem, Providence, and Boston ships brought home porcelain, Chinaware, blue Nanking earthenware, silken houserobes, lacquered trays and furniture, jade, sandalwood ornaments, and ivory bedsteads.[50]

The homes of New England merchants were decorated with Chinese and oriental articles. Many American enthusiasts started formal Chinese collections. Usually these people were retired ship captains or former American consuls in Canton, such as Edward Carrington, consul in China from 1802 to 1811, and Benjamin Wilcocks, consul from 1814 to 1820. Both of these retired

---
[47]*Ibid.*, p. 198.
[48]Perkins, *The Monroe Doctrine, 1823-1826* (Boston, 1927), pp. 40-41. Perkins concluded that "political sympathy, not economic self-interest, lay at the root of American policy."
[49]Bernstein, *op. cit.*, p. 101.
[50]Downes, *The China Trade and Its Influences* (New York, 1941), pp. 13-17.

officials had homes that were well adorned with Chinese notions. J. J. Kock, of Philadelphia, began a Chinese portrait collection in 1819. A Dutchman named Van Braam built a mansion on the Delaware River called the "China Retreat" and furnished it in authentic Chinese style down to the last detail. American interest in things Chinese continued to grow until after 1861. Due to the collections in private homes and museums, it was possible by the 1840's for people traveling in New England to learn as much of China in the seaport towns as from a personal visit to China.[51]

Widened horizons of social thought after the Revolution, to which the influx of foreign cultures contributed, were a continuation of the eighteenth-century enlightenment. The attack on authoritarian religion and fundamentalism, as seen in the interest in Deism and Unitarianism, was enlarged and supported by a growing knowledge of science and thought in other lands.[52] Geographic knowledge was expanded by the wide ranging activities of Yankee ships. The Oriental trade stimulated inquiry into the fields of meteorology, biology, and what today would be called anthropology.[53]

Overseas trade, particularly in the Pacific, indirectly stimulated the formation of foreign missionary societies in the home ports. Indirectly their activity encouraged small groups of people to acquire knowledge and appreciation of strange racial groups and religions. These contributed to the stereotypes of the South Pacific isle and the "pagan" aborigine.[54]

The rise of humanitarian reform after 1800 was given an increased area of activity in the seaport towns. Salvation of sea-

---

[51]Cole, ed., *With Perry in Japan, The Diary of Edward Yorke McCauley* (Princeton, 1942), p. 77.

[52]Curti, *The Growth of American Thought* (New York, 1943), pp. 178-184; Beard and Beard, *op. cit.*, p. 457; Morison, *op. cit.*, p. 119; Fox and Krout, *op. cit.*, pp. 226-327. The most conspicuous contribution to the American enlightenment in the field of science was Nathaniel Bowditch's *American Practical Navigator*, which formed the basis of modern celestial sea navigation. He was also a mathematician in his own right. Mathiesson, *American Renaissance* (London, 1941), p. viii; Unitarianism later during the 1840's and 1850's developed into the philosophy of transcendentalism.

[53]Curti, *op. cit.*, p. 179.

[54]Fox and Krout, *op, cit.*, p. 258.

Sea Trade in Early American Development 17

men's souls became the mission of such societies as the Marine Bible Society, established for the purpose of building havens for sailors. Two of these were the Mariner's Home and the Seamen's Bethels.[55]

Before 1812, small New England towns were becoming the cultural and intellectual centers of the country. Here secular knowledge was greater and tolerance broader.[56] Knowledge of the Orient, particularly India and China, had some later influence on the transcendentalist philosophy of the Concord sages—Emerson, Thoreau, and Alcott. The mysticism and eclecticism of the Hindu philosophers and the practical shrewdness of Confucian thought reinforced the bits of philosophy borrowed from classical and European sources. This philosophy, during the middle period, became a part of the flowering of New England or of the American renaissance, as it has been called.[57]

The contributions of the East India Society of Salem were of a less nebulous and more practical nature. Its compilations of geographic and navigational data added to the growing familiarity with the outside world. Its museum's collection of items from many areas of the earth stirred interest and provided information for a limited number of New Englanders.[58]

Maritime trade has been reviewed here as it affected the continental development along the American seaboard in the first forty-five years of independence. The seaward advance, of which these influences were merely a part, was to have more far-reaching effects in the realm of international relations and national expansion.

---

[55]Hohman, *op. cit.*, p. 107.

[56]Delano, *Voyages* (Boston, 1817), p. 256. Delano, one of the most widely traveled Americans before 1812, admitted that he had, as a result of his worldwide contacts, become more catholic in his attitude toward non-Christian religions. Phillips, *Salem and the Indies*, p. 426; Fuess, *op. cit.*, p. 10. Widened contacts resulting from the sea trade caused the people of Newburyport to be "cosmopolites in touch with wider interests than their inland neighbors."

[57]Christy, *The Orient in American Transcendentalism* (New York, 1932), pp. xi, xii.

[58]Peabody, *Merchant Ventures of Old Salem* (Boston, 1912), p. 341; Fox and Krout, *op. cit.*, p. 65.

Chapter II

The Seaborne Frontier on the Northwest Coast, 1778-1850

The present position of dominance in the Pacific, achieved by the United States at such tremendous cost, is the result, in part, of a trend that scholars and other thinking people have been observing for more than a generation; that is, the steady and inevitable extension of America's peoples and policies into the Pacific area. This urge, already incipient at the time of the purchase of Louisiana, later became articulate in the minds of a few men in high places. By the activities of a few seagoing pioneers, beginning in the first year of independence, a maritime frontier was opened across the Pacific from the North American coast to China, the Philippines, and the East Indies. Stimulated by these early contacts, official policy soon recognized the inevitable importance of an American grasp upon the Pacific slope and of a positive policy in regard to Pacific islands and borders of that ocean. The connection between these early seaward contacts and the price now demanded for Pacific security is obvious in spite of the elapse of nearly two centuries.

MARITIME TRADE, 1778-1825

Early American trade contacts with the Northwest Coast were stimulated by an event that took place in 1778 during the third voyage of the British explorer, Captain Cook. Some of Cook's men happened to engage in desultory trade with the Indians in that area, exchanging a few trinkets and metal objects for sea otter pelts. At first the furs were used to replace tattered clothing and for use as bedding and other general purposes.

The Seaborne Frontier on the Northwest Coast

When Cook's ship finally reached China, it was found that the Canton merchants were eager to get such furs and would gladly pay fabulous prices for them. Amounts for each fur that would correspond to approximately twenty American dollars were readily paid.

News of this profitable commerce spread rapidly by way of adventurers and traders to India and Europe. The first British traders appeared on the Northwest Coast in 1785 in the vessel *Sea Otter*, commanded by James Hanna.[1] During the first three years of this trade all of the ships were of British nationality.

British-American Rivalry in the Northwest. American interest in the Northwest fur trade was thought to have been stimulated in part by the agitation of an American named John Ledyard, who had accompanied Captain Cook on his third voyage. The Americans were not long in making their appearance on the coast. From 1788 until the final decline of the trade, American commerce gradually increased and by 1812 had a virtual monopoly on the sea trade along the Northwest Coast of America.

A peculiar condition of trade was responsible for this development. Under an ancient charter from the Crown, the British East India Company and the British South Seas Company held the entire Pacific area in monopoly. Individual British traders could trade in China only goods under license from one of the two monopolies. This made individual trade difficult since the license fees were all but prohibitive. Even the Hudson's Bay Company, which controlled a good part of the inland fur trade of Canada, was unable to break into the maritime aspect of the fur trade.

Since the problem of the China trade was one of obtaining a medium of exchange, the British monopolies, with their immense resources of capital, did not need to engage in the Northwest fur trade. In turn, they kept other individual British enterprises out by restrictions upon the sale in England of Chinese goods that could have been bought with Northwest Coast furs.[2] In

---

[1] Howay, "An Outline Sketch of the Maritime Fur Trade," *The Canadian Historical Association Report of Annual Meeting* (Ottawa, 1932), p. 5.
[2] *Ibid.*, p. 6.

spite of attempts of British traders to masquerade under Portuguese, French, or Danish flags, the fur trade was all but cut off from them by British monopolies.[3] About eight British vessels followed in the track of the *Sea Otter,* and the French made one feeble attempt to break into the trade after 1790.[4]

This monopolistic practice worked to the advantage of American traders. Where the British ship could carry only furs to Canton, the Americans could realize a real profit by taking China goods in exchange for Northwest furs and selling the products in America or England free of the prohibitive licensing fees on the East India or South Seas companies.

From the time of the first American ship in 1788, there were signs of the beginnings of British-American competition and rivalry. It was, perhaps, the beginning of British-American ill feeling and mistrust that finally reached a climax in the Oregon boundary controversy. As the number of American ships increased, the volume of British shipping decreased. Some statistics compiled by F. W. Howay illustrate this (see table 1).[5]

Table 1
COMPARATIVE NUMBERS OF BRITISH AND AMERICAN SHIPS
IN NORTHWEST TRADE, 1788-1814

	British Vessels	American Vessels
First ten years, 1788-1794	35	15
Second ten years, 1795-1804	9	50
Third ten years, 1805-1814	3	40

During the period of American maritime predominance, the British, likewise, were developing and expanding the activities of the Northwest Fur Company. They had established coastal fur posts on the mainland and offshore islands from Nootka Sound to the vague boundary of Russian America. A thriving coastwise traffic had been built up with small British schooners plying between the posts, collecting furs from the Indians in exchange for

---

[3]Howay, ed., *The Dixon-Meares Controversy,* Canadian Historical Studies (Toronto, 1929; reprinted by Da Capo Press, 1969), intro., p. 2.
[4]Winther, *The Great Northwest* (New York, 1947), p. 23.
[5]Howay, "An Outline Sketch of the Maritime Fur Trade," p. 7.

food, clothing, and trinkets. After 1788 an increasing number of Yankee ships began to embarrass the coastwise trade of the British. To combat Yankee competition, the English conspired to rid the coast of them. When a Yankee ship appeared in the vicinity of a fur post, they started the practice of quickly filling up canoes with liquor and sailing to the Indian villages nearby to flood the market and to incapicitate the Indians for further trading with the Yankees.[6] This is an isolated example of British and American competition, but the stories are numerous of incidents of early friction between the two nations. The British, through the instrument of the Hudson's Bay Company, seemed to realize that if the area was to be held with its lucrative trade, the Yankee mariners must be kept out.

Discovery and Exploration. American contacts on the coast, until the time of the second war with England, should be traced to illustrate how American claims to the area were reinforced and how British-American competition came about. American ships entered the area of the Northwest Coast at a time when the coast, as a vaguely defined region, was jointly claimed by England and Spain. Spain's claims were to be eliminated in 1790, three years after the first Americans appeared on the scene. Shortly after the first news reached America of Captain Cook's discovery of a valuable fur trade in Canton, a group of American merchants began financing and planning the first American voyage to the Northwest Coast. By the joint efforts of Joseph Barrell, Samuel Brown, Charles Bulfinch, and Crowell Hatch of Boston, John Derby of Salem, and John Pintard of New York, two small ships were fitted out. The sloop *Lady Washington,* commanded by Captain Robert Gray, and the bark *Columbia,* commanded by John Kendrick, left Boston Harbor late in the summer of 1787, two weeks after the signing of the United States Constitution.[7] The familiar story of their voyages is sketched in most general historical works of the Oregon territory. It need not be related in detail here.

---

[6]Bancroft, *History of the Northwest Coast* (San Francisco, 1844), vol. 2, p. 693.

[7]Winther, *op. cit.*, p. 27.

The significance of the first voyage was not in the profits obtained but in the information gained that was of use in fitting out later voyages. The Yankee traders discovered on the first voyage that much of their cargo was useless in trade with the Indians. Iron chisels, copper, and old muskets were found to be more useful in trading for furs than the baubles and trinkets that they carried. In the first voyage an attempt was also made to establish friendly and lasting relations with the Indians. The instructions from the owners of the ships to Captain Kendrick especially impressed upon him their wish that "harmony and friendship may be cultivated between you and the natives, and that no advantage be taken of them in trading but that you endeavor by honest conduct to impress upon their minds a friendship for Americans."[8] In the same instructions, the owners expressed a desire for friendly relations with Spain and for establishment of a permanent trading post ashore. It seems clear that it was the purpose of the merchants to make the Northwest fur trade a regular branch of their maritime activities. The first voyage of the *Columbia* was a test of its feasibility.

Captain Gray and Captain Kendrick exchanged ships on the coast. Gray was given orders to proceed in the *Columbia* to Canton with the furs from the Northwest Coast and to return to Boston via Cape Horn. Kendrick remained with the *Lady Washington*, shuttling back and forth between China and the coast, stopping off at Hawaii enroute. He never returned to Boston and succeeded only in selling the *Lady Washington*'s cargo at a loss in Canton. He died in Hawaii not long after Gray's return to Boston in 1790.

Losses were also incurred on the returns from the *Columbia*'s first cargo. Undaunted, the underwriters began fitting her out for a return to the Northwest Coast.[9] With Captain Gray in full command, she departed again within a few months from the time of her arrival from the first voyage. After rounding the Horn in good order she arrived in the Vancouver Island area in the

---

[8]Howay, "Hasewell's First Log," *Voyages of the Columbia* (Boston, 1941; reprinted by Da Capo Press, 1969), p. 111. Courtesy of the Massachusetts Historical Society.
[9]Winther, *op. cit.*, p. 27.

spring of 1791. During a one-year stay along the coast, a small sloop was built for work among the numerous inlets and offshore islands. A lively trade was carried on in exchange for such articles as made up her cargo—bricks, beef, gunpowder, rum, sugar, copper sheets, iron chisels, buttons, and cloth.[10] The lessons of the first unprofitable voyage had been learned. In two years the *Columbia* had a full cargo of furs ready for exchange at the Canton market.

Before returning to the China coast, Captain Gray sailed into the "River of the West," which was to have great significance in the diplomatic struggle later. The Spanish, of course, were aware of a river they called "San Roque" as a result of the explorations of Heceta and Pérez in 1775 and 1776. In the spring of 1792 the *Columbia* sailed over the great surf-ridden bar that had discouraged the entrance of previous explorers since the day of Sir Francis Drake. Gray was still in search of furs and the event, except for the navigational hazards, seemed of secondary importance at the time. It was evident, however, from the action of the natives that few, if any, white men had previously entered the river. Gray, thinking he had made an original discovery, named the river after his ship, the point north of the river mouth "Cape Hancock," and the south point "Cape Adams."[11]

The claims established by this discovery came up time and time again during the boundary negotiations from 1818 to 1846. Captain Gray himself published nothing concerning the discovery. Its importance was suddenly realized, however, when Astoria was to be returned to the United States, as provided in the Treaty of Ghent. President James Madison requested information on the discovery from Charles Bulfinch, who was still living, in order to support American claims to Astoria.[12] Bulfinch managed to find the log and took extracts from it, describing the *Columbia's* entrance into the river. The extract was later published in a Senate document and was used as supporting evidence of American claims. The influence of the *Columbia's* voyage will

---

[10]*Ibid.*
[11]Fuller, *A History of the Pacific Northwest* (New York, 1931), p. 50.
[12]*Ibid.*

be brought out in a later discussion to support the statement that the *Columbia,* on her first voyage, had "solved the riddle of the China trade." On her second, "empire followed in the wake."[13]

Economic Returns and Decline. The solution to the "riddle of the China trade" was the discovery of a medium of exchange for use at Canton. The number of ships starting for the Northwest Coast after the *Columbia*'s first voyage is proof that the search for a suitable medium of trade was successful. In 1790 the brig *Hope,* commanded by T. H. Perkins, sailed for the Northwest Coast; a brigantine, the *Hancock,* commanded by Samuel Crowell, followed two months later; and the *Columbia* started on her second voyage. In the following year, the *Margaret* departed for the Northwest Coast.[14] It would be pointless to enumerate the names and value of ships year by year. It is sufficient to say that by 1792 the Northwest Coast trade, following the pattern set by the *Columbia,* was a well-established branch of commerce.

Boston ships initiated the Northwest trade and managed to forge ahead and dominate it. The trade quickly outgrew the bauble stage.[15] Cargoes likewise had to increase in value in order to supply the Indians with useful articles, as was mentioned in the description of the *Columbia*'s second voyage.

Economic returns varied from year to year and are hard to trace due to the haphazard and individualistic nature of the voyages. The peak year was 1801, although profits remained good until 1805. By 1802 sea otter skins had declined in trade value from $120.00 to $20.00 at Canton.[16] An example of the overall profits for a characteristic year from 1801 to 1805 would vary from $40,000 to $50,000 of investment for a return profit of $150,000 to $284,000.[17] Returns on three specific voyages illustrate the range of profits (table 2).[18]

---

[13]Morison, *Maritime History of Massachusetts* (Boston, 1923), p. 51.
[14]*Ibid.*
[15]Howay, "An Outline Sketch of the Maritime Fur Trade," p. 8.
[16]Winther, *op. cit.,* p. 30.
[17]*Ibid.*
[18]Howay, "An Outline Sketch of Maritime Fur Trade," p. 11.

Table 2
CHARACTERISTIC PROFITS OF NORTHWEST COAST VOYAGES, 1791-1810

Years of Voyage	Name of Vessel	Approximate Net Profit
1791-1794	Margaret	$ 80,000
1801-1803	Caroline	73,000
1807-1810	Pearl	206,000

The returns are rather meager when it is considered that most ships were underwritten by several different merchants. The profits not only had to be split several ways but they made up the sole profit of a two- or three-year period.

During the early years of the trade, ships usually spent but one season in trading along the coast. If the trade was good, they went on to Canton. If not, it was the general practice to winter in the Hawaiian Islands. After approximately 1795 longer and longer periods were required to fill the cargoes. The trading period increased from eighteen months to sometimes as long as three years. As furs became scarce, the trading continued throughout the winter.[19] This change in the method of trade made the Hawaiian Islands of greater significance to the pursuit of the Northwest fur trade. Instead of being merely a stopping place for rest and refreshment, the islands gradually became a supply point for articles such as yams, hogs, plantains, sweet potatoes, salt, naval stores, and even for Kanaka laborers.[20] The interdependence between the Northwest Coast and the Hawaiian Islands was partially established in this way and will be discussed in more detail later.

The growing scarcity of sea otter caused another important change in the methods of the Northwest Coast trade. As the fur-bearing animals became scarce along the coast, Yankee ships began putting crews of men, sometimes Aleut Indians or Sandwich Islanders (Hawaiians), on the offshore islands of California and the Northwest Coast. These poachers would operate ashore

---

[19]Reynolds, *The Voyage of the New Hazard* (Salem, 1938), p. xiii.
[20]Howay, "An Outline Sketch of Maritime Fur Trade," p. 9.

while the ship proceeded to points along the coast, collecting furs from other parties or exchanging the usual articles with the Indians. The Boston vessel, *O'Cain,* was evidently the first Yankee ship to engage in this practice. The arrangement with Governor Baranov in 1803 for poaching along the American coast is described later in connection with Alaska contracts.

Attempts at Permanent Settlement. A logical development of the fly-by-night shore party was an attempt to establish a permanent settlement ashore. The first establishment of this kind was attempted in 1810 by Jonathan Winship.[21] Winship came from a merchant-trading family of Boston. Sailing the family vessel *Albatross,* he crossed the Columbia River bar and proceeded upstream looking for a suitable spot to erect a fort and plant vegetable gardens. On a likely location the Bostonian began erecting a blockhouse and trading post. All preparations were made to make the outpost the beginning of a thriving fur-trading town. The elaborate preparations had to be abandoned when it was discovered that they had unwittingly encroached upon the territory of the Chinook Indians. These were a tribe of "middle men" who collected the furs from inland for sale to Northwest Fur Company posts or to Yankee ships. Their threats and menacing attitude forced Captain Winship to give up the scheme and abandon his fort.[22]

Winship's enterprise anticipated by only a year the arrival of the *Tonquin,* owned by John J. Astor. The story of the founding of Astoria, its brief career in the hands of his Pacific Fur Company, and the capture of the *Tonquin* by the Indians is well known. It need not be discussed in detail here other than to point out its significance in the chain of American maritime contacts on the coast. As a financial venture it was never a success. Just as the vast plans for inland and maritime expansion were getting underway, the news of the War of 1812 came. The Astoria holding was promptly sold out to the Canadian members of the company. A British ship arrived in 1813 and formally "seized" it as a prize of war.

---

[21]Morison, *op. cit.,* p. 58.
[22]Fuller, *op. cit.,* p. 94.

The terms of the Treaty of Ghent stipulated that places and possessions taken during hostilities be returned. The question of Astoria's return was not settled until 1818, and not then until a United States naval ship was sent to assert the American claim. The controversy over Astoria was involved in the dispute over the claim to the Columbia Valley. It was the opening of the Oregon dispute. The diplomatic significance of Astoria's return is discussed later in this section. The maritime enterprise had at least resulted in an international incident that drew American interest to the Northwest Coast and awakened public interest in the Oregon boundary question.[23]

American maritime activity was checked in the entire Pacific area by the War of 1812. The war marked the beginning of the end of the Northwest Coast fur trade. Furs along the coast had long since begun to decline and after 1812 individual traders were seen less and less. The center of activity began to shift to other areas. By 1822 California and Hawaii were the scenes of increased American sea contacts.[24]

After 1812 the inland fur monopolies of Britain—the Northwest Fur Company and Hudson's Bay Company—began drawing off the inland furs and shipping them eastward via Montreal to the London market. Between 1821 and 1830 the number of American vessels engaged in the Northwest fur trade declined from thirteen to three.[25] This did not mean that American maritime trade ceased entirely. After the seizure of Astoria by the British, the control of the fur trade from the Columbia River Valley fell into the hands of the Northwest Fur Company. To combat the monopoly held by the East India Company, which virtually prohibited the use of independent British ships for the China trade, the Northwest Company officials made a business arrangement with the Boston merchant, T. H. Perkins, who had commanded the *Hope* in 1790 on one of the first fur voyages to the coast. Perkins arranged to handle all of the outside trade of the British company, bringing in supplies to Astoria and other

---

[23]Hines, *An Exploring Expedition to Oregon* (Buffalo, 1851), p. 375.
[24]Winther, *op. cit.*, p. 32.
[25]Howay, "An Outline Sketch of the Maritime Fur Trade," p. 14.

fur posts along the coast and taking the furs to the Canton market.[26] This trade was not extensive but it tended to drain off the furs again in a westerly direction.

The arrangement between the commercial house of T. H. Perkins and the Northwest Fur Company went on smoothly for about ten years. In 1821 the two British fur companies merged into one gigantic monopoly. The developments thereafter boded ill for Yankee enterprise in the Northwest. The business of T. H. Perkins was discontinued and the British monopoly began to expand in area and increase its activities. The new policy of the enlarged Hudson's Bay Company was to develop the area as well as pursue the extractive trade in furs. New subsidiaries of the company were started to develop agriculture, stock raising, lumbering, and shipbuilding. Domestic animals, vegetables, and seed were imported from California and Hawaii in exchange for furs.

Development of the inland resources caused a different sort of maritime activity to develop. Trade became a prosaic business of exchanging fish, lumber, and agricultural products for products of California and Hawaii. Although the number of American ships declined they were not entriely shut out of the trade. After 1825, however, the carrying trade had become diversified to the extent that it could no longer be called an American Northwest fur trade.[27]

In spite of the development that checked American Northwest trade after 1812, the important contacts of the earlier period proved to be invaluable antecedents for the development of American policies of westward expansion and for precedents of American claims on the Oregon country. The trade had established the first commercial relations between America, Hawaii, and China. It had filled in knowledge of a little-known corner of the world and made it a vital link in world commerce and had caused the first importation of foreign laborers to the West Coast

---

[26]Winther, *op. cit.*, p. 48.
[27]Howay, "An Outline Sketch of Maritime Fur Trade," p. 14.

of America.[28] It had stirred the first international rivalry and eventually resulted in a shift of the claims of Russia and Spain to those of America and England, which became paramount. During the thirty years of fur trade activity, it had involved exploitive and extractive methods of a highly individualistic nature, which gradually crystalized from the "early gleams of unification" into official national policy.[29]

JOHN LEDYARD AND THOMAS JEFFERSON

In the development of the theories of American expansion, the thoughts and policies of four individuals stand out. These figures, three of whom were statesmen and the fourth a naval geopolitician, are Thomas Jefferson, John Quincy Adams, William H. Seward, and Admiral A. T. Mahan. The policies of Jefferson, Adams and, to a lesser degree, those of Seward are treated in this study.

Jefferson's Early Interest. Thomas Jefferson stands as the first official proponent of American expansion to the Pacific, chiefly on the ground of his fostering the Lewis and Clark Expedition. If his inner thoughts are accurately revealed in his "Notes on Virginia," written in 1782, he apparently had an interest in the Oregon country and some vague knowledge of far western geography prior to that date. In a letter to George Rogers Clark, in 1783, he expressed the fear of British penetration into the country and proposed an expedition into the California area. In support of the feasibility of such a trip, he ventured the theory that there was a west-flowing river that joined with the headwaters of the Missouri River.[30] His vague knowledge of the West and basic philosophical interest in all unknown things were supported by a broad political and geo-

---

[28]Hines, *op. cit.*, p. 412. "A more heterogeneous mass could not be found," said the Rev. Mr. Hines in 1843, "Englishmen, Scotchmen, Americans, Germans, Prussians, Italians, Spanish, Frenchmen, Danes, Hawaiians, and Africans. An amalgam was developing.

[29]Howay, "An Outline Sketch of Maritime Fur Trade," p. 8.

[30]Schafer, *A History of the Pacific Northwest* (New York, 1918), p. 32.

graphical vision of the future of the United States.

Influence of Ledyard. With this incipient interest in the Northwest Coast area, into which he felt the American nation was destined to have a fundamental commercial foothold, Jefferson arrived in Paris to relieve Dr. Benjamin Franklin as the American minister to the Court of Louis XVI.

While Jefferson was establishing himself as the second American minister to France, John Ledyard, who had been the first American to visit the Northwest Coast of America, was exerting pressure on Atlantic Coast merchants in order to interest some of them in financing a fur voyage to the Pacific. His efforts in the East Coast ports of America served to crystalize his own ideas of the possibilities for profit on the Northwest Coast and formed a firm conviction in his mind that was later to have some influence on Thomas Jefferson's policies of Pacific expansion.

Of more immediate importance in the development of the Northwest trade was Ledyard's abortive attempts to enlist the aid of established merchants in financing a trading voyage to the Pacific. Although his attempts in America were unsuccessful, undoubtedly some interest was stirred by his efforts. It has been estimated that, in the decade after his return to America in 1783, at least thirty ships had engaged in fur trade on the Northwest Coast.[31]

In order to show adequately the influence of Ledyard on the development of the Northwest trade and resulting official policy a few incidents of successes and failures from his active life must be told. After his return from the third voyage of Captain Cook, he stayed an additional two years in the Royal Navy waiting for the Revolution to end. With the end of hostilities, he managed to get stationed on a ship bound for America. Once there, he promptly deserted and returned to the home of a relative in Hartford, Connecticut, in which he had been partially reared. For several months he remained inactive while he wrote his ac-

---

[31]Munford, *John Ledyard: An American Marco Polo* (Portland, 1919), p. 301. As was shown previously, only fifteen American ships were engaged. Munford is discussing Ledyard's influence on trade as a whole and no doubt included British ships as well.

count of the recent voyage. Though never quite completed, his *Journal of Captain Cook's Voyage* sold rather widely and, without a doubt, had some influence in familiarizing American merchants with the ways of the Northwest fur trade.

Ledyard soon tired of the confining business of writing, and early in 1784 he was in New York furthering the plan that was to be the driving force in his life—that of embarking upon a series of voyages to the Nortwest Coast for furs to exchange at Canton. In New York he walked the waterfront interviewing ship captains and pleading with merchants ashore. The Revolution had just ended and both shipping and financial support were so scarce that Ledyard was unsuccessful.

Sometime later he seemed to be on the verge of success after a visit with Robert Morris in Philadelphia. Here was a man who could help finance and fit out an expedition such as Ledyard envisioned. The plans seemed completed. Morris was convinced and the money was available. With great enthusiasm Ledyard went to New England to charter or buy a ship and to recruit seamen. A series of delays, near successes, and disappointments followed in quick succession. As each ship was chartered, the vessel would be suddenly withdrawn and sent on a safer mission. One ship was found to be old and unseaworthy. Another, the vessel of an old acquaintance, was withdrawn because the voyage was thought to be a great financial risk.

After so long a series of delays the season became too far advanced for a venture that year. In the meantime, for reasons unsatisfactory to Ledyard, Morris abruptly sent him word that his support was withdrawn. Some slight compensation for bitter disappointment was afforded, however, by the letters of introduction from Morris to a leading mercantile firm in France—written and given to Ledyard with Morris's regrets and best wishes.

How close John Ledyard's plans came to early realization in America can only be imagined. His failure can be explained by several reasons, or more likely by a combination of all of them. In the first place, the idea of a trip around the Horn to an unknown coast, involving a new medium of trade and untold risks, was in itself a revolutionary idea to merchants familiar with the

West Indies and European trade. In the early post-Revolutionary years, shipping and credit were limited to fairly familiar lines of commerce. Responsible for at least one failure in getting a ship was the personality of Ledyard himself. His unlimited optimism, his eloquent tongue, and his warm personality repelled naturally cautious, calculating ship masters.[32]

There seems to be little doubt that John Ledyard was the first American to talk of the advantages of the Northwest fur trade. If his words are to be trusted, he attested to the originality of his ideas after his interview with Robert Morris, when he enthusiastically boasted, "I take the lead in the greatest commercial enterprise that has ever been embarked upon in this country, and one of the first moment as it respects the trade of America."[33]

The influence of John Ledyard's ideas upon the thinking of East Coast merchants is as unmistakable as it is impossible to trace. At any rate, within three years from the time of Ledyard's first trip to Boston to charter a ship, the initial fur voyage had been embarked upon. Possibly the personal impression left by Ledyard and the impact of his journal of Cook's voyage, in which he sketched the possible structure of the fur trade, tended to crystalize in action during the months after his departure from America. Perhaps the arrival in America of other printed journals of Cook's voyage, written by Englishmen in official positions, also helped overcome some negative impressions left by Ledyard's unfortunate facility for exaggerating and romanticizing trade possibilities. The first voyage under Captain Kendrick was financed by gentlemen who had either seen or heard of Ledyard. The plans for the voyage correspond very closely to Ledyard's idea of how an expedition should be organized. It may well be that the influence of his ideas left behind when he departed for France was as great a contribution to American Pacific expansion as was his influence on Thomas Jefferson. On this point, Jared Sparks concluded that "he may justly be considered the first projector of this branch of commerce."[34]

---
[32]Sparks, *Life of John Ledyard* (Boston, 1855), p. 180.
[33]*Ibid.*, p. 173.
[34]Sparks, *op. cit.*, p. 182.

Important to the development of official policy in the Pacific was the meeting of Ledyard with Jefferson in Paris. As previously mentioned, when Ledyard left America for Europe he carried with him letters of introduction to a commercial house in L'-Orient, France. After a few delays and a leisurely trip via Cadiz, Ledyard was accepted by the merchants of the House of Amboy in L'Orient. His negotiations and near successes with them are not a part of the story of the American fur trade. However, it was in 1786 while Ledyard was waiting for interviews with the French merchants that he and Jefferson met and he unfolded his plans for the Northwest Coast trade.

Over a period of several months Ledyard and Jefferson met on numerous social occasions in Paris. The American minister immediately embraced Ledyard's ideas and quizzed him eagerly about all phases of the Northwest Coast of America. He wanted to know all Ledyard knew about the Indians, the forests, river courses, natural resources, and the fur supply.[35]

The reports of John Ledyard's meetings with the American minister indicate that Jefferson's early interest in the Northwest was intensified and stimulated by his contacts with the American traveler. Whether or not Jefferson conceived of an overland expedition to the coast as a direct result of Ledyard's enthusiasm is not too clear. It is known however, that, after Ledyard's plans with the L'Orient firm fell through, Mr. Jefferson suggested to him that he make a trek across Asia and an overseas trip to Russian America.[36]

Ledyard grasped this idea immediately. The plan, developed by the two of them, was an almost exact reversal of the actual Lewis and Clark Expedition of some fifteen years later. Ledyard was to get to Nootka by way of the Russian-American Coast of Alaska. From there they planned that he should follow the "River of the West" to its headwaters and then, by an easy step, proceed to the headwaters of the Missouri River, which Jefferson believed to be in close proximity; thence down to the Mississippi and overland to the newly formed United States of America.

---

[35]Munford, *op. cit.*, p. 194.
[36]*Ibid.*, p. 202.

Even though Jefferson had some previous interest in the unknown area, Ledyard's plans certainly stimulated him and clarified his thinking on the subject of America's future there. Jared Sparks, Ledyard's first biographer, concluded that Jefferson readily accepted the ideas of John Ledyard which "were deeply impressed upon the mind of Jefferson, and in them originated the journey of Lewis and Clark overland to the Pacific Ocean twenty years afterward, which was projected by him and prosecuted under his auspices."[37]

MARITIME INFLUENCES ON THE LEWIS AND CLARK EXPEDITION

The smooth link between the theories of John Ledyard and Jefferson's initiative in launching an overland exploring expedition is obvious. Yet, according to the theories of Western historians, we would be led to believe that there was no essential difference betwen the old Midwest frontier of 1805 and the frontier of the new Northwest in the 1840's. The difference is fundamental, however, when the early official interest in the area is taken in consideration. The record of early seaward approaches to the Northwest Coast, sketched previously, strongly supports the position that maritime influences were of central importance as the historic forces that shaped official policy toward the Northwest.

Jefferson's Pacific Ocean Policy. Early policy in relation to the Northwest Coast was reflected in the preliminary negotiations for the purchase of Louisiana.[38] When the area was transferred to France, Jefferson deemed it desirable, in the event of a French refusal to sell, to form a military alliance with England in order to put pressure on France. In this way it was hoped that both ends of the Mississippi would be made fairly secure. Achieving this security was a crucial national aim in 1803. For the purpose of these negotiations, Messrs. Monroe and Livingston were sent to London. They were authorized, in return for an

---
[37]Sparks, *op. cit.*, p. 202.
[38]Schafer, *op. cit.*, p. 45.

The Seaborne Frontier on the Northwest Coast

American military alliance, to object to British expansion into the area west of the headwaters of the Mississippi. To support this objection, they were to use three principal arguments:[39] (1) the desire of the United States to spread to the Mississippi River, (2) the uncertain claims of the British to the area west of the upper Mississippi, and (3) the attention the United States had paid to the Northwest Coast of America.

That this alliance did not materialize is not important here. It is significant because it shows an early official policy in regard to the Northwest Coast. It is evidence of the influence of maritime activity that gave the United States a weak but rather effective lever to apply to the international game of geopolitics, in regard to the Mississippi area and the mysterious "River of the West," involving the major powers of the world.

Instructions to Lewis and Clark. Even more concrete evidence of maritime influence over official Western policy is Jefferson's plan for the exploration of the new area purchased from France. The story of the overland trip of Captain Lewis and Lieutenant Clark is well known. Equally well known are the instructions of Jefferson to the two army officers, in which he stated that "the object of your mission is to explore to the Missouri River and such principal streams of it as, by its course and communication with the waters of the Pacific Ocean, may offer the most direct and practical water communication across the continent for the purpose of commerce."[40]

Obviously the president, in his instructions, used the word "commerce" in its broadest sense. In the letters written by Lewis, reporting his safe arrival in St. Louis on the return trip, it is clear that "commerce" means not only transcontinental trade but international trade between the Orient and North America. Some of Lewis's significant statements indicate the real meaning of Jefferson's basic instructions:[41]

1. He thought he had discovered the most practical route of commerce.

---

[39]*Ibid.*, p. 45.
[40]Schafer, *op. cit.*, p. 49.
[41]Stephens and Bolton, eds., *The Pacific Ocean in History* (New York, 1917), pp. 289-290.

2. A chain of fur posts could be erected along the Missouri to the Columbia—furs to be collected at the mouth for trans-shipment to China.

3. Furs could reach Canton before the British could get furs from Montreal to London.

4. Less bulky and nonperishable articles from China could come overland via the Columbia River in shorter time than by the present Cape Horn route.

5. Canadian furs could be drained off through an American entrepôt at the Columbia River mouth for trans-shipment to Canton.

The vast scope of activity suggested by these possibilities reflect the historic lure of the Orient. It was this lure of the China trade that Jefferson reawakened in the realm of official American policy, influenced by the dream of Pacific power, and that drew settlers to Oregon before its logical time, stretching the frontier line thin and indeed breaking it off with vast stretches of intervening plains and mountains.

The dream of Oriental trade and of the destiny of the Northwest Coast, which influenced Jefferson, came to light later in the government policies regarding the boundary dispute with England. It is reflected in the policies of John Quincy Adams, Andrew Jackson, and James K. Polk. It is shown in concrete form in the speeches and writings of such politicians as Thomas Hart Benton, in the explorations of Charles Wilkes and William Slacum, in the sacrifices and agitations of the Yankee skippers and of adventurers such as Jackson Hall Kelley, Nathaniel Wyeth, and Asa Whitney. Governmental policies, growing out of the work of such men, developed from Jefferson's hypothesis engendered by the vision of John Ledyard.

EARLY TREATY NEGOTIATIONS

The theme struck by Jefferson in his policy toward the security of the Northwest Coast is one that can be followed rather consistently through the negotiations with England regarding the Oregon boundary dispute. Diplomatic activity and the cry of manifest destiny and of "Fifty-four Forty or Fight" are familiar stories told in most American history textbooks and general histories of the West. The influence of maritime activity and the desire to control the Pacific trade is an aspect of the long period of negotiations that is less well known. Maritime influence, however, can be clearly shown to be at the basis of American policy during the Oregon controversy.[42]

It is not the purpose of this discussion to become involved in the complexities of the diplomatic negotiations nor to trace exhaustively the Oregon debates through Congress during the years of 1818 to 1846. This synthesis will attempt to demonstrate the influence of maritime trade on American foreign policy as it developed during this period.

Elimination of Spanish and Russian Claims. In order to place the influence of trade in its proper setting, a brief sketch of the principal international rivalries involved in the eventual settlement is pertinent. The Northwest Coast was stabilized politically by a series of treaties among the four leading nations of the world. Very early Spain and England came into collision on the coast. By the sweeping provisions of the Treaty of Tordesilla (1492), an island enclosing the body of water later called Puget Sound fell under the claims of Spain. This island, named Vancouver by Captain Cook, soon became the scene of British fishing and trading activities. In the same year that George Washington took over the reins of government, British traders began building temporary shacks on Vancouver Island around the shores of Nootka Sound.[43] To the Spanish, these encroachments had ominous similarity to British activities on the Mosquito Coast of Honduras. Spain took positive action to check expansion. In 1790 the news reached London of the destruction of the Nootka settlements and the capture of English ships and men. William Pitt demanded release and indemnity. These demands were accompanied by preparations for war with Spain, which had no choice

---

[42]Bell, *Opening a Highway to the Pacific, 1838-1846* (New York, Columbia University Press, 1921), p. 182. Bell observes in his conclusions that it was maritime influence that set official policy, before the agrarian and missionary impact could be felt.

[43]Bemis, ed., *American Secretaries of State and Their Diplomacy* (New York, 1928), vol. 2, p. 39.

but to back down and capitulate.[44] The significant part of the Anglo-Spanish agreement stated the land above the northern boundary of California was a "vacant area" that was agreed to be open for colonization.

The Nootka Sound agreement, in 1790, had important consequences for the future of American expansion. It came shortly after the first American seaward contact with the coast and served to forestall further Spanish dominance over the area. It was one step toward the final stage, in which England and the United States were the sole competitors for the Oregon country.

Another step in the elimination of Spanish claims to the Northwest Coast occurred in connection with the 1819 treaty with Spain over the Florida annexation. John Quincy Adams, who conducted the negotiations, was not only interested in securing Texas but was anxious to get Spain to cede her claims to the Oregon country.[45] Although the desire for Texas was unrealized by this treaty, Florida was ceded to the United States, Spanish claims to Oregon were abandoned, and the northern boundary of California was established along the latitude of forty-two degrees north.[46]

Russian claims to the area remained to be cleared. This was done by a treaty between the United States and Russia in 1824 and between England and Russia in the following year. The 1824 treaty with Russia grew out of strained relations resulting from an imperial ukase issued years before, interdicting all American trade in Russian America. Further discussion will bring out the maritime forces at play in this negotiation and the far-reaching consequences concerning American foreign policy. Suffice it to say that by the treaty of 1824 the latitude of 54°40' was recognized to be the southern boundary of Russian America. Russia abandoned her claims to Oregon and gave up the right to extend settlement below the stated latitude boundary. This negotiation further stabilized the frontiers of Northwestern America by removing the fear of Russian expansion. It left the area between

---

[44]Van Alstyne, *American Diplomacy in Action* (Stanford, 1944), p. 479.
[45]*Ibid.*
[46]Winther, *op. cit.*, p. 140.

latitude 42° north and 54°40′ north open to British and American competition. It laid the groundwork, under the doctrine of free commerce and the noncolonization principle of Adams and Monroe, for an eventual settlement between Britain and the United States in 1846.[47]

Beginning of Joint Occupation. The Oregon dispute troubled British-American relations intermittently from 1818 to 1846. Britain made no official move to secure the area for the empire. In compliance with the Treaty of Ghent, Astoria (renamed "Fort George" when captured by England during the war) was restored to American control. This was done in accordance with a general provision in the treaty calling for the return of all areas and property seized in the course of the war. During the negotiations, Lord Castlereagh was careful to point out that the restoration of Astoria did not mean that Britain was abandoning her claims to the Columbia River.[48]

The establishment of Astoria in 1811 was one of the strong American arguments for claiming that river. During the war, John Jacob Astor, reporting to the government on the state of his fur business in the Pacific, declared that Astoria could have been held if an American naval vessel had been on the scene in 1813. During the negotiations at Ghent, one of Astor's representatives was present in the corridors, eager for news, and reminded the American commissioners that Astor could reopen the Pacific branch of his fur empire if Astoria were restored. It is probably not too much to say that it was "doubtless due to Astor's warnings"[49] that, in 1814, the peace commissioners were instructed to keep the Columbia River mouth in mind. Conflicting claims over the area betwen 42° north and 54°40′ north were not pushed vigorously at the time. A modus vivendi was reached by the joint occupancy treaty signed between the United States and Britain in 1818.

Although no official British move for the occupation of the disputed land was made after 1818, the activities of the Northwest

---

[47]Bemis, *op. cit.*, vol. 4, p. 90; Goodwin, *op. cit.*, pp. 203-204.
[48]Bemis, *op. cit.*, vol. 4, p. 87.
[49]Schafer, *op. cit.*, p. 88.

Fur Company served official purposes. Foreign Minister Canning saw it as an instrument of official policy whereby the whole area could be made a vital link in the Pacific trade as well as a valuable area for colonization and development of the inland fur trade.[50] Official American policy was more clear cut. Lacking an active commercial monopoly on the ground corresponding to the Hudson's Bay Company, the United States based her claims upon the exploration of Lewis and Clark; on the Treaty of Ghent restoring Astoria and recognizing American rights in Oregon; and on the treaties with Spain (1819), Russia (1824), and Great Britain (1818).

As the Oregon dispute developed during the years between 1818 and 1846, it became evident that the issue was a clear-cut one of maritime rivalry.[51] Our maritime activity up to 1818 had convinced statesmen like John Quincy Adams and James Monroe that America could no longer afford to let another maritime power expand and fill up the vacant areas of the Northwest Coast. The American maritime stake in the Oregon territory served to introduce the question to the public mind as a vital link in the Oriental trade. For a time it was considered as the first foothold on an incipient maritime empire and as a strategic spot on the Pacific rim rather than a potential immigrant's paradise.[52]

The fact that full realization of a maritime empire did not materialize is irrelevant in terms of evaluating the motives and historic forces that guided American policy in the Northwest. From 1820 to 1846 Oregon bills were introduced from time to time. An exploratory expedition was sent to examine Oregon. Debates were held on the floors of both Houses. Books were written and magazine articles flooded the press to support the pros and cons of Oregon occupation. In all of these activities, the influence of maritime trade was strongly felt—both as antecedents of policy and to support the plea for fulfillment of unrealized possibilities of the Pacific trade.

---

[50]Winther, *op. cit.*, p. 141.
[51]*See also* pp. 41-46.
[52]Van Alstyne, *op. cit.*, p. 492.

NORTHWEST BOUNDARY NEGOTIATIONS AND CONGRESSIONAL ACTION

The House of Representatives, led by Floyd of Virginia, first took up the discussion of Oregon in 1820. It was not until two years later that he got his first hearing on the floor. To support an early American occupation of the Northwest Coast, he put forth arguments that hinged upon the importance of sea trade.
1. importance of the Colombia River to commerce
2. English competition in the fur trade
3. importance of a Columbia port for whalers
4. encouragement of Oriental trade
5. development of cross-country steamboat lines to exchange China trade via Saint Louis[53]

Floyd's bill was defeated by the arguments of men like Representative Baylies of Massachusetts, who favored the bill in theory but thought the scheme a bit too premature and visionary for practical men.

Interest of a Congressional Group. Although Floyd's bill was defeated in 1822, it is worthwhile to pause in the discussion of the Oregon debates and consider one statement quoted from his testimony in support of Oregon occupation. In reiterating the advantages of its occupation listed above, Floyd made the statement that

> ... the settlement of Oregon is to open up a mine of wealth to the shipping interests and the Western country. It consists principally of things which will purchase the manufactures and products of China at a better profit than gold and silver—it will yield a profit producing more wealth to the nation than all the shipments which have ever, in any one year, been made to Canton from the United States.[54]

This was grandiose prediction, to be sure, but prediction based on what Floyd considered sound foundations of fact. How Floyd

---
[53]Schafer, *op. cit.*, p. 96; Goodwin, *op. cit.*, p. 275.
[54]Bancroft, *Northwest Coast;* vol. 2, p. 419, n. 4, citing *Annals of Congress,* 17th Congress, 2nd session, p. 398.

got his information and what stimulated his interest is clear evidence of maritime influence on developing policy toward Western expansion. An examination of this link will be appropriate here.

Thomas Hart Benton, before being elected to the Senate, had been editor of the *Saint Louis Inquirer*. He had used the editorial columns of his paper to promote Western interests. In 1819 he became interested in the Oregon question, which, by his own admission, shows another connection with John Ledyard and Thomas Jefferson:

> All that I myself have either said or written on the subject (Oregon) from the year 1819, when I first took it up, down to the present day, when I still contend for it, is nothing but the fruit of the seed planted in my mind by the philosophical hand of Mr. Jefferson.[55]

With this vision of Oregon, Benton came to Washington in 1820 to take his seat in the Senate. He happened to be staying in the same hotel with Congressman Floyd of Virginia, Ramsey Crooks of New York, and Russell Farnham of Massachusetts. The latter two had been in the employ of John J. Astor some five years before and had been on the ground at Astoria, participating in the attempt to establish a maritime trade between the new colony and Canton. Representative Floyd had read Benton's articles in the *Saint Louis Inquirer* and he, with the other two men who had been to the Northwest Coast, naturally fell into interested conversations on the subject.[56] Floyd became enthusiastic and Benton supported him, forming, with the assistance of Crooks and Farnham, a four-man lobby with Floyd as the spokesman.

Oregon bills continued to make almost a perennial appearance in Congress after the first one in 1822. During 1824 and 1825, the year boundary negotiations with England failed, Floyd presented another bill. Many of the same arguments he had used

---

[55]Benton, *Thirty Years View* (New York, 1854), vol. 1, p. 14.
[56]Powell, "Hall Jackson Kelley," *Oregon Historical Quarterly*, vol. 18 (1917), p. 20.

in 1822 were reiterated and elaborated. The year before a letter was sent to the House of Representatives from J. B. Prevost, who officiated at the return of Astoria by the British. In it was a detailed and rather glowing description of the advantages of the Columbia River mouth as a seaport. It pointed to the spacious bays, deep waters, and excellent anchorages.[57] This letter gave supporting evidence to Floyd's plea in 1824 for the occupation of Oregon as a step in securing the Pacific trade. Floyd not only repeated his old arguments but offered detailed information on the China trade. The financial gain from the Canton trade, he argued, would justify such a step. He briefly sketched the trade, quoting the figures of 1818 on the value of exports from China. Enormous profits would pile up, he said, from a small initial investment. Goods exported from China would bring profits twenty percent higher than similar products from around the Cape of Good Hope or from Europe. To clinch his plea for Oregon, Floyd maintained that this trade, if encouraged, would prove to be a great training school for seamen—superior to the present protected and pampered cod-fisheries of New England.[58]

This bill met the same treatment as the previous one. It showed, however, the increasing pressure in Congress for the Oregon country and the important use of maritime factors in the mustering of arguments.

British-American Negotiations. Turning now from the debates in Congress to official negotiations with England, it is evident that the case for the United States leaned heavily upon her commercial contacts in the northern Pacific waters. Stimulated by the discussion in Congress, Secretary of State John Quincy Adams instructed Minister to England Richard Rush to bring up the Oregon question. Rush was to negotiate for a boundary settlement that would include the Colombia River mouth and at least a foothold on Puget Sound. His position was based on the following arguments (1) discovery of the "River of the West" by Captain Gray in 1792; (2) priority of the Lewis and Clark expedition (1803); (3) establishment of Astoria in

---

[57]Bancroft, *op. cit.*, vol. 2, p. 421, n. 8.
[58]*Ibid.*, p. 427.

1811 and its restoration by England (1818); and (4) acquisition of the Spanish claims up to latitude 54°40′ north (1819).[59]

This first attempt at negotiations failed because of the adamant position of Foreign Minister Canning. He insisted upon free navigation of the Columbia as an outlet for the Hudson's Bay Company's furs. Gray's discovery he rejected as an unofficial and weakly substantiated event. British claims on the disputed land were as strong, he said, as American in the light of the Nootka Sound agreement, which recognized British trade rights there. With the breakdown of these negotiations, joint occupation was renewed in 1827 as the only workable solution to an insoluble problem. Between 1827 and 1837 there were no official moves in relation to the boundary dispute. It seemed as though another ten years of commercial and pioneering activity were needed to bring matters sufficiently to a head to reach a settlement.

Continued Action in Congress. In spite of the inactivity in the realm of official policy during the years between 1827 and 1837, the decade was far from quiet in regard to the Oregon territory. Floyd of Virginia presented another plea for official action to save the territory. It came out on the floor of the House in February, 1828, in the form of a "memorial from citizens of the United States," asking for land grants and government aid for settlement in Oregon.[60]

Simultaneously, on the floor of the Senate, Thomas Hart Benton made a strong plea for an Oregon bill that would secure the territory to American control. He used many of the old arguments put forth by Floyd in 1822, with a significant exception. Instead of emphasizing possibilities for vast wealth, Benton urged that Oregon should be annexed to forestall foreign powers, to gain a seaport for military and naval installations, to save the fur trade and the Indians from British exploitation, to open a route between the Mississippi Valley and the markets of the Orient, and

---

[59]Schafer, *op. cit.*, p. 102.
[60]Powell, *op. cit.*, p. 21; Goodwin, *op. cit.*, p. 277. The bill was reported in behalf of the Oregon Associations, which had been organized in Massachusetts, Ohio, and New Orleans.

The Seaborne Frontier on the Northwest Coast

to send the lights of science and religion into Eastern Asia.[61] A shift in emphasis can be detected here, reflecting a fear of foreign competition in the Pacific trade rather than hopes of unlimited wealth.

Agitation of Jackson Hall Kelley. During the period of official quiet, the individual efforts of Jackson Hall Kelley are of some significance. In the memorial presented by Floyd in 1828 the name of Kelley is mentioned, and apparently he had something to do with preparing it. His biographer, Fred W. Powell, states that it was actually his work. It is known that in the same year (1828) Kelley had organized an "American Society for Encouraging Settlement of Oregon." To facilitate his recruiting he put out a circular to all "Persons of Good Character Who Wish to Emigrate to Oregon." In it he stressed the resources of the country and the possibilities of trade in these words:

> Nature furnishes many clear indications that the mouth of this far-spreading and noble river is soon to become the commercial port of that hemisphere, the great business place of nations, interchanging the commodities and productions of Western America and the East Indies . . . Lumber, ships, timber, etc., may be sent to the western coast of South America, the islands of the Pacific; breadstuffs, furs, salmon and many articles of domestic manufacture to the East Indies.[62]

In 1830 Kelly wrote a book entitled *A Geographical Sketch Of That Part Of North America Called Oregon.* The main points elaborated upon reflected the same sentiments towards Oregon that had been expressed by Jefferson and in the proceedings of Congress during the previous years. He acknowledged Jefferson's priority of idea, called England's claims to Oregon "pretentious arrogance," and called for early American occupation and the establishment of a naval base on the Columbia River and one along Juan de Fuca Straits. He thought the latter "would be of immense importance to the protection of the whale and other fisheries, and of the fur trade; and to the general control of the

---

[61]Benton, *op. cit.,* p. 54.
[62]Kelley, "A Circular to All Persons of Good Character Who Wish to Emigrate to Oregon," *Magazine of History,* vol. 16, no. 36, pp. 6-7.

Pacific Ocean, where millions of our property, are constantly afloat."[63]

As a colonizer and promoter of grand schemes Kelley was an abject failure. He attempted an overland trek in 1832, but delays and personal difficulties resulted in loss of interest among the nine thousand families who were supposed to have signed up to go. His able agent, Nathaniel Wyeth, departed alone, however, and actually arrived in Oregon with a small band of men, most of whom became permanent settlers there. Kelley himself started for Oregon with a small group the following year. After a series of mishaps, mostly due to his own fanatical and humorless disposition, his followers all abandoned him. Kelley arrived at Vancouver in 1834, alone and penniless. His stay there was futile. He spent much of his time attempting to settle certain claims of land supposedly bought by Captain Kendrick during his early voyage. This involved fruitless arguments with officials of the Hudson's Bay Company, which developed in Kelley a paranoic suspicion and hatred of the British company.

Kelley's crusade went on after his return to the East in the form of continued writing. He turned out a series of articles about the early discoveries on the Oregon coast, including documents relating to Bulfinch's (sponsor of the first fur voyage in 1792) land transactions carried out by Captain Kendrick.

The effect of Kelley's work on official policy formation is doubtful.[64] He did contribute data needed for two Congressional reports, but his flair for exaggeration, his uncritical judgments and his unbalanced statements limited his effectiveness in official circles. Both Benton and Floyd were interested in Oregon before Kelley did any writing on the subject. Doubtless he stirred interest in the first settlers to migrate to Oregon, and his writings were the first to call attention to the feasibility of overland settlement.[65]

Although Kelley was primarily interested in influencing official

---

[63] Powell, *op. cit.*, p. 32.

[64] Bancroft, *op. cit.*, vol. 2, p. 555.

[65] Powell, *op. cit.* Conclusions from the last chapter, "That Man Kelley and His Place in History."

The Seaborne Frontier on the Northwest Coast   47

policy so that Oregon would become a home for the land pioneer, it is significant to note that his interest was originally stirred by navigators and traders.[66] Being born in the home port of Captain John Kendrick, Captain Robert Gray, William Sturgis, and the Winship brothers, it seems but natural—as told in his own words —that he should be affected by the trade of the Pacific from "the perusal of the Lewis and Clark journals, personal conferences with navigators and hunters—and had become convinced that this region must, at no remote period, become of vast importance to our government of deep general interest."[67] The work of Kelley is an illustration of the influence of the sea at work as a historic force in the process of American westward expansion. However indirect, the pioneers of the Pacific Ocean trade stimulated interest in the Northwest Coast and lured the first overland "pioneers" into the vacant hinterland.

Growth of Popular Interest. During the years of Congressional agitation and attempt at a boundary settlement with England, literature of various sorts came from the press on the subject of Oregon and the Northwest Coast. A brief cross section of the years from approximately 1820 to 1840 will indicate the general nature of this influence.

The writings of Jackson Hall Kelley have already been mentioned. His efforts were carried on by pamphleteering devices and propaganda techniques to stimulate overland migration to Oregon. Benton, writing in the *Saint Louis Intelligencer,* advocated official action in the Northwest and chiefly elaborated the schemes of Ledyard and Jefferson. In 1822, there appeared in the *North American Review* an article examining the pros and cons of the question of the Russian imperial ukase. In it the author took a moderate position, stating that the United States should claim free trade privileges in the area restricted by Russia but had no claim of sovereignty on the area above latitude 49° north. Hubert H. Bancroft thought that the article was probably

---

[66]Bancroft, *loc. cit.*
[67]To a Committee on Foreign Affairs of the House of Representatives, Report 47, 25th Congress, 3rd session, no. 101. Quoted in Powell, *op. cit.,* p. 12.

written by Captain William Sturgis of Boston.[68]

Four other articles appeared in the *North American Review* during the years 1828, 1837, and 1840. They are significant in illustrating how the question of Oregon was kept before the public eye and for showing how strong was the maritime influence in forming public and official opinion on Northwest Coast policy. In the October 1828 issue a review of John Ledyard's biography by Jared Sparks appeared. In the same issue was a long article reviewing American-British relations from the Nootka Sound controversy to the failure of a boundary settlement in 1827. Ten years later in the January 1837 issue there was a review of Washington Irving's *Astoria*. The timeliness of the book was pointed out by a quotation from the book itself, showing that joint occupancy was drawing to a close (1837) and that it was regrettable that the United States had not built a chain of forts to the Oregon country to secure the coast for the control of the Pacific trade with Canton.[69]

Again, in the January 1840 issue of the *North American Review*, an article was published sketching the history of the voyages of exploration and discovery in the Northwest. The general tenor of these four articles reflected a pro-Oregon feeling, stressing the maritime antecedents of United States' claims, and revealed an underlying Anglophobia and fear of inevitable war with England over the Northwest Coast dispute.[70]

Hunt's Merchant Magazine for April 1842 ran an article by Henry Sherman, a New York lawyer. His discussion reflected the feeling that the American claims to Oregon were superior to those of England. He reviewed the discoveries of Captain Gray and the activities of John Jacob Astor's men, comparing those precedents with the discoveries of British captains, like Meares and Van-

---

[68]Bancroft, *op. cit.*, vol 2, p. 349; Morison, *op. cit.*, p. 200. Morison mentions Sturgis as an old Northwest Coast captain who made his fortune in the trade of furs to China.

[69]Irving, *Astoria* (New York, 1893), pp. 675-676.

[70]Marshall, *The Acquisition of Oregon* (Seattle, 1911), vol. 1, p. 239. According to Marshall three of the four articles, excluding the review of Sparks' biography by Ledyard, were written by Caleb Cushing of Massachusetts. The articles were unsigned.

couver. Although the fur trade had declined in importance as compared with increased agriculture and lumbering, the maritime precedents were cited to substantiate the American claim to the Northwest Coast.

It would not be safe to say that such a sampling of articles indicated the growth of the Oregon fever in the popular mind. The periodicals and the book cited were probably not read very widely in the years they were published. They do show a consensus within a limited area, among thinking people of the day. They are an idication of how the feeling toward Oregon developed up to the 1840's and how it was based upon maritime antecedents.

The Linn Report. From 1826 to the final settlement of the boundary dispute in 1846, the influence of Pacific trade over official policy became increasingly clear. Evidence for tracing this influence is found in the report to the Senate in 1838, Caleb Cushing's report to the House of Representatives in 1839, Senator Pendleton's report in 1843, and in the arguments used during the final boundary negotiations in 1844, 1845, and 1846.

During Andrew Jackson's second administration, an attempt was made to adjust the northern boundary of Texas and extend the line of the Pacific to a point north of the Bay of San Francisco. In connection with this scheme W. A. Slacum, a purser in the United States Navy who was planning a trip to the Pacific Coast, was commissioned by Secretary of State John Forsyth to proceed to Oregon. His orders, which were in the form of a letter from Secretary of State Forsyth, requested him to proceed up the "Oregon River" and obtain all possible information and statistics as to population, natural resources, and trade.[71]

Slacum arrived at the mouth of the Columbia late in 1836 and traveled up the valley visiting settlements and feeling out opinion on the justice of American claims to the area. A detailed chart of the Columbia River was also made.[72] The report was submitted to Congress in December, 1837. In it Slacum stoutly held that the United States should insist upon a boundary settle-

---

[71]*Senate Executive Documents,* No. 24, 25th Congress, 3rd session, p. 3.
[72]Schafer, *op. cit.,* p. 128.

ment that would include a seaward outlet on Puget Sound.[73]

Supporting this conclusion, he painted a dark picture of the dangers of the Columbia River bar and stressed the importance of a port on Puget Sound as a rest and supply base for whaling vessels.[74] The monopolistic practices of the Hudson's Bay Company were described in some detail. Specific examples of restrictive practices were cited.[75] He stressed the disadvantages of American vessels having to pay duties to Hudson's Bay officials in "American waters"; how the Indians often refused to sell furs to American ships for fear of the retaliation of the Hudson's Bay agents; and the obstructionism of the Hudson's Bay Company in preventing an American ship from obtaining a full cargo of salmon in the Columbia River.

Two months after Slacum's report had been submitted, the Senate unanimously approved a motion asking the Secretary of War to furnish them with all possible information on the Oregon country.[76] In June, 1838, a committee in the Senate was formed to consider a bill which would authorize the president to establish a claim of military posts into Oregon. Senator Linn of Missouri was the chairman of this committee. The Linn report of 1838 depended heavily upon what had already been said about Oregon and upon the maritime antecedents along the coast. Some of the information was supplied by Jackson Hall Kelley. Mention was made of the early explorations of Drake, Cook, Vancouver, and Gray. Monroe's statements concerning the Columbia River were quoted and statistics on trade were included.[77]

Most of the new evidence supporting United States occupation of Oregon was documented by Slacum's report of 1838. His description of the harbors and rivers between San Francisco and the Columbia River was quoted at length. Details of his discussion of the threat of the Hudson's Bay company were used to point out the disastrous results of war with England if Oregon

---

[73]*Ibid.*
[74]*Senate Documents*, No. 24, 25th Congress, 2nd Session, pp. 14-17.
[75]*Ibid.*, p. 9.
[76]Marshall, *op. cit.*, p. 199. February 13, 1838.
[77]*Senate Documents*, No. 470, 25th Congress, 2nd session, pp. 1-6.

The Seaborne Frontier on the Northwest Coast

were not secure. The Sandwich Islands (Hawaii), the report states, would most certainly fall to the British in the event of war. Without the control of the Columbia River, the United States would be without a Pacific base.[78] Another interesting enclosure of the Linn report was an affidavit from Charles Bulfinch, who had helped finance the first fur voyage to the Northwest Coast in 1792. Bulfinch had located the old log book of Captain Gray's ship and had copied for the affidavit extracts of the log, describing the entrance of the ship *Columbia* into the river that received its name.[79]

The Cushing Report. In the following year (1839) Caleb Cushing, as chairman of the Foreign Relations Committee of the House, submitted a report on Oregon corresponding to the Linn report in the Senate. It covered much of the same material, citing the precedents of Monroe and Adams, with quotations from Vattel, Judge Kent, and Judge Story. The ensuing claims to Oregon were examined in the light of precedents in international practice as to the relationship of discovery to the right of occupation. The practices of the Hudson's Bay Company were examined and found to be injurious to American interests in the Columbia River Valley.[80] Some additional information was included in the appendix of the report. More details of the discoveries of Spain, England, and America were brought out—such as Bulfinch's land purchases near the Columbia River mouth.[81]

A supplementary report was submitted on February 16, 1839, for the purpose of inquiring into the feasibility of building a military post at the Columbia River mouth. Slacum's report, with the map of Oregon and his chart of the river, was part of this supplement. Nathaniel Wyeth's memoir concerning the soil, geography, agricultural resources, and possibilities for trade also made up a pertinent part. Some naval information was furnished by Kelley. Upon Cushing's request for a memorandum, Kelley

---

[78]*Ibid.*, p. 7.
[79]*Ibid.*, p. 20.
[80]*House Reports*, 25th Congress, 2nd session, vol. 1, p. 21.
[81]*Ibid.*, Appendix.

sent an able document in which he described details of Oregon's geography, Indian life, and soil fertility.[82] On the subject of harbors, Kelley presented detailed information concerning natural facilities for defense and the navigational soundings of Gray's Harbor, Chinook Harbor, Astor Harbor, and Merriwether Bay.[83]

The Pendleton Report. The final report submitted in Congress in 1843 was, by far, the most voluminous and scholarly of all. It is known as the second report of Representative Pendleton of Ohio, who headed the Military Affairs Committee. The report accompanied a bill proposing the building of a chain of forts from Council Bluffs, Iowa, to the Pacific Ocean. Everything that had been said in his previous report in relation to trade influence was included in the final one. The second Pendleton report tended to be a cumulative and summary document of all arguments supporting Oregon occupation.

Pendleton and his associates made a complete review of the various claims to the Northwest Coast by an examination of treaty provisions. A discussion of the early discoveries presented more detail than had appeared in previous reports. For example, a quotation from Vancouver's journal was included to prove that Gray's entrance to the Columbia River was an original discovery.[84] Dates were compared to establish the priority of American claims on the Columbia River mouth. A letter from a Captain Hickey, of a British man-of-war, was quoted as evidence that Astoria had been returned to American control according to the terms of the Treaty of Ghent.[85]

The significance of the Astoria settlement was reviewed at some length. Unfamiliar information about the extent of the activities of Astor's enterprise was presented. Four obscure fur posts in the Columbia River were listed and shown to be part of the Astoria settlement. Pendleton's committee summarized the

---

[82]Powell, *op. cit.*, Appendix p. 161.

[83]*House Reports*, 25th Congress, 3rd session, vol. 1, p. 56 of Supplement.

[84]*Report of Committee of the House of Representatives*, No. 31, 27th Congress, 3rd Session, p. 14.

[85]*Ibid.*, p. 19.

The Seaborne Frontier on the Northwest Coast 53

importance of the enterprise in these words:

> The inchoate title of the United States and the exploration of Lewis and Clark was perfected by the actual settlement and occupation by Astor and his associates.[86]

Abridgements of the reports of Slacum, Kelley, Wyeth, Greenhow, and Wilkes were compared with their statements concerning trade, agriculture, and climatic conditions.[87] All seemed to be in general agreement on the advisability of occupying Oregon. A statistical chart, showing the number of ships, tonnage, value of cargo, and number of seamen arriving and departing from Honolulu from 1839 to 1841, was used as evidence to show the importance of the Hawaiian Islands to the United States Pacific trade. In the event of war with England, the Hawaiian trade would be wiped out, in which case it was held that a "depot at the mouth of the Columbia River or in the vicinity would become indispensable to the prosecution of our large and valuable trade in the Pacific."[88]

A chart on the value of the whale fishery from 1838 to 1840 and statistics on the value of fur exports from Canton from 1821 to 1840 were used as evidence to show the restrictive nature of the Hudson's Bay monopoly.[89] Further evidence against the Hudson's Bay Company was mustered by the printing of two letters in the report—one from Captain Spaulding of the vessel *Louisanne*, written in 1841; the other from Henry A. Pierce of Boston,

---

[86]*Ibid.*, p. 22.

[87]Marshall, *op. cit.*, p. 299. Pendleton's Committee requested the Senate to turn over to them the report of Lt. Wilkes, who had just returned from his Pacific expedition. It contained a significant statement from Wilkes, which became part of the Pendleton report: "'No part of the world affords finer inland sounds, or a greater number of harbors than can be found here, capable of receiving the largest class of vessels, and without danger in them that is not visible. From the rise and fall of the tides all facilities are afforded for the erection of works for a great maritime nation."

[88]*Report of Committee of House of Representatives*, No. 31, 27th Congress, 3rd Session, p. 36.

[89]*Ibid.*, p. 41. Direct trade in furs declined from $142,399 in 1821 to $2,368 in 1840.

a merchant engaging heavily in the China trade. Both letters gave accounts of the ominous, expansive plans of the Hudson's Bay Company, describing branch offices in Honolulu and plans for driving American trade from California and the Northwest Coast.[90]

Appraisal of Congressional Action. During the years covered by the three reports of Linn, Cushing, and Pendleton very little actual progress was made in settling the boundary dispute or in agreeing upon a policy regarding the occupation of Oregon. The fear of war with Britain and the remoteness of the region acted to check any premature action on the part of Congress, in spite of the enormous amount of documentary material proving the importance of Oregon in controlling Pacific trade.

It is evident that the Congressional reports did contribute to the formation of Oregon policy. They presented information in official form that committed the United States unequivocally to a boundary that would insure a foothold on Puget Sound.[91] The debates in Congress during the third session of 1842 and 1843 clearly show the influence of Pacific trade on the development of policy. Fear of the Hudson's Bay monopoly, a need for military establishments, and Indian policy were themes of the addresses in Congress. All of these aspects of the Oregon problem were described in detail in the reports previously discussed.

During the 1843 debates Senator Linn, in arguing for occupation of Oregon, quoted from the Pendleton report of the same year.[92] The letter he had received from Henry A. Pierce in 1841 was quoted to demonstrate the ominous expansion of the Hudson's Bay Company.[93] Statistical data from Pendleton's report

---

[90]*Ibid.*, p. 56. The letter from Pierce was written to Senator Linn in 1842.

[91]Marshall, *op. cit.*, p. 201.

[92]*Congressional Globe,* 27th Congress, 3rd Session, appendix, vol. 12, p. 150.

[93]Bennett, "Early Relations of the Sandwich Islands to the Old Oregon Territory," *Washington Historical Quarterly,* vol. 4, p. 126. According to Pierce's letter, the Hudson's Bay Company was making a try for the control of Oregon, Mexican California, and the Sandwich Islands. They had, he stated, by 1842 established branch offices in San Francisco and Honolulu and had contemplated others.

showing the decline of the fur trade was also used to support this argument. Linn cited Wilkes's report, too, for further support of the importance of Oregon occupation.[94] Senator Morehead, during the same session, mustered the familiar arguments in favor of occupation of Oregon. He cited extracts from Slacum's report of 1837 to emphasize the importance of Puget Sound in strengthening American control over Pacific trade and forestalling further expansion by the English monopoly.[95]

Another indication of the influence of the desire for Pacific trade upon the official policy was the changing nature of Congressional debates from the time of Senator Pendleton's report to 1846. As late as 1843 the arguments supporting Oregon occupation mustered all the available evidence to show the value of Oregon as a foothold in the Pacific. This involved, as was indicated, a strong Anglophobia as well as a specific fear of English expansion in the Pacific. Evidence of the importance of trade and the threat of Great Britain were used to refute the arguments of men who considered Oregon and the Northwest Coast as an area too remote and immature to warrant the extension of federal authority. By 1846 the debates hinged around the placement of the boundary.[96] The majority of the members of Congress were convinced by that time of the desirability of occupying the Northwest Coast and Oregon. Apparently no important antecedents of trade contacts needed to be brought up.

In the agitation for official action on the Northwest Coast from the beginning of 1818 to at least 1843, maritime activity was the dominant force serving to support policy formation. Though the volume of American trade with the coast was small after 1812, maritime activity was brisk in California, the Hawaiian Islands, and China. Oregon policy was based mainly on maritime antecedents and the hope for unrealized possibilities of trade between China and the coast. Provisional government was not extended to Oregon until 1847, but it is safe to say that American

---

[94]*Congressional Globe*, 27th Congress, 3rd session, appendix, vol. 12, p. 152.
[95]*Ibid.*, p. 230.
[96]Benton, *op. cit.*, vol. 2, ch. 157.

policy was well established by 1843, based on two main points: (1) the boundary should be run west in such a way as to include an American outlet on Puget Sound; and (2) the Columbia River must be restricted to free navigation in order to secure the Columbia Valley to American control and check the growth of the Hudson's Bay Company.

These points had been reiterated time and again and appeared in the official reports at a time when there were fewer than two thousand Americans settled in the Oregon country. The policy, then, was not based originally upon the task of making the country an immigrant's paradise, but rather of securing a strategic point on the Pacific and providing a link in the China trade.[97]

Settlement of the Boundary Dispute. The final boundary negotiations with England illustrate still further the strength of maritime antecedents in supporting the American claims to a share of the Northwest Coast. Richard Pakenham was sent over from England in 1844 to attempt a final boundary settlement. The old arguments of 1818 and 1827 were brought up again by both sides, but by 1844 a new and more persuasive one could be used by Secretary of State John C. Calhoun:

> Our well-founded claim grounded on contiguity has been greatly strengthened (since 1818) by the rapid advance of our population towards the territory . . . an emigration established at not less than 1,000 during 1843 and 1,500 during the present year (1844) has flowed into it.[98]

Population growth in Oregon became a strong talking point in the final decision on the 49° of north latitude as the boundary,

---

[97]Bell, *op. cit.*, appendix, pp. 199-200. Bell, in connection with the Whitman-saved-Oregon myth, stated that, "It would be a profitless task to prove the falsity of these assumptions, . . . to point out that the first hand information given by Commander Wilkes of the exploring expedition was of more importance than any given by the missionaries, and that the boundary adjustments were not determined by the presence of settlers. . . . All this was as obvious and well known then as today . . . Unfortunately, it is not too well known even now. . . ." (1921).

[98]Schafer, *op. cit.*, p. 181.

The Seaborne Frontier on the Northwest Coast

but for proof of American claims to the Columbia River Valley, the old claims resulting from Pacific trade activities were recalled. Calhoun, writing to Pakenham in September, 1844, stated that:

> Our claim to the portion of the territory drained by the Columbia River may be divided into those we have in our proper right and those we have derived from France and Spain. We ground the former, as against Great Britain, on priority of discovery, and priority of exploration and settlement. We rest our claim to discovery, as against her, on that of Captain Gray, a citizen of the United States, who, in the ship *Columbia* of Boston, passed its bar and anchored in the river, ten miles above its mouth, on the eleventh of May, 1792; and who, afterwards, sailed up the river twelve or fifteen miles, and left it on the twentieth of the same month, calling it "Columbia," after his ship, which name it still remains.[99]

The Lewis and Clark expedition was cited as a basis for priority of claims of discovery. Claims of France, ceded by the Louisiana treaty, and claims of Spain, ceded by the Florida treaty, were mentioned to prove that the United States had acquired the titles of those two countries on the Northwest Coast.[100]

While negotiations were pending, James K. Polk, was elected to carry out the rallying cry of "Fifty-four Forty or Fight." After he was inaugurated he showed little interest in supporting the extreme claims to the 54°40′ latitude boundary of the Oregon territory. His first annual message to Congress, December 2, 1845, officially recorded the Oregon policy that he was to pursue. The message asked that he be authorized to establish a line of military posts to Oregon, to establish an Indian Agency, and to establish an overland mail to receive nautical intelligence.[101] Recommending that joint occupancy be terminated, Polk reaffirmed the principles of President Monroe (John Quincy Adams, actually) and applied it to the territory between the 49th parallel

---

[99]*House Executive Documents*, No. 2, 29th Congress, 1st session, pp. 146-153. Quoted in Bartlett, *Records of American Diplomacy*, p. 226.
[100]Bartlett, *op. cit.*, p. 227.
[101]*Congressional Globe*, 29th Congress, 1st session, appendix, p. 3.

and the mouth of the Columbia River. In his message he stated:

> Existing rights of every European nation should be respected, but it is due alike to our safety and our interests, that the efficient protection of our laws should be distinctly announced to the world as our settled policy that no further European colony or domination shall, without consent, be planted or established on any part of the North American continent.[102]

This was a vague statement in regard to the Northwest, but apparently it was clear that Polk meant that the territory south of the 49th parallel should be closed to further foreign expansion. When the treaty arrived from England in 1846, Polk passed it quietly on to the Senate without a single remark. The cry of "Fifty-four Forty or Fight" was quickly silenced and the treaty placing the boundary along the 49th parallel was approved.

The acceptance of the compromise line of 49° north was due, in part, to the position taken in Congress by moderate men like Benton and Calhoun. They were affected very little by the extreme demands of the "fifty-four, forty line," but judged the treaty on its merits as based on sound historical antecedents.[103]

President Polk, on the other hand, might have been persuaded to accept the compromise line in 1846 because of disquieting letters from Minister McLane in London. McLane's letters to the President told of extensive naval preparations going on in England after Polk's bold message to Congress in December, 1845.[104] At any rate, McLane received instructions to make clear to the British that a peaceful settlement was still possible. This was soon followed by the arrival of the treaty from England, which Polk transmitted to Congress. The boundary line of 49° north latitude, thus established, was actually the only sound one that could have any substance in fact based on settlement or by maritime antecedents of exploration and trade.

---

[102]*Ibid.*, p. 4.

[103]Van Alstyne, *American Diplomacy in Action*, p. 502; Goodwin, *op. cit.*, p. 389.

[104]Pratt, "James K. Polk and John Bull," *Canadian Historical Review*, vol. 24, p. 345.

RUSSIAN-AMERICAN CONTACTS

In 1728 Vitus Bering discovered and explored the strait dividing Asia and the North American continent. The American continent was occupied from the East after 1740 by individual Russian fur hunters.[105] They spread down in haphazard fashion and carried on an exploitive and opportunistic trade along the Aleutian chain. In the last year of the eighteenth century, the disorganized efforts of the Russian trappers were recognized by the imperial Russian government. The Russian-American Fur Company was formed in 1799.

The governor of Russian America from 1790 to 1818 was Alexander Baranov, an aggressive and hard-dealing Russian, who was ambitious for the future of Russian expansion in America and for the profits of the Russian-American Company. His term in office marked the most active period of Russian operation in Alaska and the Aleutian Islands.[106]

It was not long after the first appearance of American ships on the Northwest Coast that they were touching at the ports of Sitka and New Archangel. The first contact, in 1803, was made by the Boston vessel *O'Cain*, commanded by a Captain O'Cain. Baranov's colony, due to the indifference of the Russian government, was continually short of shipping and food supplies. To fill this need, Baranov was glad to make a deal with Captain O'Cain to return to the Northwest Coast and California for a load of furs.[107] Baranov furnished Aleut Indian hunters and O'Cain furnished the ship. The catch was to be returned to New Archangel, where it was to be split. The arrangements apparently worked to their mutual advantage, for the *O'Cain* is recorded to have been chartered again in 1807 for the same purposes, and again in 1809 and 1810 for fur hunts to the Northwest Coast and California.[108] Other American ships were engaged similarly in the Russian fur trade. In 1810 the *Albatross*, owned

---
[105]Winther, *The Great Northwest* (Princeton University Press, 1946), p. 82.
[106]Dulles, *China and America* (Princeton University Press, 1946), p. 82.
[107]Chevigny, *Lord of Alaska* (New York, 1942), p. 21.
[108]Bancroft, *History of the Northwest Coast* (San Francisco, 1884).

by the Winship brothers of Boston, was supplying Russian America with furs under charter.[109]

During the brief operations of John Jacob Astor's ships in the Pacific, there were considerably more Russian-American contacts. It was Astor's aim to monopolize the maritime phase of the fur trade and to devise a scheme with Baranov whereby the Russian-American and the Pacific Fur Companies would be in virtual control of the fur supply of the Pacific.[110]

Although Baranov was too wary to make a formal agreement, Astor's ships did some business with his fur posts. The *Enterprise* is recorded to have sold $23,883 worth of goods to Russian America in 1809. Astor's other ships, the *Pedler* and *Foster*, were supposed to have traded between the Russian settlements. The *Enterprise* freighted furs to Canton and the *Pedler* took supplies to Fort Ross in California.[111]

Basis of the Non-Colonization Principle. These early haphazard contacts appeared to be the beginning of a profitable and friendly relationship. As the trade developed, however, the converse proved to be true. The inception of the maritime fur trade caused a shift in the structure of commerce. Originally the Russian company had shipped its furs eastward along the Aleutian chain to be transshipped by land into China by way of the Siberian border towns of Kiakhta and Irkutsk.[112] When the maritime trade started, ships began calling more frequently at Sitka in the Aleutians. The result was that American traders could ship the Russian furs more expeditiously by sea to Canton, thereby underselling the furs that arrived by the devious route the Russians were obliged to use. Another feature obnoxious to the Russians was the American's ability to trade for the furs at the Aleutian posts ridiculously cheap articles such as old Revolutionary muskets, defective flour, and salt beef—all vitally needed in the barren islands.[113]

---

[109]*Ibid.*

[110]Irving, *Astoria* (Putnams [Hudson Edition] 1893), p. 502.

[111]Howay, "An Outline Sketch of the Maritime Fur Trade," *Canadian Historical Report of Annual Meeting* (Ottawa, 1932), pp. 5-14.

[112]Chevigny, *op. cit.*, p. 16.

[113]*Ibid.*, p. 154.

The Seaborne Frontier on the Northwest Coast

Out of the difficult position in which the Russian-American Company found itself, came the well-known imperial ukase of 1821. By its provisions, all foreign commerce was restricted in the North Pacific holdings of Russia. The pertinent excerpts are quoted to indicate its sweeping provisions and its significance to American trade:

> The pursuit of commerce, whaling and fishery, and of all other industries on all islands, posts and gulfs including the whole northwest coast of America, beginning from Bering Straits to 51 degrees north latitude, also from the Aleutian Islands to the eastern coast of Siberia as well as along the Kurile Islands from Berings Straits to the South Cape of the Island of Arup, viz. to the 45 degree 50 minute north latitude, is exclusively granted to Russian subjects . . . All transgressors' vessels are subject to confiscation along with the whole cargo.[114]

Both England and the United States objected strongly. Meanwhile, Russia took no steps to enforce the ukase. Although the United States and Britain preferred to pursue independent policies, both took substantially the same position. The arguments presented by John Quincy Adams contain some interesting statements of American policy in regard to the Oregon country. He wrote to Henry Middleton, minister to St. Petersburg, in July, 1823, stating the American position: "The right of the United States from 42° to 49° on the Pacific Ocean we consider as unquestionable."[115] He enumerated the United States' claims established by Captain Gray's discovery, the Lewis and Clark Expedition, and the settlement of Astoria. Included in the note was a statement that was to receive much elaboration in subsequent years: "This territory is to the United States of an importance which no possession in North America can be to any European nation."[116]

We can recall that Adams was the architect of the Florida treaty of 1819, in which he was careful to acquire the Spanish

---

[114]Bartlett, *Record of American Diplomacy, Documents and Readings* (New York, 1947), p. 168.
[115]Bancroft, *op. cit.*, p. 357, n. 19.
[116]Bartlett, *op. cit.*, p. 171.

claims to the West Coast north of the forty-second parallel. During the same summer that he stated United States policy to Minister Middleton, he made it clear to the Russian minister in Washington that the United States would contest Russian expansion and that the United States no longer considered the American continent open for new colonial establishments.[117] Five days later the same ideas were communicated to Minister Rush in London. In December, 1823, Secretary of State Adams sketched an overview of American foreign policy, using words similar to the ones communicated to the Russian minister six months previously. In the annual report to Congress a few days later, Monroe took them over bodily and inserted them in his message of December second.[118] The statement was formulated in these familiar words:

> The occasion has been judged proper for asserting as a principle in which rights and interests of the United States are involved, that the American continents, by the free and independent condition which they have assumed and maintained, are henceforth not to be considered as subjects for future colonization by any European powers.[119]

This statement was the first part of what later came to be known as the Monroe Doctrine. The Russian ukase of 1821 grew out of an attempt to control American Pacific trade. The official statements of Adams and Monroe were answers in the form of official policy. It is evident, in the light of the maritime antecedents, that the protection of Pacific trade was a strong historic force in formulating a doctrine that was destined to have hemispheric scope.

Background of the Alaskan Purchase. By the repudiation of the imperial ukase of 1821, further Russian hopes of expansion in North America were checked. By the agreement of 1824, the Russian boundary was established along latitude 54°40′ north,

---

[117]Perkins, *Hands Off: A History of the Monroe Doctrine* (Boston, 1944), p. 31.
[118]*Ibid.*, p. 51.
[119]Bancroft, *op. cit.*, p. 357.

and the right to trade as well as free use of fishing grounds was guaranteed to American vessels. Commercial reciprocity was also established. American ships continued touching at New Archangel and Sitka throughout the negotiations, although the volume was never important in the total amount of American Pacific trade. Slacum reported in 1836 that, on the average, two ships a year touched Russian-American ports.[120] In return for manufactured goods from Boston and Hawaii, Americans received bills of exchange on the St. Petersburg house of the Russian-American Fur Company. The balance of trade was still against the Russian establishments. They could not produce articles of sufficient value to exchange for needed supplies on an equal basis with the American traders. The reciprocity provision of the 1824 treaty was therefore unworkable since the American traders could hold a virtually unchallenged position in the carrying trade.[121]

The grievances growing out of unfavorable trade with Americans were seen to be the origin of the ukase of 1821. Partially out of that ukase grew the dictum of American hemispheric protection. Also from the grievances of Russian trade grew the final withdrawal of Russia from the North American continent.

Official Russian policy had never strongly supported the fur settlements in America. From the time of Catherine II to the final sale of Alaska, it was a political and economic burden to the imperial Russian government. During the final negotiations for its sale, Baron Stoekl wrote a letter to the Russian Minister of Finance enumerating the reasons why Alaska should be sold to the United States, in which he remarked:

> Should Alaska be thrown open to the Yankees, they would soon exhaust it. If they close their ports to us, we are lost; if we open our ports to them we are equally lost.[122]

---

[120]*Senate Documents*, 25th Congress, 2nd session, vol. 24, p. 18.
[121]Mazour, "The Russian-American and Anglo-Russian Conventions of 1824-1825; An interpretation," *Pacific Historical Review*, vol. 12, p. 308.
[122]Golder, "The Attitude of the Russian Government toward Alaska," *The Pacific Ocean in History*, ed. Stephens and Bolton (New York, 1917), p. 269.

This statement reads like a succinct review of Russian-American trade relations since the days of John J. Astor. It is an illustration of how conditions that made the Russians willing to abandon Alaska grew out of the antecedents of the early contacts between the Russian-American Company and Yankee sea traders.

RAILS TO THE PACIFIC

Another important American development also had its roots in maritime antecedents of the Pacific trade. This was the early agitation during the years from 1845 to 1850 that eventually resulted in the building of a railroad line across the country.

Early Interest of Asa Whitney. The work of one man was chiefly responsible for the stirring of public interest in a Pacific railroad and of launching the first debates in Congress concerning official policy in regard to its building. Asa Whitney, a retired merchant, is a man whose name is mentioned in texts and general histories of the West. He is given credit for initiating the first railroad scheme deserving of widespread notice. Fuller, in his *History of the Pacific Northwest,* generalized that "of those who first proposed a railroad from the States to the Pacific Coast, the most influential were not so much interested in the development of the West as in control of the China trade."[123] After 1829 there were many schemes for building a railroad line across the continent but none of the promoters worked at the idea as deliberately and systematically as did Whitney.[124] A look at his work will clearly show that he was motivated by the idea of Pacific trade.

It was coincidental that Whitney's railroad planning and agtiation overlapped two events of great national importance— the opening of four new treaty ports in China in 1844, and the annexation of Oregon in 1847. Whitney, however, was not stirred to his vision of a transcontinental railroad by these developments. He was on his way to China in June, 1842, with a scheme already

---

[123]Fuller, *A History of the Pacific Northwest* (New York, 1931), p. 318.
[124]Brown, "Asa Whitney and His Pacific Railroad Publicity," *Mississippi Valley Historical Review,* vol. 20 (September 1933), p. 209.

in mind. His movements in China are obscure. It is known that in Singapore he read of the signing of the British-Chinese treaty of Nanking. During the next two years he moved about China collecting information and statistics concerning the Chinese trade with America and Europe.[125] He left for America shortly after the signing of the Cushing treaty of Wanghai in March, 1844. His sojourn in China must have been successful. On the return voyage Whitney organized his materials and formulated his plans for a transcontinental railroad. Upon his return to New York, instead of going back into business, he moved to Washington where he could exert a steady and skillful pressure on the national Congress. During the next five years, he launched a one-man publicity campaign of memorializing Congress and stumping the country.

Pressure on Congress. Whitney's memorial was presented to Congress in January, 1845. In it he sketched the substance of his railroad plans. Congress was to set aside a strip of land sixty miles wide from some point west of Lake Michigan to the Pacific Coast via South Pass—one strip going to San Francisco, the other to the mouth of the Columbia River. Proceeds of the land sales were to finance the building of the road. A commission of private citizens was to be appointed by Congress to manage the land sales. Upon completion of the road, and after a twenty-year lapse of time, all unsold land was to revert to members of the commission as compensation for their services. Realistic senators observed that Whitney and other members of the commission would be close to eighty years of age before any compensation reached them. The plan was examined, but appeared to be too altruistic to be accepted.

While Congress was discussing the first memorial, Whitney went to work on his publicity campaign. Railroads were only fifteen years old at the time and he realized that his plan depended upon a job of educating the public. He had to make them see both the need and feasibility of a transcontinental railroad. After Congress adjourned in March, 1845, Whitney sent a letter to the *National Intelligencer* asking for volunteers to accompany

---

[125]*Ibid.*, p. 209.

him on a scouting trip over part of the proposed route.[126] The letter was copied by other papers. His plans were much publicized by this means. The northern route, he explained, was selected mainly because it would shorten the time between New York and China from 150 days (at the most) to approximately thirty days. The railroad line to the part of the coast claimed by the United States would also facilitate a quick concentration of military might for the purpose of domniating "the Pacific and Indian Oceans and even the Chinese seas."[127]

Whitney actually departed on his exploratory tour in June, 1845, accompanied by several volunteers from various States. They left from a point near Milwaukee and took a swing up the Missouri River and back to Saint Louis. A long letter was published in a Saint Louis newspaper that was copied in the *New York Commercial Advertiser* in October, 1845.[128] Much editorial space was given to it and this proved an important means whereby Whitney spread his arguments of the China trade and Pacific control as talking points for a Pacific railroad.

When Congress reconvened in 1846, Whitney presented a second memorial reiterating his early arguments about the China trade, but sharpening his statements considerably by firsthand knowledge obtained from his brief exploring trip. He included statistical information about land elevations, grade ratios, and general topographical data.[129] On the last day of the session, July 1, 1846, the Senate committee on public lands, to which Whitney's memorial had been referred, brought in a bill providing for setting aside lands requested by Whitney. Of the fifty-one pages that made up the committee's favorable report on the memorial, almost one quarter were devoted to a description of China and the East Indies, describing in detail the trade needs and potentialities of the markets in various Oriental countries and Pacific islands.[130]

---

[126]*Ibid.*, p. 212.
[127]Cotterill, "Pacific Railroad Agitation," *Mississippi Valley Historical Review*, vol. 5, no. 4 (March, 1919), p. 397.
[128]Brown, *op. cit.*, p. 213.
[129]Cotterill, *op. cit.*, p. 400.
[130]*Report of Committee,* 29th Congress, 1st session, no. 466, pp. 1-51.

The Public Lands Committee approved every basic argument presented by Whitney. The route proposed was practical, they said, citing the precedent of the Lewis and Clark Expedition.[131] They agreed that the plan would be advantageous to military control of the Pacific, would direct trade from China, Australia, and the Pacific islands toward the United States, would develop fisheries and naval power, and would also stimulate land settlement along the railroad land grant. A long appendix contained statistical charts, showing the value of imports and exports for China, India, East Indies, Australia, and the Philippines with the principal nations of Europe. Charts showing the present length of steamship lines from Europe to the Orient were compared with the distance over the route proposed by Whitney—that of Europe to the Orient via North America. The statistics were provided, of course, by Whitney, and the concluding remarks of the committee reports reflect his influence and summarize the heart of his theory of a transcontinental railroad:

> By the aid of a small portion of the public lands, the committee believes the United States can possess the channels of speedy and safe communications through which will pour a continued rich and fertilizing stream, a large portion of the commerce of the Oriental world.[132]

In the same session, the House Committee on Roads and Canals also produced a favorable report. The first session of the Twenty-Ninth Congress ended in 1846 without any concrete proposals being adopted. Sectional interests began to be felt, such as Thomas Hart Benton's opposition based on disagreement over the location of the eastern terminus.

Publicity Campaign. After the adjournment in July, 1846, Asa Whitney embarked on a long "stumping tour" of the country. He delivered addresses in Pittsburgh, Cincinnati, Louisville, Saint Louis, Terre Hause, Indianapolis, Dayton, Columbus, and Wheeling. He was well received, although some opposition was encountered. His publicity campaign began to stimulate opposing

---

[131]*Ibid.*, p. 4.
[132]*Ibid.*

plans. Benton preferred the eastern terminus to be Saint Louis, Steven A. Douglas wanted Chicago, and Southern senators preferred Memphis.

Congress paid little attention to Whitney's railroad plans throughout the next session. Whitney nevertheless continued his attack throughout the country by widespread speaking tours. The results of this phase of his campaign is shown in the favorable reception given him in the state legislatures. During 1847 ten different legislatures adopted resolutions approving Whitney's railroad plans.[133] In the following year he presented another memorial to the Senate and again there was a favorable report from the Public Lands Committee. Again Benton attacked the scheme. Again it was killed in the Senate, in spite of widespread approval in the New England and Midwestern states.[134] No more progress was made through 1848.

The session of 1849 was a busy one in which various routes were considered. It also marked the peak of Asa Whitney's efforts in railroad agitation. He published a pamphlet in that year, entitled *A Project for a Railroad to the Pacific*. In it he summarized all of the arguments he had used in his memorials to Congress. Much of his earlier themes were strengthened by statistical data. He included a chart on page 22 showing how the balance of trade had run against the United States in 1846 to the amount of five million dollars. The balance was made up in specie or in notes on London houses. "Ten million bushels of corn," he declared, "could pay this balance if it could be gotten there." Here was the theme of Jefferson, elaborated by Benton and used by Whitney as support for the building of a railroad to the Pacific.

Apparently the pamphlet was well received by the reading public. It won the approval of periodicals such as *Hunt's Merchants Magazine, DeBow's Southern Review,* and the *North American Review*. The New York Chamber of Commerce drew up a resolution advising Congress to accept the Whitney plan.[135]

---

[133]Brown, *op. cit.* p. 216.
[134]Cotterill, *op. cit.*, p. 405.
[135]Brown, *op. cit.*, p. 216.

The Seaborne Frontier on the Northwest Coast

Congressional Reaction. After 1849 opposing sectional interests blocked Congressional action. Whitney made one more appeal in 1850, but the negative results indicated that further discussions could lead only to a political impasse. After that he was through, living quietly until the 1870's practically in the shadow of the national capitol. Although he seemed to have failed, it is clear that he had a plan that stimulated a unanimous demand for a railroad and that it was sectional interests on the eve of the Civil War that blocked its realization. This situation was recognized by Congress, itself, as late as 1850:

> Mr. Whitney, the projector of the stupendous enterprise, has been untiring in his efforts and energy in making the subject known to the public, and urging it upon the consideration of Congress, and from the favorable reports of different committees of both Houses, as also from the very favorable impression he has made upon the minds of the members and upon the public at large, it was expected that some definite action would have been taken before this. In the meantime, sectional and local interests and personal jealousies have reared themselves in opposition and possibly placed in danger this, the only feasible plan, for the great work may now be defeated forever.[136]

The sectional snarl finally ended in a bill in 1853 providing for the original railroad surveys of the three principal routes undertaken by the army engineers before the Civil War.

The arguments used for the original campaign for a Pacific railroad now seem absurd. They were based on two plans growing out of the China trade:

1. the hope of connecting the breadbaskets of the Middle West and the markets of the Atlantic states with Oriental trade
2. the hope of making the European-Oriental flow of trade along the proposed railroad "tribute" to the United States.

The China trade never lived up to these hopes, and the railroads, when finally built, never served as a link in the European

---

[136]Report of Committee of Both Houses,"*DeBow's Southern Review,* December, 1850, p. 4.

trade to China to the extent dreamed of by Whitney. It is significant, however, that as late as 1878, when J. J. Hill was laying plans for the Great Northern Railroad, he had visions similar to those of Asa Whitney. Also significant is the emblem adopted as a symbol of the Northern Pacific Railroad. It was the "familiar Yin and Yang symbol of the Far East."[137]

Whitney's plan, developed by James J. Hill, a corollary of the vision of Ledyard and Jefferson, was perhaps a vestigial appendage of the historic quest for a northwest water route to the riches of the East.

---

[137] Latourette, *The United States Moves Across the Pacific* (New York, Harper & Row Publishers, Inc., 1946), p. 14.

Chapter III

American Policy Toward China

The initial urge to develop the Pacific Northwest, as was indicated in the last chapter, came from the need to solve the "riddle of the China trade." Seaborne trade and official policy toward China established the antecedents for the annexation of Oregon, California, Hawaii and expansion to Japan. Trade was responsible for the early adoption of the Open Door policy in China and a long-abiding attitude of friendliness for the Chinese people and their de jure governments. Foster Rhea Dulles recognized this in pointing out that the American attitudes toward China did not originate in Hay's Open Door note, Stimpson's declaration of policy in 1932, or in the Washington Conference of 1922. "The nineteenth century holds the clue to the underlying policy which these declarations and treaties were supposed to implement."[1] Similarly K. S. Latourette has observed that "The fateful December 7, 1941, was not an accident. It came as a consequence of a long chain of events which go back into the seventeenth and eighteenth centuries."[2]

SCOPE AND STRUCTURE OF THE EARLY CHINA TRADE

American contacts with China and the East Indies resulted directly from colonial experience and conditions existing during the immediate post-Revolutionary period. With the end of hostilities American shipping, no longer able to trade with ports protected by English monopolies and now subject to the tonnage and tariff duties levied on all foreign commerce, was shut off from

---

[1]Dulles, *China and America*. Introduction, p. iv.
[2]Latourette, *The United States Moves Across the Pacific*, Preface, p. vii.

the markets of the West Indies.³ Some ships had been lost and others had rotted during the war; a new start was necessary.⁴ These two conditions forced American ships to seek markets wherever they might be found. In a short five years after the end of the war American ships were seen in virtually every deepwater port of the then civilized world. The Pacific trade of America developed during this period of maritime expansion.

The policies of economic nationalism adopted by the Federalists (see page 10, Chapter I) bore abundant fruit in the form of increased tonnage and expanded markets. A phenomenal growth in the merchant fleet occurred after 1789. The total tonnage in that year was 123,438 tons. Three years later it had increased more than threefold to the figure of 411,438 tons. This is said to be a growth without parallel in the history of the commercial world.⁵ A period was opening in which the total American deep-sea tonnage would reach its highest mark in proportion to population. During the years from 1789 to approximately 1828 American ships carried over 75 percent of the total American commerce. The highest percentage was reached in 1794, when American vessels carried 90 percent of American imports and 80 percent of the exports.⁶

This was the era of famous Pacific voyages characterized by their incredible risks, enormous profits, or, sometimes, stunning losses. The Yankee merchant skipper was in his heyday. He was the seagoing pioneer who established the first American contacts in the Pacific. His work, though he was probably unaware of its import, would correspond both in time and function to the Indian scout of the midwest frontier or the mountain man of the Rocky Mountain and Pacific coast area.

Early Routes. The important developments in the Pacific trade before 1815 can be traced through local histories of Salem

---

³Latourette, "Early Relations Between United States and China, 1784-1844," *Connecticut Academy of Arts and Sciences*, vol. 22 (August, 1917), p. 12.
⁴Marvin, *The American Merchant Marine*, pp. 34-35.
⁵*Ibid.*, p. 43.
⁶*Ibid.*, p. 44.

and Boston—the two ports involved. By tacit agreement the Pacific Ocean was divided into two vague areas in which the ships from each port operated almost exclusively. An imaginary line starting from the coast of China, running along the 20th degree of latitude, bending southward to the equator below Hawaii, and extending to the 120th meridian west, would roughly delineate the two trading areas.[7] To the north of the line lay the sphere of activity of the Boston ships, including the Pacific coast of the Spanish Main, the Northwest Coast, Alaska, the Hawaiian Islands, and Canton. To the south of the line, the area of Salem's maritime trade included the Dutch East Indies, the Philippines, the South Pacific islands, and Canton.

The favorite route of Boston ships took them around the continent of South America and along the western coast. Their ultimate goal was the Canton market, but the type of trade pursued resulted in varying routes through the Pacific. If the Boston vessel was bound for the Northwest Coast for fur, she usually would sail "broad off" Cape Horn, touching the Hawaiian Islands before sailing back in a northeasterly direction for the American coast. If a smuggling voyage was anticipated, the vessel invariably proceeded from port to port along the western coast of South America and upper California. Sometimes a combination smuggling-fur trading voyage was carried out. In this case, nearly every port of the Spanish Main was contacted before the ship sailed to the Hawaiian Islands in preparation for a season of fur trading along the coast. When the cargo was complete, whether it was fur, hides, or specie, the inevitable route to Canton was taken by way of the Hawaiian Islands, through the strait between the Philippines and Formosa, the China Sea, and to Macao at the mouth of the Pearl River in China.

Salem skippers preferred the eastern approach to the Pacific. The route used by most of these ships took them to Capetown by way of the West Indies or the Cape Verde Islands. From South Africa there was usually a stopover at the Isle of France (Mauritius). Some trading was done along the coast of India and Ceylon, but the usual route from Mauritius took Salem ships on the long

---

[7]Morison, *Maritime History of Massachusetts*, p. 84.

trek across the Indian Ocean for a landfall on Java Head, which marked the entrance to the Sunda Straits. After the passage of the Straits, the vessels proceeded to the Philippines, South Sea Islands, or Canton, depending upon the type of voyage.

Different types of voyages resulted in variations from the two general trade routes just described. Sealing voyages from Massachusetts and Stonington, Connecticut, took the ships to the Falkland Islands, Massa Fuero Island, and Juan Fernandez Island off the tip of South America.[8] Some of the early traders and whalers from Salem and Boston took a low southerly route from Capetown that brought them in contact with Tasmania and the subcontinent of New Holland.[9] From the western side of the ocean other whalers, after rounding Cape Horn, sailed among the Marquesas and Society Islands en route to the Hawaiian Islands and the northern whaling grounds.[10]

Most American ships returning from Canton followed the Cape of Good Hope route. They were carried south across the South China Sea by the northeasterly monsoons. They then worked their way along the Borneo coast toward the Sunda Straits, usually making a stop at Anjur, Java, for supplies. After clearing the dreaded Strait of Sunda, the long voyage across the Indian Ocean was often broken at Madagascar and Capetown. On the next leg of the journey, Saint Helena Island or Ascension in the South Atlantic were the usual stopping places. After rest and refreshment were obtained, the Yankee trader took departure from these small points of land and "squared away" for Cape Cod.[11]

---

[8]Phillips, *Salem and the Indies* (Boston, 1947), p. 189; Delano, *Voyages*, (Boston, 1817), p. 306. Sealing in 1801 in Juan Fernandez and Massa Fuero Islands is vividly described.

[9]*Ibid.*, p. 460. Delano's voyage to New Holland is a good example of this activity; Fanning, *Voyages to the South Seas and Pacific Ocean* (New York, 1938), chapter 6. The voyage of the *Hope* 1806-1808 is also a good example of this route, although Fanning was a New Yorker sailing a New York vessel.

[10]Dulles, *Lowered Boats* (New York, 1933), pp. 55-57.

[11]Morison, *op. cit.*, p. 68; Quincy, *Journals of Major Samuel Shaw* (Boston, 1847) pp. 293-335. Details of the return route most often used by Yankee ships was described in Shaw's journal of his third voyage.

American Policy Toward China

Cargoes. Risk and individualism were the keynotes of the early China voyages. Before 1840 the vessels were incredibly small —rarely over five hundred tons and varying in length between sixty and one hundred twenty-five feet.[12] The voyages themselves could truly be called "tramp" ventures. Specie was scarce during the years of early nationality. A medium for the Canton market had to be found in numerous ports and by a variety of ways. Salem ships would often turn over their cargoes three or four times. Yankee products, such as fish, lumber, rope, and rum could be exchanged for wine in the Madeira Islands or for sugar in the West Indies. A cargo of opium or tobacco might be taken in exchange in some eastern Mediterranean port. At Mauritius, crossroads of the European-Oriental trade, manufactured goods, specie, or bills of exchange on London or Amsterdam could be exchanged.[13] The Yankee ship, with a small accumulation from each transaction, might then have a cargo that could be sold on the Island of Sumatra for pepper, in the Philippines for rice or Manila hemp, or in Canton for tea, silk, and chinaware. The ship that rounded Cape Horn similarly tramped from port to port, moving a part of its cargo at each stop, arriving at Canton with a salable accumulation of articles obtained by barter en route. It was a haphazard and risky business, often depending upon the fortunes of competition, market, and weather, or on the whims of Chinese tastes.

First Chinese Contacts. Shortly after the signing of the Treaty of Paris in 1783 a Boston vessel, the *Harriet* (55 tons), commanded by Captain Hallet, departed for Canton with a cargo of ginseng.[14] By a turn of fate Captain Hallet met the captain of a British East Indian vessel during the stopover at Capetown. So profitable an exchange was offered by the Englishman that Hallet traded his cargo for the British cargo of Chinese tea. The *Harriet* then returned to Boston with the purpose of her voyage accomplished. Although the first voyage fell short of

---

[12] Forbes, *Notes on Ships of the Past* (Boston, 1887), p. 18.

[13] Delano, *op. cit.*, pp. 204-205. Delano touched this island numerous times and described its importance as a world emporium.

[14] An odoriferous plant that was thought to be useful in restoring lost youth.

reaching the Pacific Ocean, the vast possibilities for future profit were demonstrated.[15]

A New York vessel was to be the first actually to reach Canton and initiate the China trade. The *Empress of China,* whose name appears in most general histories of American trade, was fitted out as the name suggests—specifically for the Canton trade. It was an experimental voyage. The cargo was selected from items which, it was hoped, would please the Mandarin tastes. Captain Green of the *Empress* sailed from New York in 1784 with "sea letters" from Congress addressed to emperors, kings, "republics," princes, dukes, earls, barons, lords, burgomasters, and counselors.[16] The all-inclusive nature of the official letters of introduction shows that a bartering tramp voyage was planned and broad contacts with a variety of principalities were anticipated. Although profits were realized from the first voyage,[17] the lasting result was that commercial relations were established that led to later official action. Samuel Shaw of Boston served as supercargo of the *Empress of China*. During the next years he was active in the China trade and an important figure because his writing attracted governmental interest to China for the first time. In all, he made three voyages to China. On his second he was appointed honorary consul. Unofficial though his status was, he remained until 1794, writing reports back to the United States government about the condition of trade and giving freely of aid and advice to American traders, who began coming to Canton in increasing numbers.[18]

---

[15]Morison, *op. cit.,* p. 44.

[16]Dulles, *China and America,* p. 2.

[17]Latourette, "History of the Early Relations Between the United States and China, 1784-1844," p. 15. About 25 percent, approximately $30,000.

[18]Morison, *op. cit.,* p. 66; Quincy, *op. cit.,* p. 129. Shaw wrote the following letters to officials in the government (appendix pp. 337-360): John Jay, May 1785, describing first voyage of the *Empress of China;* John Jay, January 1787, describing details of trade, Hong system, and status for foreign trade; President Washington, December, 1790, describing the extent of American trade with Batavia. Some of his documents were used by President Van Buren in 1841 as he formulated official policy (see p. 105 of this work).

American Policy Toward China 77

The year after the return of the *Empress of China*, five American ships departed for Canton. To show the parallels between the China trade and the Northwest Coast fur trade, it is interesting to note that in 1787 the third China trader was returning from Canton as the brig *Columbia* and the sloop *Lady Washington* were en route to the Northwest Coast. By the time Captain Gray in the *Columbia* reached Canton in 1789 with the first load of American furs, fourteen other vessels from Salem, Boston, and New York had preceded her. Thus, by 1789, five years after the first voyage, fifteen Yankee ships were engaged in the China trade.[19]

The business of carrying on trade at Canton was a rather complicated process. Chinese intercourse with the outside world was in the hands of Hong merchants, who were men of wealth and influence—usually highly esteemed and respected by Chinese and foreigners alike.[20] Foreign ships were required to anchor at Whampoa, a point upstream from the Portuguese establishment at Macao. As each foreign ship arrived at the designated anchorage, a Chinese official, or *hoppo*, boarded the vessel, measured her depth and beam, and determined the tonnage duties to be paid. Usually the hoppo's job was considered a sinecure, from which the agent could receive lucrative gifts and extort bribes from foreign traders who were anxious to be freed of annoying tonnage fees and other obstacles.[21] The boarding of the hoppo involved the usual ceremony and protocol of measuring the ship, exchanging pleasantries, and of giving gifts and bribes for all members of the agent's family.[22]

---

[19] Dulles, *China and America*, p. 3.

[20] Peabody, *Merchant Ventures of Old Salem* (Boston, 1912), p. 66; Quincy, ed., *op. cit.*, appendix, pp. 349-350. Shaw also attests to this opinion.

[21] Latourette, "History of the Early Relations Between the United States and China, 1784-1844," p. 25.

[22] The following have rather full accounts of the Hong system; Morison, *op. cit.*, chapter 6; Abend, *Treaty Ports*, pp. 6, 16; Phipps, *China and the Eastern Trade*, section on American trade; Quincy, ed., *op. cit.*, pp. 173-178, Appendix, p. 342. The best accounts are found in the journal and in a letter to John Jay written in January, 1787, which is found in the appendix.

When the formalities with the hoppo were completed, the cargo was turned over to the Hong merchant. After agreements were made concerning the price of the cargo to be exchanged, it was lightered by sampans twelve miles up the Pearl River to the Hong's warehouse in Canton. The China goods gained in exchange were carried downstream and loaded aboard the foreign ship for the return voyage.

Into the pattern of trade and lines of commerce described, the American traders eagerly settled. The American-China trade, as has been mentioned, was well established by 1790. Before 1800 most of what later became American insular possessions had been visited by Salem or Boston ships.[23]

Trade of Salem. Salem commerce was never large in the Pacific. The favorable trade areas were the West Indies, the Mediterranean, the Isle of France, India, and the East Indies. Occasionally a ship would touch the Philippines or Canton. In the long list of Salem merchants, such as John Fiske, George Crowninshield, John Norris, and Simon Forrester, Elias Hasket Derby stands out as the supreme example of the successful man of commerce, even though he never went to sea.[24]

Derby had been active in commerce in colonial days. During the Revolution he had both profited greatly and sacrificed much in smuggling and fitting out privateers. After the war most of his ships, like the rest of Salem's fleet, were occupied in trade in the Western Hemisphere and along a thin line to the East Indies. One notable voyage was started in March, 1796, when the Derby ship *Astrea* sailed for Manila with Captain Prince in command and Nathaniel Bowditch as navigator and supercargo (a notable combination). The *Astrea* followed the usual route of the Salem ships passing through the Sunda Straits and, after a slight brush with Malay pirates, anchored in Manila Bay in October, 1796.[25]

One thing that made the voyage of the *Astrea* notable was the work of Nathaniel Bowditch. It was during the long, idle days at sea that he did much of the mathematical computation

---

[23]Morison, *op. cit.*, p. 94. The one exception was Guam, visited by a Yankee ship in 1801.

[24]Phillips, *op. cit.*, ch. 7.   [25]Peabody, *op. cit.*, p. 116.

that later became the basis of his book, *The Practical Navigator*, still the basis of modern celestial navigation. The other notable point about this voyage was that it opened up the Manila trade, which continued from that year. During the stay of the ship at Manila, Captain Prince and Bowditch lived ashore with a Philadelphia gentleman named Kerr, who acted as middle man for handling the *Astrea* cargo. Spanish wine and specie that made up part of her lading bought a mixed cargo of indigo, hemp, molasses, sugar, hides, and pepper.[26]

The search for a medium of exchange at Canton took Salem ships into the Fiji Islands, in voyages as novel as they were dangerous. Here was found an unusual article esteemed by the Mandarins in China, called "beche de mer," or sea cucumber. This small sea plant was gathered on the beaches of the islands by the Salem crews and dried and prepared for the Canton market. This involved both hard work in the broiling tropical sun and imminent risk of attack from savage Fiji Island cannibals. Similarly the quest for nests of a small sea bird living among the rocky caves of the South Sea Island shores proved both risky and profitable. The nests were relished by the Mandarins as a flavoring for soup.

Tracing the numerous fly-by-night voyages to the South Sea Islands would be superfluous. The important result was that the islands became familiar territory to New England men who accumulated information and sailing directions for use by later mariners.[27] Whaling captains, who began entering the Pacific

---

[26]*Ibid.*, p. 118. The pepper was bought from Borneo pirates trading among ships in Manila Bay.

[27]Morison, *op. cit.*, p. 117. In 1789 a Salem Marine Society was formed for collecting nautical information and sailing directions. Blank sheets of sea journals were furnished to each skipper in which he was to fill in new information as to discoveries, reefs, etc. At the end of the voyage they were deposited in the Marine Library at Salem.

Delano, *op. cit.*, ch. 26. Much of this 598-page narrative is made up of minute sailing directions and information about the South Sea Islands and peoples. Details of hunting sea cucumbers and birds nests are included. He also gave information about the Chinese customs and attitudes—much of it from firsthand knowledge.

Latourette, "The History of the Early Relations Between the United States and China, 1784-1844," p. 59. The trade of Salem vessels in search of beches de mer and edible birds' nests continued until 1837 but generally in the same areas as the early ones.

in great numbers after 1820, made use of much of the information and added more of their own. It was the beginning of a growing body of knowledge about a little-known sea that helped form and strengthen American concepts of strategic control of the Pacific.[28]

The voyages of Richard J. Cleveland are an example of the trade of Salem before 1812. He left Salem in 1797 on a voyage which proved to be a series of voyages that kept him away from home for seven years.[29] During that time he circled the globe three times, touching the Cape of Good Hope, India, China, Northwest Coast, Mauritius, Copenhagen, Havre, Rio de Janeiro, California, Hawaii, Canton, and eventually Boston. This assortment of place names on the globe, named in order in which he visited them, indicate how he traced and retraced his steps in pursuing the China trade by collecting cargoes all over the world. Names of other Salem men, such as Nathaniel Silsbee, could be mentioned.[30] Their voyages to China followed much the same pattern as the ones described. All followed the usual route to obtain a medium of exchange. The apogee of Salem commerce was reached during the first ten years of the nineteenth century. It is estimated that in 1807 five percent of the total federal revenue was coming from the commerce of Salem.[31]

Trade of Boston. Early Boston voyages in the Pacific did not achieve the broad geographical range of the navigators of Salem. Instead the Boston traders built up extensive commercial contacts in Canton and originated the early American contacts between the American Pacific coast, Hawaii, and the China coast.

The voyage of John Boit, Jr., is an example of the early

---

[28]Albion, *The Rise of the Port of New York, 1815-1860* (New York, 1939), p. 207. Early discoveries often resulted in naming of Pacific Islands. For example, Fanning, in 1797 on the *Betsy,* named Fanning Island, Washington Island, and Palmyra Island.

[29]Cleveland, ed., *Voyages of a Merchant Navigator,* ch. 3.

[30]At nineteen years of age he commanded a ship on a voyage to the island of Mauritius and returned less than two years later with 500 percent profit. Later he became a senator from Massachusetts.

[31]Peabody, *op. cit.,* p. 248.

strengthening of ties with China—started by the voyages of the *Columbia* on which he had been a mate. In 1794 Boit was on his way to the Northwest Coast again in command of his own vessel, the sixty-foot sloop *Union*.[32] He followed the early route of the *Columbia* and brought his small craft safely back to Boston harbor with a profitable cargo.

Four years later, in 1798, Willaim Sturgis, son of a Cape Cod shipmaster, shipped out as a deckhand on the ship *Eliza*, which was owned by his wealthy relative, T. H. Perkins. The *Eliza* was engaged in the Northwest Coast-Canton trade. Five years later Sturgis returned as commander of a fur ship, the *Caroline*. He stayed in the fur trade long enough to complete his third voyage. After returning to Boston a wealthy man, he combined with a Boston merchant and established the commercial house of Bryant and Sturgis, which came to be well known in the Pacific trade. After the War of 1812 the house of Bryant and Sturgis reopened the Northwest fur trade and originated the hide and tallow trade from California.[33]

The seagoing career of John Suter is a good example of a slightly later period. Raised and educated in the ways of the sea by a Boston harbor pilot, he began his seagoing adventures at the age of seventeen. The events of the turbulent years of privateering and impressment during the sea war with France were firsthand experiences for him. After spending a term in a Brest prison and becoming a pressed seaman on a British man-of-war, he returned to Boston and shipped out on the *Alert* for the Northwest Coast and Canton. His next voyage in 1804 saw him as a mate of the *Pearl* on a similar voyage. On the third voyage of the *Pearl* he was in full command. It was an adventurous trip in which the ship was attacked by Indians on the coast. The defense must have been successful, however, since

---

[32]Morison, *op. cit.*, p. 74.

[33]Morison, *op. cit.*, p. 69. Captain Sturgis wielded considerable influence in Massachusetts' affairs; he occupied a seat in the Great and General Court, joined the learned societies, and lectured and wrote on Oregon (Dana, *Two Years Before the Mast*, pp. 85-86). His commercial house dominated the hide and tallow trade. By 1836 it was bringing in two-thirds of the manufactured goods to California.

the returns from the goods exchanged at Canton sold at auction in Boston for more than $206,000.[34] Suter continued in the Canton trade until the British patrols during the War of 1812 made it necessary to sell his last ship at the Hawaiian Islands. After his successful sea career, he retired to Boston and lived to a ripe old age on the wealth he had earned from the Pacific trade.

The China trade, with its chances for tremendous profits, held the incentive that stimulated men of ability to go to sea in the early years and establish American contacts in the Pacific. Commanders of the early Yankee vessels, such as Boit, Sturgis, and Suter, received an annual salary that in itself was not inconsiderable. In addition to their set wage, the skippers were allowed cargo space by the owners of the vessels, ranging from one-half to five tons for individual speculation on the "captain's account." Nor was this all. On the net proceeds of the voyage, captains also received from one to eight percent. The chance for enormous wealth, as it was measured in that day, naturally attracted the most capable New Englanders from Boston, Cape Cod, and Maine. It was not difficult for a competent and fortunate ship's captain to clear $25,000 on a single voyage.[35] This figure is probably high for the average, but usually profits from voyages tended to have a pyramiding effect—a part of the proceeds from a particular venture being invested on the "captain's account" for the next voyage.

In spite of financial failures, of which a few are recorded,[36] the brevity of the seagoing career of a typical Yankee skipper is testimony of the lucrative nature of the business in which he was engaged. In the early trade before 1812 a man rarely spent his entire life at sea. Quick profits and early retirement ashore were the rule. By the time the average Yankee mariner was thirty he had either left the sea in discouragement—usually joining the

---

[34]*Ibid.*, p. 71.

[35]Morison, *op. cit.*, p. 77.

[36]*Ibid.*, pp. 47, 52, 54, 92. In these pages are described nonprofitable voyages caused by a variety of reasons, such as poor markets, Indian attacks, and piratical attacks; Cleveland, ed., *op. cit.*, p. 100 ff. Cleveland, after making a fortune from his seven-year voyage (see p. 80), was obliged to go to sea again to recoup losses incurred from nonprofitable voyages in which he had invested.

growing westward migration, had been lost at sea, or had retired a wealthy man still in the prime of life.

Financial gain, to be sure, was the incentive that sent individual Americans all over the world in the years after 1784. Although the wealth brought back to the Eastern seaboard made its contribution to American development (see pages 7-12, in Chapter I), it was the incidental contacts established in the Pacific, of which the seafarers were unaware, that were later to be of more significance to the nation. Commercial ties originally established by them justify this tribute: "These master seamen of the young republic were as truly pioneers as their kinsmen who, with axe and rifle on their backs, at the same time were pouring through the passes of the Alleghenies to subdue the West. . . . Seamen then were almost the only wide and constant travelers. They were in an especial sense the eyes and ears of the nations."[37]

TRENDS AFTER 1812

Haphazard and individualistic as the voyages were in the early years, the beginnings could be seen of the system of placing commercial agents ashore. The first step in this development began immediately after the voyage of the New York ship *Empress of China*. Captains and supercargoes of five American ships that had followed in its track cooperatively rented a warehouse in Canton for handling the season's business.[38] This was the first American interest ashore set up along side of the factories of the English, French, Dutch, and Danish.

It will be recalled that Major Samuel Shaw had been the supercargo on the *Empress of China* in 1784. After his return to Boston in 1794 he combined resources with a wealthy merchant to form the China trading house of Shaw and Randall. Similarly in 1803 T. H. Perkins, who had financed ships engaged in the

---

[37]Marvin, *op. cit.*, p. 76.
[38]Peabody, *op. cit.*, p. 69.; Quincy, ed., *op. cit.*, pp. 173-178. From firsthand observation Shaw sketched the status of foreign trade, the description of Canton, and society and relations among Americans and foreigners as well as between Chinese and foreigners.

Northwest fur trade, established the branch house of Perkins and Company in Canton. This agency became one of the most famous of China trade branch houses. A sixteen-year-old clerk, John Perkins Cushing, took over its management and became over a thirty-year period, one of the most wealthy and well-known American merchants in Canton.[39]

Changed Routes and Cargoes. Early establishments ashore were the precursors of the change that occurred in the China trade after 1815. The eighteenth-century seamen had traced out the main sea routes. There was no great change in that respect. But a change had occurred in the type of products exchanged at Canton. Seals and sea otter along the Northwest Coast declined. A sandalwood trade from the Hawaiian Islands boomed through the 1820's and soon died out. Direct voyages from America by way of the Isle of France or Cape Horn became the general practice.[40]

Direct voyages from the ports of Salem, Boston, New York, Philadelphia, and Baltimore meant that China-bound vessels carried a salable cargo in their holds. This was another change in the methods of China trade which reflected a growing American industrial power. In the place of furs and beches-de-mer the China vessels began to carry such American-made products as shoes and textiles. There was also a change in the articles imported from China. European imitations ruined the market for Chinese willoware, and nankeens and silks became less popular as 1840 approached. As a result teas became the predominant United States import from Canton by 1834.[41]

The change was not sudden and complete. American ships continued to tramp from port to port en route to Canton. The

---

[39]Latourette, "History of the Early Relations Between the United States and China, 1784-1844," p. 134. John Cushing was a third cousin of Caleb Cushing, negotiator of first official treaty with China in 1844.

[40]*See also* page 73-75.

[41]Phipps, *op. cit.*, p. 314. Silk, satin, and crepes decreased by one-third between 1818-1834. Tea increased by over one-half, making up nearly seven-eighths of the total American imports ($8,333,000).

old specialties of Salem and Boston were continued but to a lesser extent. Salem vessels continued in the Sumatra pepper trade and the South Sea Island trade but gradually ceased its maritime activity as the Civil War approached. Boston ships continued to touch the fur posts along the Northwest Coast but also began to carry English goods to Canton. The house of Perkins began to engage heavily in the opium trade from Smyrna to Canton. As the scope of trade increased, the commercial houses of Perkins, Sturgis, and Russell were consolidated in 1823 into the gigantic Russell and Company of Canton, which carried on the largest volume of Boston trade in China.

Rise of New York. After 1812 the trade with Canton settled down to a prosaic business pattern. With the establishment of commercial agents ashore, the old supercargo of the earlier years was no longer needed. Paralleling this change was the rise of New York City as an entrepôt for China goods. With the increased value of cargo for direct voyages and increased size of ships, Salem and Boston began to relinquish their position in the Canton trade.[42] The New York companies having agents in Canton included Thomas H. Smith, N. L. and G. Griswold, O.

---

[42]Albion, *op. cit.*, p. 207. New York ships also had their period of individualistic tramping of the world, though to a lesser extent than the Salem and Boston vessels. There are three such examples, two of which had some significance for later American policy in the Pacific. Edmund Fanning (discoverer of the Fanning Islands) commanded a sealing voyage to the South Pacific in 1816. He was seized and thrown into a Chilean prison for smuggling. He stoutly objected and later claimed that his protestations to Washington resulted in stationing a United States naval vessel in Chilean waters. In 1819 Captain Pendleton commanded a group of vessels to the Shetland Islands in quest of seals. He sent one of his captains, Nathaniel Palmer, to investigate floating ice to the southward. It proved to be a part of the Antarctic continent, which was later called Palmer's Island. Nathaniel Palmer became in time a China clipper captain for Lows of New York. In 1824 Captain Morrill commanded a schooner on a sealing voyage to New Zealand. After a futile search he proceeded to Manila to fit out for a beches-de-mer hunt. En route he discovered two groups of islands and named them after the builders of the ship—Bergh and Westervelt.

W. C. Olyphant,[43] and Russell and Company.[44]

The importance of the China trade declined after 1820, although its total volume continued to climb. In 1830 the China trade was still fairly well distributed among the various New York shippers; but by 1840 the commercial house established by Seth Low, originally of Salem, surged ahead and assumed a leading position.[45] By 1860 the trade with China was securely in the hands of New York shippers. In the total Oriental trade, however, whihc included China, India, the Philippines, and the East Indies, the ports of New York and Boston were evenly matched.[46]

During the fifteen years preceding the Civil War the competition for trade in a declining market between the commercial houses of Boston and New York caused the tremendous drive for speed in passages to China. During the 1830's, driven by this incentive, China merchants, such as the Lows, Howland, and Aspinwall of New York, began ordering a faster, roomier vessel.[47] As a result a type of vessel emerged called the "China clipper." After 1837 the length of passages to China approached the one-hundred-day mark. It was the forerunner of the California clipper or the vessel that was to receive the true appellation of the "clipper ship" during the 1840's and '50's.

Opium Trade. In a sketch of the American-China trade a word should be said about the traffic in opium as it existed before its restriction treaty. The traffic, however, was less important in American commerce than in its effect on the early political relations between China and America. Opium was a familiar item in China that had gained popularity before the

---

[43] An Olyphant ship in 1837 attempted to break into Japan for trade but failed.

[44] Albion, *op. cit.*, p. 199. This company was made up of a majority of Boston men. Warren Delano became a Russell partner. He had a daughter named Sarah, who later joined him in China; eventually she married James Roosevelt and became the mother of a president.

[45] *Ibid.*, p. 81. The elder Seth Low had moved from Salem in 1834 and formed the importing business of Low and Sons. One of the sons resided in Canton with Russell and Company agents.

[46] *Ibid.*, p. 203.

[47] Forbes, *op. cit.*, p. 36.

first American ship made its appearance in Canton. The trade was in the hands of the East India Company, which monopolized the trade between India, the chief source of the drug, and China. Records show that American ships first imported opium into Canton around 1804.[48] The letters of T. H. Perkins of Boston to the commander of one of the company ships reveal that one or two opium voyages were attempted between India and the East Indies.[49]

The restrictive policy of the East India Company resulted in American merchants seeking sources of opium in the markets of Asia Minor, Turkey, and the Levant. Between 1805 and 1819 American ships dominated the Mediterranean-Canton opium trade. Nearly every commercial house in America engaged in it as a means of relieving the drain on the silver and specie supply. There was apparently no moral stigma attached to dealing in opium in the early nineteenth century. Prominent among merchants in the opium trade were Augustine Heard, the Wilcocks brothers, Christopher, and T. H. Perkins, all of Boston. Olyphant and Company of New York was the only commercial house that refused to handle opium. The house of T. H. Perkins ranked at the top among opium merchants.[50]

Compared to the English commerce the amount of opium handled by Americans was very small. Between 1805 and 1807 it is estimated that the value of opium carried to Canton varied between $50,000 and $100,000 per season. This represented from 102 to 150 chests of opium per year as compared to 4,000 imported by the ships of the East India Company.[51]

Sporadic attempts at controlling the opium trade were made

---

[48]Quincy, ed., *op. cit.*, pp. 238-239. Shaw tells of the British opium trade through Macao in the late 1780's, describing the system of smuggling and bribery of Chinese officials. This is related to his second trip to Canton. American trade was not sufficiently established to take part.

[49]Stelle, "American Trade in Opium Prior to 1820," *Pacific Historical Review*, vol. 9, March, 1940, p. 429.

[50]*Ibid.*, p. 433. Letters from Perkins to his agent, John Cushing, and to his various ship captains were examined by the author. They reveal that Perkins was the foremost opium importer in Canton.

[51]*Ibid.*

by the Chinese government, but with little effect. The Hong merchants were forbidden to handle the opium directly. Abortive attempts by the Chinese government to cut off the illicit trade increased the risks and resulted in more concentration of the trade in the hands of more wealthy China houses in America. T. H. Perkins continued to lead, but John J. Astor's firm became a rival after 1812.[52]

Although the amount of opium carried by Americans to Canton was never important in the total value of imports, it increased during the seven years following the War of 1812,[53] after which the market became depressed by an over supply. English merchants continued to dominate the opium trade after 1820, American participation in it being inconsequential.

Later treaty negotiations between China and the western powers resulted directly from the abuses of the opium trade. For England the trade was a major item of her total volume of imports to China; for the United States it was an incidental branch of commerce. This contrast is reflected later in the treaty negotiations from 1842 to 1844, which show the United States as having the stronger position in Chinese opinion in terms of good will and cooperation.

Statistical View. The structure and principle trends of the China trade from its inception to the year 1860 have been discussed thus far in general terms. A few statistics for imports, exports, and amount of tonnage for the years 1795 to 1860 illustrate vital relationships, growth, and decline.[54] The following figures show the general trends in the China trade, the relationships between exports and imports, relationships between China trade and total American trade, and the importance of Chinese

---

[52]*Ibid.*, p. 441.

[53]*Ibid.*, p. 442.

[54]Figures from 1795 to 1833 are from: Pitkin, *A Statistical View of Commerce*, 1817 and 1835 editions. Figures from 1840 to 1860 are from: "Annual Report on Commerce and Navigation," *Senate Executive Documents,* 26th Congress, 2nd session, 1840; *ibid.*, 29th Congress, 1st session, 1845; *ibid.*, 31st Congress, 2nd session, 1850; *ibid.*, 34th Congress, 2nd session, 1855; *ibid.*, 36th Congress, 2nd session, 1860.

American Policy Toward China

trade in relation to other principal American trade areas.

The exact money values and tonnages involved in the China trade are difficult to establish. Statistics were compiled by Phipps and Pitkin[55] in a variety of places and ways. They used customhouse records at Canton (after an American consul was established), individual estimates of commercial agents in Canton, and federal customs returns. Before 1820 the *amount* of imports and exports was based on the *value* of imports and exports.[56] In spite of the protective policy of the federal government in regard to the China trade, the customhouse records used by Pitkin (and included after 1821 in the "Annual Reports of Commerce and Navigation") were a fairly accurate indication of the total value of the Chinese trade. Nankeens direct from China were exempt after 1816 from the duty applying to cotton cloth; thus it is likely that this part of the trade is not recorded. Teas, however, which compromised nearly seven-eights of the total as early as 1834, received an assessment from the beginning. By the Tariff Act of 1816, tea was assessed the preferential duty of twelve to fifty cents per pound in contrast to fourteen to sixty-eight cents on teas from ports other than Canton.[57]

The figures in Table 3, representing the total value of American imports and exports in vessels engaged in the China trade, are subject to another inaccuracy. Much of the early tramp trade went unrecorded save for the accounting of individual merchants and the obscure supercargoes. No systematic record of these exists. Goods listed as exports to China may have been disposed of and replaced—perhaps many times along the way—at such places as Capetown, India, Isle of France, Manila, California, the Northwest Coast, and Australia. Similarly the value of imports from Canton might include articles picked up on return voyages from Batavia, Manila, the Hawaiian Islands, and South American and Mexican ports.[58]

---

[55]Phipps, *op. cit.*; Pitkin, *op. cit.*, 1817 and 1835 eds.
[56]Pitkin, *op. cit.* (1835), p. 163; Table A, p. 164.
[57]*Ibid.* (1817), p. 357.
[58]Pitkin, *op. cit.* (1835), p. 253.

Table 3

COMPARATIVE VALUE OF
AMERICAN WORLD TRADE AND AMERICAN CHINA TRADE

Year	Place	Value of Exports from United States	Value of Imports to United States
1795	World	$47,855,556	$69,756,258
	China	1,023,242	1,144,163
1801	World	$93,020,513	$111,574,876
	China	877,276	4,558,356
1807	World	$108,343,150	$138,574,876
1805	China	3,558,815	3,842,000
1816	World	$81,987,000	$147,100,000
	China	2,527,500	4,220,000
1833	World	$87,500,000	$108,118,311
	China	8,362,971	8,225,375
1840	World	$132,085,940	$107,141,519
	China	1,009,966	6,640,829
1845	World	$114,646,606	$117,252,564
	China	2,275,995	7,285,914
1850	World	$151,898,720	$178,183,318
	China	1,605,217	$6,593,462
1855	World	$275,156,846	$261,468,520
	China	1,719,429	11,048,726
1860	World	$400,122,296	$362,100,254
	China	8,906,118	13,566,587

Table 4 indicates the relative value of the China trade in terms of the amount of shipping involved as compared with the total amount of American tonnage registered in foreign trade for selected years.

Table 4

AMOUNT OF SHIPPING ENGAGED IN THE CHINA TRADE FOR SELECTED YEARS

Year	Number of Vessels	Tonnage in China Trade	Tonnage Registered in Foreign Trade
1801	33	5,887	—
1802	34	8,409	—
1803	32	8,314	—
1805	34	10,159	794,341
1816	30	10,209	800,760
1833	59	22,467	750,026
1840	—	18,000	900,000
1845	—	39,000	1,095,172
1850	—	39,000	1,585,711
1855	—	156,000	2,535,136
1860	—	155,000	2,546,237
1946	—	—	120,000,000

Table 5 indicates the decline in the amount of foreign specie used by American traders from 1821 to 1833, and how after 1840 a growing amount of domestic produce (both goods and specie) dominated the value of exports to China.

Table 5

GROWTH OF DOMESTIC PRODUCE AS EXPORTS TO CANTON

Year	Total Exports	Value of Domestic Produce	Value of Foreign Produce	Value of Foreign Specie
1821				$3,902,025
1833				895,985
1840	$1,009,966	Approx. half	Approx. half	
1845	2,275,995	$2,079,341	$196,654	
1850	1,605,217	1,485,961	119,256	
1855	1,719,429	1,533,057	180,372	
1860	8,906,118	7,170,784	1,735,334	

Table 6 shows the growth in importance of the China trade in relation to trade with other countries.

Table 6

RANK OF CHINESE-AMERICAN
TRADE IN WORLD COMMERCE

Year	Imports to the United States	Exports from the United States
1835	Great Britain	Great Britain
	France	France
	Cuba	Cuba
	Mexico	Mexico
	China (fifth)	European countries
		South American countries
		China (fourteenth)
1860	China (sixth)	China (seventh)

An overall picture of the extent and relative value of the China trade can be seen in spite of the gaps and inadequacies of statistical information. The value of exports and imports (Table 3) and amounts of tonnage (Table 5) indicate that it was scarcely more than a trickle in relation to the total world trade of America. In value it ranged from two percent to three percent of the total of American world trade (exports and imports); in tonnage never over one percent. An inconsistent but gradual overall growth is also noticeable from 1795 to 1860 with an increase in percentage of exports to the Chinese market in relation to other American overseas markets (Table 6).

BEGINNINGS OF OFFICIAL POLICY, 1831

It is an accepted fact that the sea traders and commercial agents preceded and paved the way for American expansion and extension of official policy in the Pacific. For the first twenty years of the trade (approximately to 1820), the federal government remained aloof, issuing sea letters (letters of introduction to foreign rulers: see page 76), and performing the constitutional function of regulating commerce in general. Very few people in the United States had more than a vague conception of China

American Policy Toward China

and its relation to their country. China trade grew in its early stages without the benefits of a paternal government (save for the tariff and tonnage policy) and was stimulated only by the desires for profits of a limited number of merchants of the east coast ports.

Obstacles to Trade. The China trade of America went through its early years of growth in a world situation that was continually subjected to boarding parties or capture by war vessels of the major belligerents, England and France. Confiscation and press-gang seizures were not unusual results of such incidents.[59]

If the European powers were at peace—a rare occurrence between 1795 and 1812—pirates were a continual menace to the unprotected Yankee trade. Along the lines of commerce, on the fringes of civilization, were freebooting principalities and strongholds. In the Caribbean and South Atlantic as late as 1820 attacks on unarmed ships were not uncommon.[60] The pirates swarming in the waters around Sumatra, Borneo, the Celebes, and Lintin Island near the China coast were a more serious obstacle to the China trade. Occasionally a pirate ship was encountered in the Indian Ocean. These encounters with Oriental pirates were taken as matters of course in the trade—incidents that occurred so frequently that they received only casual mention in ships' logs.

An obstacle in itself to American trade was the attitude toward Americans and foreigners in general held by the Chinese Mandarin class. They considered traders very low on the social scale. In addition to being traders, white foreigners were considered to be an inferior race. The fact that these white people appeared periodically at Canton to trade was proof to the ruling class that they could not live without the products of China.

---

[59]Latourette, "The History of the Early Relations Between the United States and China, 1784-1844," pp. 49-51. Latourette summarizes this after an examination of government documents and letters of protests from American consuls.

[60]Bowen, *America Sails the Seas* (New York, 1938), ch. 18. Fear of piracy and actual incidences of it are expressed in the firsthand accounts of the following seafarers: Cleveland, *op. cit.;* Fanning, *op. cit.;* Dana, *op. cit.;* and Quincy, ed., *op. cit.*

Trading with foreigners, then, was an act of compassion to be regulated by Chinese whims.[61]

In keeping with this attitude, strict laws forbade foreigners from leaving areas set aside for them in Canton and Whampoa. Foreign traders were forbidden to bring the two articles deemed essential for secure living—women and firearms. There were no chances for friendly contacts to break through the almost complete isolation of foreigners. Trade in this atmosphere, though lucrative, was sometimes hindered by discriminating tariff and tonnage policies, graft, and whimsical imperial decrees.[62]

The early obstacles—danger of piratical attack, capture and confiscation by belligerent ships, inequalities and graft, and the Chinese attitude toward foreigners—were aggravated by the indifference of the United States. Britain had been protecting commerce by naval ships and treaties for years. Americans, ranking second in the China trade, were subjected to discrimination and dangers due to the lack of policy of their government.[63] Not until an overt act resulted in death and property loss did the United States first take action.

First Official Interest. In February of 1831, a Salem vessel, *Friendship*, was attacked by Sumatran pirates while lying at anchor in the roadstead of Quallah-Battoo, a small Malayan principality on the western coast of Sumatra. There was some loss of life and confiscation of cargo worth about $30,000. Five months later, in July, 1831, Messrs. Silsbee, Pickman, Stone, and Jackson of Salem addressed a letter to Washington asking for naval measures to punish the Malayan pirates.[64] The letter was not the determining factor in sending the naval expedition, but it furnished invaluable information regarding sailing directions for the Su-

---

[61]Dulles, *China and America*, p. 13; Quincy, ed., *op. cit.*, pp. 167-171. Shaw complained about the haughty Chinese attitude and the obstacles to free trade and cultural relationships.

[62]Dulles, *China and America*, p. 13.

[63]Marvin, *op. cit.* The abuses of American shipping resulting from the naval wars of France and England and pirate activities in the East Indies are discussed in some detail in chapters 4, 7, and 10.

[64]Reynolds, *Voyage of the United States Frigate Potomac* (New York, 1835), p. 19.

matran coast and the political status of the Malay States.[65]

This far-away incident coincided with the planned cruise of the frigate U.S.S. *Potomac* to the Pacific to relieve a ship and join the Pacific squadron. When the news of the attack reached official circles, the sailing orders of the *Potomac* were changed from the Cape Horn to the Cape of Good Hope route. In that way the frigate would reach Sumatra quicker and also be able to stop off at Capetown, South Africa, where the commander would be able to obtain all possible information concerning Quallah-Battoo in order to determine his course of action on the coast of Sumatra. Commodore Downes was put in command of the *Potomoc*. The ship was disguised as an unarmed merchantman and, in company with the tender *Peacock*, departed for the Sumatran coast.

In the light of information received from the Salem merchants and additional information picked up at Capetown, the commodore decided that the best policy upon reaching Quallah-Battoo would be to launch a sudden and overwhelming attack without preliminary threats or negotiations. Accordingly, at dawn on May 30, 1831, an amphibious assault was delivered. The shore guns were quickly silenced and the important forts destroyed by cannon brought ashore from the ship. A detachment of seamen, led by an advance wave of marines, swept throught the village, inflicting heavy losses among the Malay forces and driving the inhabitants of the town back into the jungle. The local ruler was sought out the next day. Chastened and penitent, he gave apologies for the attack on the American ship *Friendship* and gave promises of future peaceful attitudes toward American traders.

This severe and arbitrary action on the part of Commodore Downes received some criticism in official circles at home. Considered from the standpoint of conditions in Sumatra and the accepted practices of other western nations, it was doubtless the only feasible course to obtain results. Other nations of Europe, as France, Holland, and Denmark, having less at stake in the Oriental trade, periodically sent armed vessels to look after trade interests in the East Indies.[66] But the American trade had been

---

[65] *Ibid.*, p. 533.
[66] *Ibid.*, p. 122.

carried on for nearly forty years without the shadow of protection from the American navy. The Malay principality itself, in an early stage of culture and political growth, eked out a parasitic existence from lone, unprotected traders. The use of naval force seemed, at the time, more effective than the usual instrument of negotiations and treaty.

Emergence of China Policy. The vengeance by the *Potomac* was the first overt act of official nature in connection with the Chinese trade.[67] Although isolated attacks on pirate strongholds can hardly be called official steps in developing policy toward the Pacific area, the basic instructions from the secretary of the navy, Levi Woodbury, to Commodore Downes foreshadowed such such a development. In regard to the operation at Quallah-Battoo, Downes was given much discretion by the vague and innocuous wording of his orders. It seemed to be almost an incidental part of his mission. The broad scope of the Pacific ocean as a trade area was conspicuously stressed. He was instructed to visit Macao (a port of Canton) and all of the islands along his track to the South American coast that were frequented by whalers and merchantmen.[68] In connection with the China merchants he was instructed to "give any temporary aid or relief in your power without involving this country in any hostilities with the regular and authorized authorities of China."[69]

This was an early expression of a thread in Chinese policy that is consistently seen throughout the early treaty negotiations of 1844, 1858, 1868, and to the John Hay statement of the Open Door policy. It placed the United States in the position of a nation interested in furthering trade relations and at the same time scrupulously maintaining both the integrity of China and friendly relations with her as an independent nation. It was the beginning of the policy of avoiding overt acts of hostility

---

[67]Dulles, *China and America*, p. 12. Naval ships had circumnavigated the world and contacted China before the voyage of the *Potomac* in 1831. In 1819 the frigate *Congress* visited Canton. In 1839 the *Vincennes*, on a world cruise, also touched Canton. No concrete results were forthcoming from these contacts, however.

[68]Reynolds, *op. cit.*, appendix, p. 529.

[69]*Ibid.*

toward China and yet not being indisposed to pressing every advantage of trade, whether it be by treaty or through coercion of China by another foreign power.

J. N. Reynolds, a secretary to Commodore Downes who joined the ship after it had reached the Pacific station, pieced together the story of the *Potomac's* voyage by personal conversation with officers and men, official orders, and ship's logs. His conclusions and observations were not from firsthand acquaintances but from reliable primary sources. His book painted the commercial picture in the Pacific pointing to the growing American trade, lack of marine hospitals, and absence of naval power to protect the commerce.[70] He quoted a letter from J. C. Jones, consul at Honolulu, asking Commodore Downes for a naval ship to control desertions from whalers and merchantmen in the islands. Based on the records concerning the voyage of the *Potomac,* Reynolds concluded that more naval protection was needed in the Pacific and that the time had come for awakening interest in China among the American people.[71]

BACKGROUND OF THE CUSHING MISSION 1834-1844

Events as they transpired in Canton during the late 1830's were to result in an aroused American interest in China and direct governmental policy in relation to the China trade. Growing British-Chinese tension during the decade resulted in incidents that radically changed the status of American trade in Canton. In 1834, as a result of the breaking of the monopoly held by the British East India Company, the British official, Lord Napier, arrived in Canton to take over his duties as first chief superintendent of English trade. The old conflicts based on the Chinese doctrine of barbarian inferiority began to be felt immediately.

---

[70] See note 64, this chapter.
[71] Reynolds, *op. cit.,* p. 385. "There is now a fundamental principle in commerce and that is, a thorough and extended knowledge of the dispositions, habits, and necessities of the people, and of the natural capacities and resources of the country where we have commercial intercourse. At no period of our history had this knowledge of China been so essential to our interests as at the present moment."

Napier's attempt to communicate directly with the resident Chinese viceroy was repulsed. Likewise his violation of the rule that made the Hong merchant an intermediary proved unfortunate when he attempted to go directly to Canton to negotiate about matters of trade. Without the force of the British fleet, which had not been sent to China as yet, Lord Napier was forced to withdraw to Macao.[72] He found he was an official without status or a means of direct negotiation with Chinese officials of equal rank in spite of his important position in the British imperial system.

Disturbances in Canton. The opium trade gave rise to the first overt act of violence between England and China. In 1839 the Chinese governor of Canton, aroused by the growing traffic in the illegal drug, confiscated all the stocks of opium in the foreign warehouses. The British were hit the hardest.[73] Captain Charles Elliott, the new chief superintendent of the British trade, ordered all British merchants to withdraw from Canton to Macao.[74] Large units of the British fleet soon appeared and waged an informal and undeclared war throughout 1840 and 1841. The Chinese forts along the Canton River were destroyed and the British fleet and Imperial Marines moved north along the coast capturing Amoy, Tinghai, Chinhai, Ningpo, and Shanghai.[75] When Nanking was threatened, China sued for peace.

During the hostilities the American consul in Canton, Peter Snow, advised the American traders to withdraw in protest to Macao along with the British merchants. The advice was ignored and American trade went on as before. American traders and merchants maintained a strict neutrality and profited greatly by the temporary English withdrawal from Canton.[76]

In spite of the profits gained by American merchants during the Opium War, the arbitrary seizure of goods by Chinese offi-

---

[72]Dulles, *China and America,* p. 19.
[73]See page 87 for comparison of English and American opium traffic.
[74]Dulles, *op. cit.,* p. 20.
[75]Abend, *op. cit.,* pp. 37-38.
[76]*Ibid.,* p. 21. The opium seizure was hardly an issue of dispute with American merchants since opium imports amounted to approximately three percent of the total American imports in 1840-1841.

cials began to convince Americans in China that trade could not be carried on much longer in the old ways. Dependence upon Chinese whims, lack of official protection, and the growing volume of trade all tended to arouse the American merchants in Canton to the realization that governmental aid and protection were necessary. The chain of events after 1839 clearly illustrate how the incentive of the Pacific trade and the influence of people participating in it helped the formation of official American policy toward China.

Pressure on Congress. A memorial from leading American merchants in Canton, addressed to Congress, appeared in 1839. Leader in the movement was R. B. Forbes, agent of a Boston house in Canton. The memorial was a review of the general trade conditions, abuses of the Chinese government, a sketch of the opium trade, and an appeal to Congress for a commercial agent to be sent out to negotiate a trade treaty. Naval protection was also requested. The memorialists asked that trade be put on a "safe and honorable footing" based upon: (1) direct communication with the imperial capital at Peking; (2) fixed tariff duties; (3) a bonded warehouse system for duty-free reexporting; (4) liberty to trade at ports other than Canton; (5) compensation for American losses incurred at the start of the Opium War; (6) punishment of American offenders under English and American law "until the Chinese laws are distinctly made known and recognized"; (7) negotiation of a commercial treaty and provision for naval protection. The memorial, dated May 25, 1839, was signed by Russell Sturgis, W. Delano, Jr., A. A. Low, Edward King S. S. Rowe, and James Ryan.[77]

This memorial had no immediate effect upon Congress, but it is interesting to note that a series of official acts followed in quick succession. Also of interest is the similarity between the points in the memorial and subsequent treaties between China and the United States.

It had been the policy of the United States government before

---

[77]*House Documents*, No. 40, 26th Congress, 1st session, pp. 1-6; cited in Clyde, *United States Policy Toward China, Diplomatic and Public Documents 1839-1939* (Durham, N. C., 1940), pp. 5-6.

1840 to let American merchants shift for themselves in China. The memorial of the Canton merchants had followed shortly after the arrival of the British fleet in Chinese waters. Six months after the formulation of the Canton memorial, Secretary of the Navy Pauling, in November, 1839, placed Commodore Kearny in command of an East Indian squadron with a set of more far-reaching instructions than those issued to Commodore Downes in 1831[78] (see pp. 95, 96). He was to proceed to Canton over the route the *Potomac* had used[79] and, upon his arrival, was to give all lawful and necessary assistance to Americans in Canton. He was admonished to respect the laws of China and to impress upon her the deep feelings of friendship extended to her by the United States. American trade was to be protected and the opium trade was to be stopped.[80]

Work of Commodore Kearny. Commodore Kearny arrived off Macao in March, 1842 as the Opium War was drawing to a close. The historic old warship *Constellation* was his flagship, which, with two other frigates, made up the East India squadron.[81] Kearny's course of action is of some importance for the energetic way in which he carried out his instructions and for the precedents and ground work established by his negotiations with the Chinese officials.

Soon after his arrival he took up the problems of trade presented to him by the American merchants. There were claims for damages against the Chinese government and claims of the Chinese governor of Canton against Americans accused of smug-

---

[78] Alden, *Lawrence Kearny, Sailor Diplomat* (Princeton, 1936), p. 139.

[79] *Senate Documents*, No. 139, 29th Congress, 3rd session, p. 6. Commodore Kearny stopped off at Quallah-Battoo en route to Canton to "show the flag." He addressed a letter to the Rajah expressing friendship and also veiled threats of force in the event of a repetition of an incident similar to the *Friendship* massacre.

[80] Alden, *op. cit.*, pp. 139-141. Protection of the China trade during the Opium War was the primary aim. His instructions, however, contained orders to view the whale fisheries of New Zealand and New Holland and to visit the Hawaiian Islands, Society Islands, and others frequented by American whalers.

[81] *Ibid.*, p. 129.

American Policy Toward China 101

gling opium.[82] Kearny apparently made an earnest effort to remove the abuse of fraudulent use of the American flag. The case of the schooner *Ariel* is an example of a ship carrying the American flag while engaging in the opium trade. Kearny captured the schooner and found it to be a ship of illegal American registry.[83] Although Kearny exerted some real pressure on the Chinese for settlement of damage claims, his attempts at checking the opium trade were probably more effective in demonstrating the American attitude than in achieving results.

Kearny's arrival in China preceded by five months the signing of the Chinese-British Treaty of Nanking, in August, 1842.[84] It was in connection with this negotiation, rather than in protection of American merchants, that he made his greatest contribution to the formation of American policy in the East. His instructions contained nothing specific as to what his course of action should be in regard to the changed status of English commerce following a victorious war with Chinese. He was intelligent enough to realize, however, the importance of such an event when it happened. As soon as the terms of peace were known he dispatched copies of the treaty to Washington by various sea and overland routes to insure its safe arrival.

Between the time of the end of the Opium War and the arrival of the British treaty commissioner, Kearny took a most important step in the development of American policy. In October, 1842 he wrote to the Chinese governor of Canton, Ke,

---

[82]*Senate Documents*, No. 139, 29th Congress, 3rd session, pp. 1-47. The scope of his work in straightening out mutual trade abuses is shown in his letters to the American consul stating his opposition to the opium trade and his request that the consul issue a proclamation prohibiting it. He wrote letters to the governor of Canton, Ke, concerning instances of Chinese piracy and obtained right to punish future cases. Some vague satisfaction was gotten on the question of claims for damages against Chinese and irresponsible soldiers in the case of riots and firing on American boats and ships.

[83]Forbes, *op. cit.*, p. 22. The schooner had been built in Boston in 1841 for the China trade and taken out by an American captain. By 1843 her registry had lapsed and she was illegally freighting opium from points in the East Indies to Canton.

[84]Alden, *op. cit.*, p. 164.

expressing the hope that before a final treaty was drafted United States trade would be placed on "the same footing as the merchants of nations most favored."[85] Soon a reply came back from Governor Ke agreeing in vague and flowery phrases,[86] though no definite commitments were made until a few weeks after Kearny's squadron had departed for the Hawaiian Islands. Then came a letter from the imperial high commissioner (for the Nanking negotiations) and the governor of Canton (the same Ke). Addressed to the American consul in Canton it referred to Commodore Kearny's original request for equal treatment in commercial affairs and stated that each of the foreign nations would be allowed to trade at newly opened ports of Fuchow, Amoy, Ningpo, and Shanghai.[87]

Extreme claims have been made for the importance of Commodore Kearny's letter requesting equal treatment with other foreign countries in trade relations. It has been claimed that he was responsible for the most-favored-nation clause in the Treaty of Nanking. His biographer, generalizing cautiously, stated that "he took the first steps in founding a definite American policy for China."[88] This was a policy that antedated Perry in Japan by ten years and was equally far reaching. Kearny did succeed in making a favorable impression upon the Cantonese at a critical time. He secured a just settlement of claims and made friends with Chinese officials. Regardless of the controversy as to the origin of the most-favored-nation clause, he urged upon the Chinese commissioners at the time of the Nanking negotiations equal rights, which were granted because the American traders were on the scene.[89]

---

[85] *Senate Documents*, No. 139, 29th Congress, 1st session, p. 21.
[86] *Ibid.*
[87] Alden, *op. cit.*, p. 181.
[88] *Ibid.*, p. 130.
[89] The question as to who was the originator of the most-favored-nation clause has resulted in a controversy: (1) A Professor Tsaing, who had access to the original Chinese documents in Peking, says the Chinese had decided to include a most-favored-nation clause, while Kearny's letter merely put it on the agenda (*Chinese Social and Political Review*, vol. 15, no. 30 (October, 1931); (2) Thomas Kearny, Esquire, of New York says

This concept of equal rights became the basis of American policy with minor variations throughout the nineteenth and into the twentieth century. Kearny's reports to his superior officers served to keep the government fully informed as to the current situation in China during a critical time. It had unmistakable influence on policy formation.[90] His China mission is a direct link between abuses suffered by the American merchants in Canton and the sending of the first official emissary from the United States. As Kearny's biographer put it, "his representatives prompted the sending of the able Cushing commission . . . that made permanent and official what had been informally secured."[91]

Agitation for a China Mission. Before official policy had been formed to the point of sending a diplomatic mission to China, however, a series of events transpired at the policymaking level. They can be traced in official documents and are interesting for showing the influence of trade on the gradual development of American-Chinese policy. On January 7, 1840, two months after Commodore Kearny had received his instructions regarding the China trade (see page 100), Pickens, of the House Foreign Affairs Committee, brought up a resolution asking the president for all available information concerning the effect of

---

the commodore's work alone was responsible ("Commodore Lawrence Kearny," *New Jersey Historical Society*, vol. 50, no. 2 [April, 1932]; also in "Tsaing Documents," *Chinese Social and Political Science Review*, vol. 16, no. 1 [April, 1932]); and (3) A Mr. Martin, member of the Hong Kong legislative council, states that the most-favored-nation clause was a result of policy of a farsighted American on guard against discrimination (Martin, *China*, 1844, vol. 1, p. 414). All of these authorities are cited in Alden *op. cit.*, p. 185.

[90]*Senate Documents*, No. 139, 29th Congress, 3rd session, pp. 1-47. Just before his departure, in a letter to Daniel Webster, Kearny pointed out the evils of letting merchants act as official consuls. His letters to the secretary of the navy kept the government posted on the military situations during the Opium War and conscious of the necessity of keeping a fleet in China. He also supplied information about the extent of the opium trade, piracy, and the nature of relations between Chinese and Americans in Canton.

[91]Alden, *op. cit.*, p. 185.

the opium trade on American commerce and the Chinese policy of the British government. Furthermore, it was asked that the secretary of the treasury submit statistics on the American-China trade for the years from 1821 to 1839 in regard to tonnage, specific duties, and number of ships involved.[92]

A prompt reply came back from President Van Buren on February 25, 1840. In a special communication to the House of Representatives he sent along all of the information in the form of a compilation of letters from China to Secretary of State John Forsyth. The mass of detail included in these communications conveys a general picture of confusion and insecurity of American trade interests in Canton.

A few examples will illustrate this picture. The American consul, Snow, writing to Secretary Forsyth, described the execution of a Chinese opium dealer in front of the American factory in Canton in 1838. Snow also included newspapers and memoranda about the extent of the opium trade and incidents of ill-feeling between the Hong merchants and Canton officials. Snow, in one of his letters to the secretary of navy, suggested the stationing of naval vessels on the China coast. An 1839 edict of the Chinese governor in Canton prohibiting the opium trade was included. Letters from Commodore Reed to the secretary of the navy in 1839 detailed the obstacles to trade, the futile attempts to stamp out the opium trade, and the need of fleet protection on the China coast. A later letter from Snow to Secretary of State Forsyth gave illustrations of the haughty attitude of Chinese officialdom and the impossibility of dealing with them on a basis of equality.[93]

More evidence concerning the China trade was supplied to Congress on April 9, 1840. A memorial from leading Salem and Boston merchants was received and was referred to the House Committee on Foreign Affairs.[94] It stated a curious combination of desire for both protection and freedom in the China trade. It

---

[92]*Congressional Globe*, 26th Congress, 1st session, January 7, 1840, p. 172.

[93]The message of the president indicating these impressions is included in *Executive Documents*, No. 119, 26th Congress, 1st session, pp. 1-85.

[94]*Executive Documents*, No. 170, 26th Congress, 1st session, pp. 1-4.

American Policy Toward China 105

emphasized the necessity of a naval force to protect American ships and advised against interfering in the Chinese-British war or of sending a diplomatic mission until more knowledge was available concerning the customs of the Chinese. The merchants simply wanted a China policy regulated by a treaty that would remove the fear of pirates and prevent attacks from the Cantonese, while at the same time not inhibiting their freedom of action in commercial affairs.

In December, 1840, President Van Buren supplied additional information to the House of Representatives on the question of the British blockade of Chinese ports. In this communication, letters from the American minister in London, Mr. Stevens, to Secretary of State Forsyth indicated that the British expected to blockade Chinese ports but that it would affect American trade very little.[95] An exchange of letters between Stevens and Lord Palmerston brought out the existence of a blockade and the vague guarantee of American neutral rights. "Unless extreme measures deem it fitting, only Chinese vessels will be seized."[96]

Early in the following year, January 25, 1841, President Van Buren sent another message to both Houses of Congress. In it he reviewed the political and commerical relations from 1790 to 1840. It was referred to the Foreign Affairs Committee of the Senate and to a similar committee in the House of Representatives.[97] Extracts from the letter from American consuls to the secretaries of state brought out the main abuses and obstacles to American trade that were encountered during this period. The principal communications were Samuel Shaw's commission from President Washington (1790); a letter from Consul Carrington to J. Q. Adams (1805) attacking the Hong system as an obstacle to trade; letters to President Madison requesting funds for a salaried consul and a paid public physician (1807); consular letters to Secretary of State J. Q. Adams concerning the raiding and seizure of American ships by Chinese pirates

---

[95]*Executive Documents*, No. 34, 26th Congress, 2nd session, pp. 1-4.
[96]*Ibid.*, p. 4; *Executive Documents*, No. 71, 26th Congress, 2nd session, pp. 1-83.
[97]*Ibid.*, p. 60.

(1817); documents of the Terranova Affair⁹⁸ (about fifty percent of the total eighty-three pages devoted to that incident); edicts of the imperial government and documentary evidence about the opium trade (1839); and letters of Snow to Secretary of State Forsyth citing opium troubles and hindrances to trade resulting from the Opium War. Snow reiterated the general feeling among Americans in China by stating that "the magnitude of our trade strongly claims protection, and we are fondly hoping that [the] government will consider it of sufficient importance to make this a naval station."⁹⁹ The part of Van Buren's message treating with conditions in China was principally a compilation of communications reporting contemporary events. There was very little pressure for naval protection and no specific mention of the need for treaty protection.¹⁰⁰

The next significant link in the chain of official events was a section of President Tyler's annual message to Congress on December 31, 1842.¹⁰¹ He sketched the main incidents in the recent Opium War in China, expressing the opinion that other

---

⁹⁸While serving on the American vessel *Emily* in 1821, an American sailor named Terranova got in an argument with a Chinese woman who had come out in a small boat to sell vegetables. During the dispute the woman fell overboard and drowned. Terranova was eventually tried in a farcical manner by a Chinese court on board the *Emily*, condemned, and put to death. The affair not only caused ill feeling between the Chinese and Americans, but it convinced many Americans that the Chinese laws were inadequate for settling disputes in a manner in keeping with Western standards of justice. Chinese law proved to be following too closely the ancient doctrine of an eye-for-an-eye in spite of moral issues or extenuating circumstances.

⁹⁹*Executive Documents*, No. 71, 26th Congress, 2nd session, p. 60.

¹⁰⁰Adams, ed., *Memoirs of John Quincy Adams* (Philadelphia, 1876), vol. 10, p. 445. Some Congressional debate had taken place as early as 1841. J. Q. Adams, in March of that year, took the point of view that the time was not ripe for a full diplomatic mission. He thought it unwise to attempt to mediate in the opium controversy between England and China.

¹⁰¹Agitation for official action in China was not stilled between the two presidential messages (Van Buren's in 1841 and Tyler's in 1842). It will be recalled that letters from Commodore Kearny concerning the situation of American trade in China kept coming in to the secretaries of navy and state from early in 1842 until the following year.

American Policy Toward China   107

nations would have to pursue individual policies to obtain equal status with Great Britain in the China trade. Statistics showing the value of direct trade with China for the years 1831 to 1841 were included to emphasize the importance of the American commercial stake in China. President Tyler's message was a concise summary of the pertinent communications, memorials, and official statements that had been exerting influence on official thinking since the mission of Commodore Downes in 1831. The most relevant statement of Tyler was the passage in which he went on record as "being of the opinion that the commercial interests of the United States require at the present moment a degree of attention and vigilance such as there is no agent of this government on the spot to bestow."[102]

The insecurity of the American interests in China, in spite of actual prosperity, had been made apparent to the policymakers. Tyler stated the need for official action in these words: "I recommend to Congress to make appropriation for the compensation of a commission to reside in China to exercise a watchful care over the concern of American citizens . . . and empowered to hold intercourse with the local authorities, and ready, under instructions from this government, . . . to address himself to the high functionaries of the Empire, or through the Emperor himself."[103] Tyler's message of December 31, 1842 was of tremendous significance. It was more than a recommendation for a Chinese treaty. Trade conditions in Hawaii and the desirability of official connections with the islands were mentioned. It reflected a general Pacific advance on the part of the United States.

In the House of Representatives the debates concerning Tyler's recommendation dealt not with the advisability of a China mission but with the amount of appropriation necessary to accomplish it. There was no serious questioning of Tyler's basic policy.[104] The wording of the appropriation bill is interesting for

---

[102] *Executive Documents*, No. 35, 27th Congress, 3rd session, p. 3.

[103] *Executive Documents*, No. 35, 27th Congress, 3rd session, p. 3.

[104] *Congressional Globe*, 27th Congress, 3rd session, appendix, p. 325. It passed the House February 21, 1843 by a vote of 96 to 59. Nine thousand dollars was appropriated for Cushing's salary and forty thousand dollars for the expenses of the mission.

its reflection of basic United States policy in China. The appropriation was for a mission to establish "the future commercial relations of the United States with China on *terms of equal reciprocity.*"[105]

THE CUSHING MISSION, 1844

The Cushing mission to China and the successful negotiation of the Treaty of Wanghai are familiar landmarks in American Pacific foreign policy. Its connection with maritime trade in the past and its importance to future commercial expansion in China is obvious. The general histories, in discussing the development of the United States as a world power, rarely fail to mention the Chinese-American treaty but scarcely tie it up with the previous events in China or establish a logical connection between the treaty provisions of Wanghai and American policy in China since that time.

Cushing's Interest in the China Trade. Caleb Cushing, as it turned out, was a fortunate choice as head of the diplomatic mission. Edward Everett, minister to England, was chosen originally but refused for fear of being "kicked upstairs" to make room for Daniel Webster in London. Cushing, therefore, was not selected unanimously and unequivocally for his sympathetic views toward New England commerce or for any other particular qualification.[106] Yet as a member of the Foreign Affairs Committee of the House of Representatives he had shown intense interest in developing a governmental policy that would strengthen the United States in China. It was he who moved, after the petition of the Canton merchants was referred to his committee, that the president provide Congress with all available information concerning conditions of American trade in Canton.[107] Again, in 1842, a few weeks before Tyler's decisive message to Congress concerning Pacific policy, Cushing had sent a long letter to the president recommending that a mission be sent. In it he revealed his strong Anglophobia—a feeling that doubtless had much to do

---

[105]Fuess, Claude M., *Life of Caleb Cushing* (New York, Harcourt Brace Jovanovich, Inc. 1923), vol. 1, p. 408. Italics added.

[106]Fuess, *op. cit.*, vol. 1, p. 411.

[107]*Ibid.*, vol. 1, p. 404.

American Policy Toward China 109

with guiding American policy in general. The Open Door idea can be detected in this letter: ". . . we can, only by the extent of our commerce, act in counterpoise to . . . England, and thus save the Chinese from that which would be extremely inconvenient for them, viz., the condition of being an exclusive monopoly in the hands of England."[108]

The early background of Caleb Cushing is also of some importance for the fact that he grew up in an atmosphere of ships and commerce in Newburyport, Massachusetts. J. N. Cushing, his father, followed a familiar pattern—went to sea as a youth, became wealthy, and settled down ashore as a shipowner and merchant. Between 1830 and 1848 he sent ships out to Russia and north European ports. Young Cushing's first memories were heavily conditioned by the shipping-class point of view.[109] It is likely that he often heard Thomas Jefferson dubbed a Jacobin scoundrel and his policies termed the ruination of the country.

Cushing's Instructions. Cushing received his commission and orders on May 8, 1843, as soon as news of the end of the Opium War was received and the provisions of the British-Chinese Treaty of Nanking were made known.[110] His instructions, in a long letter from Secretary of State Webster, were a statement of American policy based on antecedents and designed as a guide for future relationships between China and America.[111] Cushing was furnished with figures on the value of the export trade of the United States to China up to 1842 and was instructed that a leading object was to obtain access, on a basis of equality,

---

[108]Dulles, Foster Rhea, *China and America: The Story of their Relations Since 1784* (Copyright 1946 by Princeton University Press), p. 24. Letter from Cushing to Tyler, December, 1842.
Reprinted by permission of Princeton University Press.

[109]Fuess, *op. cit.*, vol. 1, p. 21; Dulles, *China and America*, p. 22. In carrying out the China mission Cushing probably had a narrow view, seeing it only as a measure to forestall British monopoly. Opposed to this concept was the view represented by J. Q. Adams, who saw the basic fallacy of Chinese arrogance in following a policy of seclusion in an already interdependent world. Adams *op. cit.*, vol. 11, p. 30.

[110]Kuo, "Caleb Cushing and the Treaty of Wanghai," *Journal of Modern History*, vol. 5 (March, 1933), p. 34.

[111]*Senate Documents*, No. 138, 28th Congress, 1st session, pp. 1-9.

to the four new ports that had been opened recently by force of British arms.[112]

A basic aim was to impress the Chinese with the peaceful intentions of the United States. Cushing was to mention the fact that America had no foreign colonies and desired none. He was content to contrast the policy of force used by England and the peaceful desires and acts of cooperation, characteristic of American action in the past.[113] Cushing was to establish direct communication with Peking, if possible, and to remove the tribute-bearing-nation concept from the Chinese attitude. As to the obnoxious "Kowtow" ceremony before the Chinese emperor, the orders were vague, urging him only to maintain a status of equality with Chinese officials.[114] In establishing such equality Webster stated that Cushing "would be conducting Chinese intercourse one step further toward the principles which regulate the public relations of European and American States."[115]

Another of Cushing's instructions concerned the control of the opium trade. In a separate letter from the State Department, sent just before his departure, he was told of the rumor that the American consul, R. B. Forbes, was dealing heavily in opium.[116] Cushing was instructed to investigate.[117]

Cushing's instructions outlined a broad policy, many of the details and much of the spirit of which were not realized until several decades later. A Chinese scholar, P. C. Kuo, has stated the principal aim in these words: "stripped of all verbiage [he was to] negotiate a treaty with China whereby the same privileges as had lately been acquired by the British would be secured for the American merchants."[118]

---

[112]*Ibid.*, p. 2.

[113]*Senate Documents*, No. 138, 28th Congress, 1st session, p. 4.

[114]*Ibid.*

[115]*Ibid.*, p. 5.

[116]*Senate Documents*, No. 138, 28th Congress, 1st session, p. 7.

[117]Kearny had suggested divorcing commerce and consulate work the year before. This suggestion to Cushing was a step toward the policy of having a disinterested person in the office of consul.

[118]Kuo, Ping Chia "Caleb Cushing and the Treaty of Wanghai, 1844," *Journal of Modern History*, vol. 5 (March, 1933, University of Chicago Press), p. 35.

Treaty of Wanghai. The Cushing mission arrived in China in February, 1844 and established headquarters at Macao.[119] A series of delays followed, while Cushing spent much energy in a futile exchange of letters with Acting Viceroy Ching at Canton, in which Cushing attempted to get recognition as a fully accredited representative from the United States.

The Chinese envoy, Kiying, finally met with Cushing on May 16, 1844 in a small temple at Wanghai near Macao. Negotiations were obstructed for a time by Cushing's insistence on free access to Peking. Such a concession would have been unprecedented in the history of Chinese relations with "barbaric" countries, and Commissioner Kiying bent every effort toward forestalling it. At first consideration it would seem Cushing was holding up more important negotiations to gain a minor point in his instructions. When Cushing finally abandoned the demand, however, negotiations went on quickly, resulting in the final signature in July, 1844. Apparently the Chinese commissioner had been so distracted by Cushing's insistence on a Peking visit that he was quite willing to make any other concession to check that one.[120]

The treaty signed at Wanghai was the first articulate expression of American Eastern policy as it had developed since 1784. It was to form the basis of a policy that has in various forms survived to this day. Early in the negotiations Cushing wrote a letter to Commissioner Kiying in which he sketched broadly

---

[119]The description of the preparations for the mission, the equipment, Cushing's ornate uniform, the elaborate naval fleet, and the narrative of the trip make an entertaining story. It is told in some detail in general works on Chinese-American relations such as Dulles, *China and America;* Latourette, "History of Early Relations Between the United States and China"; firsthand accounts, such as the diary of Cushing himself, used by Fuess in his *Life of Caleb Cushing,* and *Senate Documents,* No. 67, 28th Congress, 2nd session, pp. 1]-104.

[120]Kuo, "Caleb Cushing and the Treaty of Wanghai, 1844," p. 52; conclusions in *Senate Executive Documents,* No. 67, 28th Congress, 2nd session, p. 60. In a letter to Secretary of State John C. Calhoun in July of 1844, Cushing sketched his efforts to get to Peking and concluded that insistence would be inadvisable before the treaty was actually secure; insistence on a Peking visit presented the alternative of prostration before the emperor or war with China.

the provisions of the proposed treaty.[121] It was an outline of American policy toward China. The three main ideas suggested were: (1) cordial and lasting friendship between the two countries; (2) unwillingness of the United States to annex any Chinese territory; and (3) complete and free reciprocity. The reciprocity guarantee was, of course, purely an academic question since China had no control over her exterior commerce with the world. The other two principles have been guiding themes in American policy since that time. The treaty, however, in the form in which it was finally passed was in reality a long list of concessions (thirty-four articles) granted to the American commercial interests in China.[122]

Significance of Wanghai. The treaty afforded a firm American foothold in Asia. The United States promised to uphold the laws of China (Article XXIX and XXXII), but Article II extended to the United States all concessions and privileges granted to other foreign countries. Here was the familiar most-favored-nation clause which, according to Clyde, was "fundamental to American policy in China from that day to the present."[123] The other major concession was included in Article XXI, providing that Americans accused of crimes in China be dealt with in accordance with the laws of the United States.

During the negotiations at Wanghai a small incident took place that first brought the question of extraterritoriality into Chinese-American relations. A group of Chinese broke into an American garden at a factory in Canton. In the course of the ensuing riot one Chinese, Sue Aman, was killed by the Americans as they defended themselves.[124] Mr. Cushing, being the senior official of the American government near the scene, was asked to examine the case. He recommended a course of action to the American consul, Forbes, in a letter in June, 1844: "Accordingly I shall at one and all refuse application for the surrender of the

---

[121]*Senate Executive Documents*, No. 67, 28th Congress, 2nd session, pp. 41-42.

[122]Miller, *Treaties and Other International Acts of the United States*, vol. 6, pp. 559-579; Clyde, *United States Policy Toward China*, pp. 13-21.

[123]Clyde, *op. cit.*, p. 13. Reflections of Commodore Kearny's instructions are seen in this treaty stipulation; see pp. 99-102.

[124]Kuo, "Caleb Cushing and the Treaty of Wanghai, 1844," pp. 44-45.

American Policy Toward China   113

party who killed Sue Aman; which refusal involves the duty of instituting an examination of the facts by the agency of officers of the United States."[125] This, according to Mr. Kuo, is the first expression of the theory of extraterritoriality in regard to China.[126]

In September of the same year Cushing wrote a long letter to John C. Calhoun on the subject of extraterritoriality. It was a closely worded legal document, as between lawyers, citing precedents established in other areas of American trade contacts, such as the Levant, Italian cities, and North Africa. Mr. Cushing took the point of view that logical magistrates in countries "outside the limits of Christendom" should exercise no legal authority over the lives and properties of American citizens. Although this principle was stated in the Treaty of Wanghai no machinery, such as an American judicial system and suitable places of confinement and punishment, was set up to put it into force. Extraterritoriality as stated by Cushing at this time was later recognized in international law.[127] It was a principle that would plague Chinese-American relations until well into the twentieth century.

The final treaty was submitted to Congress, along with all of the letters and documents in connection with its negotiation, in January, 1845.[128] With his recommendation for ratification, President Tyler submitted a recommendation for new Congressional law to implement the theory of extraterritoriality.[129] He further recommended the establishment of a permanent minister with full diplomatic powers as well as paid consuls in all five treaty ports as the British had. Cushing had advised the secretary of state, Calhoun, of the advisability of such measure in October of 1844 before Tyler's 1845 communication to Congress.[130]

[125]*Senate Documents*, No. 67, 28th Congress, 2nd session, pp. 65-66.
[126]Kuo, "Caleb Cushing and the Treaty of Wanghai, 1844," p. 45.
[127]Fuess, *op. cit.*, vol. 1, p. 439.
[128]*Senate Executive Documents*, No. 67, 28th Congress, 2nd session, pp. 1-104 contain all documents and letters but not the treaty.
[129]*Senate Executive Documents*, No. 58, 28th Congress, 2nd session, p. 2.
[130]*Ibid.*, p. 14. No such measure was passed until 1855 when salaried consuls with judicial authority were set up in the five treaty ports. Griffin, *Clippers and Consuls* (Ann Arbor, 1938), p. 51.

The successful negotiation of the treaty with China was a major triumph in Cushing's career, which was distinguished and not devoid of other achievements. His mission climaxed a series of events that tended to drive Chinese affairs increasingly into the realm of official policy. Much general interest was also stimulated by the negotiation. During the autumn of 1845 Cushing toured the larger cities of the East Coast of America speaking on China and Chinese policy. He was in demand as a lyceum lecturer rivalling, according to his biographer, Wendell Phillips and Edward Everett.[131]

Caleb Cushing's work has been evaluated in various ways. It apparently stimulated the sending of similar missions from other countries. The French delegation arrived in Macao before Cushing had completed his negotiations.[132] K. S. Latourette concludes that Chinese seclusion and the policy of holding western nations at arm's length was advantageously attacked by Cushing.[133] But Foster Rhea Dulles, writing after the successful conclusion of a war fought directly over our Pacific commitments, took long-time Chinese interests into account and offered a less optimistic commentary on the Treaty of Wanghai.[134] For a century, he said, it proved to be a barrier to Chinese attempts to wield more independent power over their own affairs. At the time it seemed advantageous to China to avoid further political and military pressure; actually it loosed a chain of other pressures, culminating in the Open Door. This evaluation is probably the sounder from the standpoint of subsequent American policy in China.[135]

---

[131]Fuess, *op. cit.*, vol. 1, p. 453.

[132]*Senate Executive Documents*, No. 67, 28th Congress, 2nd session, p. 88.

[133]Latourette, *The United States Moves Across the Pacific* (New York, 1946), p. 144.

[134]Dulles, *China and America*, p. 30.

[135]Clyde, *The Far East*, New York, 1948. This work gives a full textual treatment of Oriental development resulting from western contacts. American policy, resulting from maritime antecedents is traced down to the post-World War II period. It is a convenient summary and reference for further study. Clyde, *United States Policy Toward China* is a convenient compilation of essential documents in tracing American policy and its applications.

THE WANGHAI POLICY TO 1898

Maritime commerce as a conditioning influence on American policy toward China has been suggested and traced to the year of the signing of the Treaty of Wanghai, 1844. Although an exhaustive review of foreign relations is beyond this study, some later incidents involving the policy established at Wanghai will be reviewed. They are:

1. Taiping Rebellion and Treaty of Tientsin, 1858
2. Seward-Burlingame Treaty, 1868
3. The Open Door, 1898-1902
4. Annexation of the Philippines

Developments in China after Wanghai. According to Article XXXIV of the Treaty of Wanghai, provisions were made for a revision of the treaty within twelve years after its ratification, but reexamination of Chinese-American relations proved necessary long before the twelve-year period had expired. The provisions of Wanghai were not faithfully carried out by either side. Opium smuggling by Americans continued in the face of American obligation to check it. The Chinese attitude toward westerners was little changed. American representatives were still barred from Peking. A growing antiforeign feeling was rising in the vicinity of Canton.[136] It was becoming obvious, after the enthusiasm over the fancied triumph of Cushing's mission had died down, that long-standing habits and attitudes of the Chinese could not be changed appreciably by a mere half-century of foreign contacts and one treaty. As a result of the Treaty of Wanghai, the new treaty port of Shanghai began to surge ahead. The first American, a representative of Russell and Company, arrived in 1846.[137] By 1853 there were 271 foreign residents in Shanghai and about seventy-one American ships a year entered there.[138] By 1854 the principal American firms, such as Russell,

---
[136]Dulles, *China and America*, p. 48.
[137]Griffin, *op. cit.*, p. 258.
[138]*Ibid.*, p. 257.

Heard, or Gideon Nye and Company, had established branch houses in the foreign section of Shanghai.[139] Canton remained supreme in total volume of trade until 1860, although Shanghai was gradually drawing away the volume of commerce from 1845 on; Canton was still leading in tea exports by 1849, but Shanghai led in silk exports by that time. Canton remained the chief mart for Indian products, making it primarily important to the British. Shanghai, being closer to California than Canton, was more important to American trade.[140]

Growing discontent with the old Manchu dynasty combined with a deepening antiforeign feeling to precipitate an open revolt in 1849 in the vicinity of Canton. A Chinese visionary revolutionist, under the influence of Baptist missionary Issacker J. Roberts, organized a rebellion and succeeded in conquering a portion of the Yangtze Valley and setting up a regime at Nanking.[141] This movement, known as the Taiping Rebellion, had a profound effect upon American trade and eventually upon Chinese-American relations. Trade was disrupted by the military operations in and around the tea-growing areas inland from Shanghai, affecting the sea trade of both Canton and Shanghai.[142]

Work of Humphrey Marshall. During the Taiping disturbance of 1849 the merchants in the treaty ports at first favored the rebels, hoping that the United States would recognize the de facto Nanking regime. It was thought that business could be put on a sounder footing, with closer adherence to treaty provisions and less antiforeign feeling. Into this situation came Humphrey Marshall, appointed consul at Shanghai in 1853. Marshall immediately concluded that the revolution was a threat to American commerce. He predicted the eventual overthrow of the Manchu dynasty, and in his letters to Secretary of State William L. Marcy he suggested that a "sustain-China policy" be followed

---

[139]*Ibid.*, p. 252.

[140]*Ibid.*

[141]Dulles, *China and America*, p. 49.

[142]Griffin, *op. cit.*, p. 252. The volume of foreign trade climbed again in 1860, but the opening of the Yangtze Valley and growth of Shanghai made Canton, by 1860, of secondary importance to American commerce.

American Policy Toward China

to protect American trade and at the same time to check any possible foreign aggressions in China.[143]

The letters from the American consul painted a dark picture of China. He described on one hand the corrupt imperial government, and on the other the inefficient, ignorant rebel regime. The military operations, he said, were a farce and Chinese apathy toward the issues in the rebellion made China vulnerable to foreign encroachments. Marshall underlined this threat by describing the actual and potential danger of Russian dominance in China. Troops were drawn up along the border and a Russian fleet was at Hong Kong watching the Perry expedition in the vicinity of Japan. They held an actual monopoly over the trade entering China by way of the mountain passes at Kiachta and Muzaban. Marshall warned that China in her present state of weakness could fall easily under a British-Russian protectorate in the area of the Yangtze River. Russia, he added, could suppress the rebellion—the price exacted for which would:

> nullify the projects of the United States for the future and materially annoy us in the present by disturbing the fisheries which are now opening their treasures to our hardy mariners in the North Pacific. . . . I think then almost any sacrifice should be made by the United States to keep Russia from spreading her Pacific boundary. . . . It is my opinion that the highest interests of the United States are involved in sustaining China—maintaining order here, and gradually engrafting on this worn out stock the healthy principles which give life and health to governments, rather than to see China become the theater of a widespread anarchy, and ultimately the prey of European ambition.[144]

This statement is a restatement of the principles of Wanghai —maintenance of Chinese friendship and support of a Chinese government friendly to the United States. Marshall went so far as to suggest peaceful "interference" to protect American rights and the eventual good of the Chinese people. Actual intervention,

---

[143]*House Executive Documents*, No. 123, 33rd Congress, 1st session, pp. 99-102; cited in Clyde, *United States Policy Toward China*, pp. 22-29.

[144]Clyde, *United States Policy Toward China*, p. 26; cited from *House Executive Document*, No. 123, 33rd Congress, 1st session.

he recommended, should look to the following outcomes: (1) amnesty for rebels; (2) freedom of passage for citizens of treaty nations throughout Chinese territory; (3) creation of a Chinese foreign affairs department; (4) opening of the Yangtze River to steam navigation; and (5) subscription by the emperor to the laws of nations. These suggestions to the secretary of state hint at the advisability of forestalling Russia and, as a corollary of "interference," suggested the right of the United States to intervene in the event of threats to American lives and property.

Shortly after Marshall's arrival in 1853, Shanghai was overrun by the Taiping rebels. The imperial officials fled, leaving the customs collection in a chaotic state. Marshall took a strong stand, insisting that the duties and tariffs be collected as before and turned over to the imperial government at some later date.[145] The action led to further control of Chinese customs and set a precedent for Marshall's successor, Robert M. McLane.

McLane and Chinese Customs Collections. Marshall was relieved by McLane early in 1854. McLane's action in the question of customs collection further developed Marshall's original plan and was the origin of a Foreign Inspectorate of Chinese Maritime Customs. Since September of 1853 collections had been generally suspended, and McLane took the initiative in formulating a scheme to put them back on an efficient basis. In a letter to Secretary of State Marcy in June, 1854, he enclosed the minutes of a conference held in Shanghai between Chinese, English, and American commissioners that outlined the essence of the plan:[146]

1. Absence of reliable officials who knew Chinese language impeded customs collections. Provisions for removing this obstacle were given.

---

[145]Dulles, *China and America*, p. 52. The American customs were actually collected under his direction until the imperial government could take over again.

[146]*Senate Executive Documents*, No. 22, 35th Congress, 2nd session, pp. 122-123; cited from Clyde, *United States Policy Toward China*, pp. 30-34.

2. Personnel of a customs inspector board made up of a foreign chief inspector, Chinese and foreign subordinates, linguists, writers, and clerks were provided for.

3. Foreign powers were to have power to appoint the head customs inspector.

4. Foreign consuls were to adjudicate actions of customs inspectors as to tenure, graft, extortion, and general conduct of business.

5. An auxiliary department of inspectors was set up for surveillance of records.

6. An armed revenue cutter was provided out of proceeds of customs and manned by a foreign master and a majority of foreign sailors.

The establishing of the foreign customs board, like the provision of extraterritoriality in the Treaty of Wanghai, was another step in a series of foreign encroachments upon Chinese sovereignty. American support of the plan was in keeping with the basic policy of demanding equality of treatment with other foreign nations. The Chinese emperor approved it because it seemed, at the time, a way to protect Chinese trade interests during a period when the country was in a particularly weak position internationally. Customs control proved to be a sore spot later on when the foreign countries proved reluctant to give it up. Like extraterritoriality the system survived until well into the twentieth century and was finally abandoned in 1930.[147]

Originally Robert McLane had been sent to China to investigate the possibility of a de facto recognition of the Nanking government of the Taiping revolutionists. After his arrival he saw that Humphrey Marshall, whom he had relieved as consul, had taken the correct position, as far as American trade was concerned, in supporting the old Manchu dynasty in Peking. It had been hoped by the United States government that the Treaty of Wanghai could be revised. Chances of this seemed to fade when the revolutionary government in Nanking demanded tribute before opening negotiations. The imperial government in Peking

---

[147] Dulles, *China and America*, p. 174.

remained as aloof as always in spite of McLane's efforts to uphold Chinese functions in the board of customs collections.

The Parker Interlude. McLane resigned the consulate in 1856 and was succeeded by Dr. Peter Parker. An imperialist of the Perry school, Parker had been a medical missionary in China long before the Treaty of Wanghai, had memorialized Congress, and talked to government officials about the need for official action in China long before it happened. On the Cushing mission he had acted as Chinese secretary or official interpreter. In December, 1856, writing to Secretary of State Marcy, Dr. Parker urged that the revision of the Treaty of Wanghai was desirable due to the continued abuse of American traders, the attitude of contempt toward Americans, and the adamant refusal of the Peking government to receive foreign representatives.[148]

In March of the following year Parker sent another communication to the State Department, strongly advocating the use of naval force. Formosa, he suggested, should be seized as reparations for damages to American trade incurred during the Taiping rebellion. He cited the importance of the island as a useful spot for refueling steam vessels and as a strategic point in war. Precedents of England's St. Helena, Ceylon, and Singapore were used as supporting arguments. A letter was enclosed to W. M. Robinet, a China merchant, describing the wealth of Formosa—the coal mines, agricultural wealth, and the amount of exports in 1856 amounting to $1,654,000. The Parker document was not considered particularly able. Some of the evidence was rather shaky and all of it was too obviously weighted in favor of the Formosa seizure to have much influence upon the State Department.[149] The policy suggested by Parker's letter was rejected by Marcy, who assured him that President Pierce would never consent to the use of force against China. Persuasion, instead, would be the keynote. The Parker episode is unimportant except in showing the reapplication of America's consistent policy of avoiding overt acts of war against the territory and peoples

---

[148]*Senate Executive Documents*, No. 22, 35th Congress, 2nd session, pp. 1081-1083.

[149]*Ibid.*, pp. 1092-1093.

American Policy Toward China

of China. This was stated in the first article of the Treaty of Wanghai. It was to be pursued consistently during the efforts to revise the treaty.

Treaty of Tientsin. The Treaty of Wanghai was revised by the Treaty of Tientsin in 1858.[150] Four years previously the British had sought American cooperation in securing a treaty revision. In 1857 the British wanted military cooperation and use of joint force, if the need arose, in revising the earlier treaties (Nanking, 1842, and Wanghai, 1844). This was, of course, rejected because it smacked too much of a military alliance. The "Arrow War" had broken out late in 1856 between England and China. William B. Reed was appointed American Envoy Extraordinary and Minister Plenipotentiary a few months later.[151] President Buchanan declared American neutrality. The events that followed were reminiscent of the background of the Wanghai negotiations.

Reed was sent to China to keep a watchful eye upon developments and gain by peaceful means what England, France, and Russia were in the process of getting by war. He was instructed to consult with representatives of foreign countries and to maintain friendly relations with them, but hold to strict neutrality. The Chinese were to be assured of the peaceful intent of the United States. Opium smuggling was to be disavowed. American losses resulting from the Taiping Rebellion were to be dissociated from British losses. Every effort was to be made to separate in the Chinese minds the aims and methods of England and the United States. In this framework Reed was instructed to enlarge the provisions of the earlier treaty on the following points:[152]

1. access to Peking and direct recourse to authorities over foreign affairs
2. extension of commercial scope, now limited to five ports

---

[150]*Ibid.*, pp. 1-16. Instructions and letters involved in the negotiations are included here.

[151]*Ibid.*, p. 1. Instructions dated May 30, 1857.

[152]*Senate Executive Documents,* No. 30, 36th Congress, 1st session, pp. 1-16.

3. reduction of the tariff on domestic Chinese goods from the interior

4. religious freedom for all foreigners in China

5. extension of treaty benefits to all civilized powers of the earth

6. suppression of piracy

Reed spent unprofitable months in China while the British and French were fighting at several points along the coast. He had no success in pushing his negotiations through until after Canton had been captured by assault, later in 1857, and the forts at the mouth of the Peiho had been battered down, in 1858. The incident in which Reed, along with the Russian representatives, steamed up the Peiho in an unarmed ship, following the British and French attacking force as the latter silenced the forts on shore, was symbolic of American policy in China up to that time. The United States was unwilling to make active war on China but was not averse to following in the path of British aggression, and, as at Wanghai after the Opium War, thereby profiting by negotiating a favorable treaty.[153]

It would be unprofitable to enumerate the provisions of the treaty that resulted from the negotiations at Tientsin. Most of the articles dealt with items that had been covered in the Treaty of Wanghai. In general each one restated the established principles and enlarged the concessions granted to American traders and missionaries. For example, duties and tonnage dues were restated stipulating the methods of collection; rights of American citizens to rent property were restated; protection of stranded and wrecked vessels was guaranteed; interior tariffs (transit duties) were set down in definite amounts; transshipments from treaty ports were allowed; and freedom of religion and religious teaching was reaffirmed.[154]

The approval of the Treaty of Tientsin showed that there was

---

[153]Bemis, *op. cit.*, vol. 5, p. 375. Bemis says that American policy in China was as timid as it was assertive in the Western Hemisphere.

[154]Clyde, *United States Policy Toward China*, pp. 39-58; cited from *Senate Executive Documents*, No. 30, 36th Congress, 1st session, pp. 1-16.

no basic change in American policy as it had developed under the influence of trade interests since the beginning of China trade. The fundamental most-favored-nations principle established in the Treaty of Wanghai was reaffirmed[155] and the principle of extraterritoriality was restated in practically the same form.[156] By this treaty and the incidents revolving around its negotiations, America had demonstrated again that she had no desire for territorial aggrandizement in China but only a desire to promote trade on a basis of equality and to protect the lives and property of her citizens.

The Burlingame Mission. According to the provisions of the Treaty of Tientsin foreign countries were allowed direct diplomatic access to Peking. As a result, subsequent negotiations between China and the United States were carried on with a minimum of pressure and without aid of English or French military support. The next important diplomatic negotiation that was illustrative of American policy produced the Seward-Burlingame Treaty, signed in July, 1868.[157] It further developed principles suggested at Wanghai. Anson Burlingame pursued a cooperative policy based on the belief that the treaty nations had an identity of interests in China. He followed the historic policy of using restrained pressure to accomplish national aims without resort to force. His methods were in keeping with the spirit of the instructions issued to previous diplomats, such as Commodore Kearny, Caleb Cushing, and William B. Reed.[158]

The Burlingame Treaty reassured the Chinese emperor that, in spite of foreign ownership and rental of properties in the treaty ports, he had in no way relinquished the basic principle of eminent domain.[159] This clause was a step toward the principle of territorial integrity of China which became basic to American policy at the turn of the century. It had been hinted at in previous diplomatic instructions and letters to American represen-

---
[155]*Ibid.*, Article XXX.
[156]*Ibid.*, Article XI.
[157]Clyde, *op. cit.*, pp. 79-85.
[158]*Ibid.*, p. 59.
[159]*Ibid.*, p. 84, Article I.

tatives in China. Direct intervention for the purpose of political control of China was disclaimed. The way was left open, however, for direct American aid in developing construction and engineering works in the event that the emperor appealed to the United States for such aid. To maintain an equality of status in trade and commerce, the most-favored-nation principle was mentioned again in connection with the treaty.[160]

CONTINUATION OF THE OPEN DOOR POLICY, 1898-1941

American policy toward China, as it had developed up to the year 1898, was to change very little as the competition among foreign countries and the scramble for spheres of influence in China came to a head near the turn of the century.

Threats to China. Charles Denby, minister to Peking, wrote to Secretary of State John Sherman in the last month of 1898 warning the American government of the dangerous foreign pressures being exerted upon China.[161] He saw the territorial integrity of China threatened and urged a more aggressive United States policy to bolster Chinese resistance to foreign encroachments. A clause in the Treaty of Tientsin was cited that provided for the "good offices" of the United States in smoothing unsatisfactory relations between China and other countries.[162] Although the suggestion was rejected by the State Department, it was another link between the Open Door, as it was soon to be proclaimed by Hay, and the historic policy of equality of commercial status demanded by the United States as early as 1842.

The Open Door and Philippine Annexation. China's insecure situation, growing more precarious as 1900 approached,

---

[160]*Ibid.*, p. 85. In a letter from Secretary of State Seward to Minister Ross Browne, in Peking, in September, 1868, Seward mentioned the desirability of applying the most-favored-nation principle in the event that England negotiated for tariff modifications and enlarged commercial privileges.

[161]*Department of State Dispatches from China,* vol. 103, No. 8858; cited in Bartlett, *The Record of American Diplomacy,* pp. 408-409.

[162]Dennett, *Americans in Eastern Asia* (New York, 1941), p. 409.

American Policy Toward China

coincided with Admiral Dewey's conquest of the Philippine Islands. Whatever the reasons for the original plans for attacking the Spanish fleet in Manila Bay, the final decision for demanding the acquisition of the Islands at the peace conference would seem to involve America's traditional policy in Asia. Senatorial debates, examining the pros and cons of annexation, covered every economic, legal, and moral ground but, as Tyler Dennett concluded, "was settled without any clear understanding by the American people of the relation of Hawaii and the Philippines to the still larger question of American policy in Asia."[163] If this broader view of the Philippine acquisition can be accepted, it is sound to conclude that the islands became part of the American western empire by virtue of the antecedents of historic Pacific contacts that had, by 1899, made it impossible for the United States to withdraw from the Philippines after the defeat of Spain. The fear of foreign aggression against China and the ominous possibility that the Philippines might share the fate of Korea were American power not to fill the vacuum left by Spain made annexation a logical outcome of an imperialistic war. Annexation was not a departure from historic policy but indirectly an effort to keep the door open in Asia. It was a development of the "sustain China" policy advocated by Humphrey Marshall in 1858 and enlarged in scope to a "sustain Asia" corollary.[164]

Hay's Open Door Statement. While Denby's recommendations were being rejected, the Hay statement of the Open Door policy was being prepared. Almost a year and a half before Minister Denby's note to Secretary Sherman, W. W. Rockhill, John Hay's private secretary, had sent a memorandum to Hay from China in which he sketched the activities of foreign countries and made some recommendations as to a course of action.[165] He described the strong military forces of foreign countries in China and their spheres of influence, railroad connections, and dangers

---

[163]*Ibid.*, p. 632.

[164]*Ibid.*, p. 631; Griswold, *Far Eastern Policy of the United States* (New York, 1938), p. 26. The point of view is taken that annexation resulted from a combination of forces—imperialism, foreign threats, and a sustain-China doctrine.

[165]Griswold, *op. cit.*, pp. 475-491. Rockhill papers, cited in Clyde, *op. cit.*, pp. 201-217.

of a partitioning of China. Support of these developments, Rockhill said, would be suicidal to American interests in China. In the light of the existence of spheres of influence, the United States should get assurances from the various countries involved that the eqaulity of treatment in the treaty ports would not be disturbed. He suggested that the most-favored-nation principle should be guaranteed in the event of newly opened ports and that "we should insist on absolute equality of treatment in the various zones."[166] Rockhill outlined further the activities of England, France, Germany, and Russia and indicated their willingness to agree to equality of commercial privileges. He thought the time was ripe to press for the Open Door principle.

When John Hay became secretary of state he restated Rockhill's memorandum, in practically the same wording, in the form of the first Open Door note on September 6, 1899.[167] In the second Open Door note of July 3, 1900, Secretary Hay stated American policy as being one designed to work concurrently with other powers to open Peking, protect American life and property, and maintain a peaceful China. The pertinent quotation from his communication states the guiding principles of American relations in China which had been applied in various forms since Kearny's mission in 1842.

> The policy of the government of the United States is to seek a solution which may bring about permanent safety and peace to China, preserve Chinese territorial and administrative entity, protect all rights guaranteed to friendly powers by treaty and international law, and safeguard for the world the principle of equal and impartial trade with all parts of the Chinese empire.[168]

---

[166]Clyde, *op. cit.*, p. 208.

[167]*Ibid.*, p. 214.

[168]*Foreign Relations*, 1899; cited in Clyde, *op. cit.*, p. 215. This basic policy of the United States is traceable from 1900 to 1941 in fairly clearcut fashion throughout a series of diplomatic incidents between the United States and Japan over issues involving China. The Open Door policy and the ideal of a sovereign China is seen in the following incidents: Restatement of Policy, 1903; The Root-Takahira Notes, 1908; Japanese Demands, 1913-1919; Washington Treaties, 1922; Recommendations of Extra-territoriality; The Manchurian Incident, 1931-1934; the exchange of notes during the period of undeclared war, 1937-1939; and the Japanese and American proposals for peace, 1941.

American policy toward China, at first preoccupied with the problem of encouraging trade, was influenced strongly by merchants, naval officers, and commercial consuls in China. The American government had always hesitated about making political commitments—even during the profitable years of trade in the nineteenth century. The taste of the China trade turned a bit sour after 1900. The unlimited possibilities for profit, which seemed to be apparent throughout the nineteenth century, were never quite realized. Instead American policy turned to the purposes of maintaining (1) the territorial integrity and national sovereignty of China and (2) the equal rights of the United States in China.[169] Official policy, as a result, became so preoccupied with maintaining equality of treatment of American citizens that very little effort was made in removing the basic conditions for existing inequalities. Equality as used in the treaties meant rights of seamen, treatment of missionaries, and equal opportunities for American businessmen.[170] Haste to obtain quick gain obscured the means of obtaining real equality among Asians and foreigners in China. Exploitation and bitterness resulted.

The principle of commercial equality nevertheless became almost a moral doctrine in American foreign relations. In the preamble of the first American treaty (the French Treaty of 1778) appeared the first statement of the principles of equality and reciprocity, and the most-favored-nations concept.[171] It was good revolutionary thought and in keeping with the fundamental doctrine of the rights of man expressed, in fact, in the Declaration of Independence two years previously. The United States' ultimatum for peace in 1941 and Japan's unequivocal answer to it dramatized this moral issue of equality of rights. The policy and aims of the United States had become so deeply involved in China that the ultimate price that had to be paid for national security was a fight to the finish with Japan.

---
[169]Van Alstyne, *op. cit.*, p. 461.
[170]Griffin, *op. cit.*, p. 351.
[171]Moore, *American Diplomacy*, p. 107.

Chapter IV

The Seaborne Frontier in California, 1796-1850

At the same time that American policy toward China was taking form, American merchant ships were making contacts in Spanish California that soon attracted official attention to that area. Here, as farther north, "sailing vessels, like the covered wagons which they preceded to California by four decades, served during the westward movement as a conveyor of United States interests to the Pacific coast."[1]

EARLY SEA TRADE WITH CALIFORNIA

Until well into the fifteenth century California was thought to be an island. Spanish conquistadors, looking out from the Mexican side of what is now called the Gulf of Southern California, named the dry rugged land on the other side "Baha California." The yearly treasure galleon from Manila, laden with spices, silks, and gems from the Orient and Indies, made its landfall on a bold and rocky headland and bore away to the south to discharge its riches at Panama City or Acapulco. On the southern leg of the voyage this bit of coast disappeared from view and, due to the lay of the land, no more was sighted until the steep coast of southern California became visible. The point of landfall, now named Cape Mendocino, was plotted on those early charts as an island of uncertain proportions and of unknown character, known as "Alta California."

Sea stories and Indian legends, both fabricated and true, surrounded this land with mystery and awe. It was thought to be

---

[1]Ogden, *The California Sea Otter Trade* (Berkeley, 1941), preface, p. v.

a land of bliss, flowers, and riches, inhabited by a race of beautiful and warlike Amazons. Subsequently, difficult coastal and overland explorations by the Spanish dispelled this myth. By the end of the 1780's the area that later became California had been charted and explored.

Obstacles to Trade. This legendary history of California has significance for the background of the American seaward approach to its coasts. Figuratively speaking, California was indeed an "island" so far as early American migration was concerned. It was shut off to the eastward by formidable deserts and mountains. At first the approaches by sea were equally difficult. The route around Cape Horn was the only feasible approach and northwesterly winds made the Pacific leg of the voyage a long uphill beat to windward that discouraged seaborne visitors. Another barrier, though probably the least effective, was the Spanish law forbidding trade with foreign ships along the California coast. The adventurous Yankee skippers and their profit-seeking employers at home flagrantly violated these commercial restrictions. American ships in the China trade began using California ports as convenient places for obtaining fresh supplies. The ports quickly developed into profitable trading points.

A variety of commercial activities attracted American navigators to the coast of California before the discovery of gold in 1849. The fur trade of the Pacific Northwest involved incidentally the ports of California. The voyage of the first fur ship, the *Columbia,* stirred some interest in Mexico; in fact, the California governor was instructed to seize her if she illegally entered any California port.[2] Another activity involving California was the sea otter trade that sprang up in 1784 and attracted Americans from 1796 to approximately 1814. There was also an illegal trade of miscellaneous goods that paralleled the sea otter trade and was almost entirely in the hands of American nagivators and supercargoes.[3] American whalemen, who started cruising the Pacific

---

[2]Cleland, "The Early Sentiment for the Annexation of California," *Texas Historical Association Proceedings* (reprint from *The Southwestern Historical Quarterly*), vol. 18, nos. 1, 2, 3 (1914), p. 3.

[3]*Ibid.,* p. 4.

after 1820, began touching California ports on the way to and from the whaling grounds. After 1822, when Mexico became independent of Spain, the hide and tallow trade developed. This was a legally recognized branch of commerce, carried on almost exclusively by Boston firms and vessels.[4]

In a brief overview of the commercial activities of California, which later had effects on American foreign policy, the threat of foreign invasion should not be ignored. As early as 1812 the Russians had an establishment at Bodega Bay and had made earnest efforts to secure a trading post in the San Francisco Bay area. There was also the constant threat of English competition and eventual annexation of California.[5]

Since trade with the Spanish ports was illegal before Mexican independence, Yankee vessels engaged in the Northwest fur trade carried letters of introduction to Spanish officials in the event of mishap or heavy weather—"'par mal tiempo,' which exigency was pretty sure to exist if the land breeze smelt sea otterish."[6] The illegal trade with California began, then, as a branch of commerce subsidiary to the fur trade in the Puget Sound region.[7] Captain Ebenezer Dorr, in the *Otter*, established the first American contact in Monterey in 1796. He left ten men ashore to hunt sea otter while the ship traded elsewhere.[8]

California-Alaskan Contacts. From 1803 to 1812 most of the American participation in the sea otter trade was done in connection with the Russian monopoly in Alaska—the Russian-American Company.[9] For a period of four years after 1812 American cooperation with Russian traders was abandoned and the Yankee

---

[4]*Ibid.*, p. 5.

[5]*Ibid.*, p. 7.

[6]Morison, *Maritime History of Massachusetts* p. 60. Copyright (©) 1969 by Samuel Eliot Morison. Reprinted by permission of the publisher, Houghton Mifflin Company.

[7]*See* Chapter II.

[8]Ogden, *op. cit.*, p. 33. The first permanent residents brought in by Americans were several Australian convict women whom Dorr left ashore in Monterey.

[9]*Ibid.*, pp. 45-57. Names of American ships and personalities are mentioned, as is their activity in poaching along the Pacific coast as far south as San Diego. This trade was also discussed in relation to Russian-American contacts in Chapter II.

merchants became ocean tramps. Chinese goods and articles of American manufacture were esteemed by the Californians and mission residents. Direct contact on shore between American sailors and California residents resulted in closer commercial ties as well as incidents with Mexican customs officials.[10] Illegal and unsatisfactory as this form of commerce was, it was highly profitable to both Americans and Californians. The Spanish in California proved eager to break out of the iron-bound mercantilism of the Spanish empire, reinforced by laws made in Mexico City. The early American trade drove a wedge between the government in Mexico City and the loosely held province of California.[11]

Trade During Spanish and Early Mexican Rule. From 1812 to the end of Spanish rule, individual Yankee ships carried on a sporadic trade in sea otters. When the Mexicans revolted from Spain in 1821 the ports of the old Spanish main were opened to foreign trade. In 1821 the mercantile house of Marshall and Wildes in Honolulu fitted out its first ship, the *Eagle*, exclusively for the sea otter trade.[12] In the same year the Boston firm of Bryant and Sturgis fitted out its first ship to exchange Chinese goods for sea otter in California. Other firms, such as that of John Jacob Astor of New York and T. H. Perkins' agent in Canton, tried their hand at the trade. The merchants involved had small fleets of vessels engaged in an established relay system;[13] one ship carrying China goods from Canton to Hawaii, another from Hawaii to California and South America and still another from the States to Hawaii or from Hawaii to California or Canton.

Until 1830 the sea otter, valuable in the Canton trade, mainly accounted for American interest in California. Gradually, in the

---

[10]*Ibid.*, p. 74. In 1816 it was reported that sixteen Americans were in jail in Santa Barbara for smuggling and poaching sea otter.

[11]*Ibid.*; Rives, *The United States and Mexico*, vol. 2 (New York, 1913), pp. 24-44. In the sections cited the author develops the point that American contacts hastened the decline of Mexican rule; that inept Californian officials, secularization of missions, and lax ties with Mexico all left a wide-open field for aggressive American enterprise.

[12]Ogden, *op. cit.*, p. 86.

[13]*Ibid.*, p. 94.

early 1830's, due to indiscriminate slaughter, the sea otter became scarce.[14] After the decline of the fur trade, horses, cowhides, and beef tallow were taken in exchange for China goods and American products.[15]

During the early years of Mexican independence government officials made strong attempts to control the activities of Americans along the coast. Although trade was legal when carried on through proper customhouse channels, indiscriminate poaching along the beaches and offshore islands was frowned upon. Between 1826 and 1830 the Mexican government, viewing the influx of Yankee ships as a real threat to their nationality, adopted a policy of strict licensing of Russian and American hunters. No seagoing vessels were allowed to hunt sea otter. Under these regulations, one-half of the profits from each individual venture were required to be left in the hands of native Mexicans, and a majority of men engaged in hunting were required to be Mexican nationals.[16]

The restraining influence of Mexican law was moderately effective until approximately 1830, after which Amercian pressure gradually increased. Men of American citizenship—deserters from whalers or merchant ships and men from Jedediah Smith's overland expedition—infiltrated the coast in search of sea otter. Between 1830 and 1842 ships, usually fitted out in the Hawaiian Islands and partially owned and manned by men of spurious Mexican citizenship, challenged the California laws. The *contrabandista* came with the dual purpose of poaching sea otter and of smuggling China and American goods ashore.[17] It became the practice of these ships, which were actually American, to hire Northwest Coast Indians to do the dangerous work of killing otters close in shore or of landing smuggled goods. On several occasions the Indians were attacked by the Mexicans and killed or driven off, but the mother ship could not be touched. The Mexican government found that it was hindered by the lack of

---

[14]*Ibid.*, p. 145. Overland trappers from the States introduced the use of guns in hunting sea otter, hastening their disappearance.
[15]*Ibid.*, p. 90.
[16]*Ibid.*, p. 119.
[17]*Ibid.*, p. 132.

patrol vessels and the tenuous lines of control from the distance in Mexico.

In addition to the particular trade in sea otters, a casual and less clear-cut type of trade was carried on from 1800 until the Mexican revolution in 1821. At first it was subsidiary to the Northwest fur trade. American ships were treated with some friendliness when they put in at California ports under stress of weather, or with low supplies and sickness aboard. The good faith of the early contacts was soon destroyed, however, when smuggling became the prime objective. The Northwest Coast ship *Betsy* made the first call of this kind in 1800.[18] In that year the usual value of a cargo destined for trade on the Northwest coast was approximately $25,000; yet vessels are recorded to have sailed for the Northwest Coast and Canton with ladings valued at $450,000.[19] The explanation for the vast difference in value of some cargoes is obviously that these vessels were equipped for a smuggling voyage along the California coast before touching the fur posts in the Puget Sound region. A cross-section view of this incidental trade of the Yankee ships shows that scarcely a year passed between 1800 and 1821 in which at least one American vessel did not smuggle goods along the California coast.[20] In nearly every instance at least one man deserted or was left ashore to recuperate from shipboard diseases.[21]

Characteristic of the illicit trade in miscellaneous products before Mexican independence is the cooperative voyage of Richard J. Cleveland and William Shaler. Sailing the vessel *Lelia Byrd,* they rounded the Horn in 1803 and traded among the

---

[18]Howay, "An Outline Sketch of the Maritime Fur Trade," *Canadian Historical Association, Report of Annual Meeting* (1932), p. 12.

[19]*Ibid.*

[20]Bancroft, *History of California*, vol. 2, (San Francisco, 1884), pp. 2-95. By an examination of the official Spanish records of ship contacts along the California coast, Bancroft pieced together a chronological account of the activities of American traders from approximately 1801 to 1821. It is a rather dull recital of names of ships, names of men, destinations, and cargoes.

[21]*Ibid.*, p. 95. In 1818 one American ship's captain left his Hawaiian common-law wife and her child in California.

Spanish ports of South America.[22] Their contact with California was merely a small incident in a worldwide trading voyage (see page 80). Cleveland first stopped at San Diego on the pretext of needing supplies. Some of his men, while on shore buying sea otter skins, were captured. After boarding a few skins, the *Lelia Byrd* ran out under the Spanish guns guarding the entrance, cleared the fort by a broadside from her own guns, and made her escape to sea.[23] The two traders then took their vessel north along the coast and carried on a friendly and lively trade with the Spanish missions between San Diego and Cape Mendocino. The *Lelia Byrd* eventually sailed on to Hawaii and Canton. Shaler, like Cleveland an intelligent observer, estimated that American traders by 1804 were spending $25,000 annually along the coast in illegal trade.[24]

AMERICAN TRADE DURING THE MEXICAN ERA

In December of 1821 the California trade was thrown open to foreign vessels. A direct trade with Boston quickly sprang up. The new era coincided with the beginning of the decline in sea otters and of the increase in ranching and cattle grazing. A brisk commerce in hides and tallow soon developed. These superseded otter skins as incentives for American trade and, until the discovery of gold, formed the main economic base for the external commerce of California.[25]

---

[22]Cleveland, ed., *Voyages of a Merchant Navigator* (New York, 1886), pp. 90-100. Both Cleveland and Shaler wrote journals of their voyage—two of the few firsthand accounts of early American trade with California.

[23]*Ibid.*, p. 94. This obscure incident facetiously became known later as the "Battle of San Diego." Shortly after the annexation of California, Commodore Biddle sent Cleveland a letter referring to the "'Battle of San Diego" and offered him the honorary governorship of the territory on the strength of his "conquest" in advance of Fremont and other Mexican War heroes.

[24]Bancroft, *op. cit.*, vol. 2, p. 23, taken from footnote 7, citing Shaler's "Journal of a Voyage Between China and the Northwest Coast of America, Made in 1804," *American Register*, pp. 137-175.

[25]Rives, *The United States and Mexico* (New York, 1913), vol. 1, pp. 115-116. The need for supplies forced Mexico to recognize foreign trade. This marked the real beginning of American dominance in California.

The Seaborne Frontier in California

Hide and Tallow Trade. A Boston vessel, *Sachem*, of the firm of Bryant and Sturgis, arrived on the coast in 1821 and took off the first cargo of hides and tallow under the new system of trade.[26] William Gale was the supercargo of the vessel. His arrival with the first hide ship is of some significance because he returned on a subsequent voyage, remained ashore as agent of his Boston firm, and became an influential American resident of California.[27] His pressure for annexation and his influence on American policy will be noticed later.

In every year after 1821 there is a record of foreign ship arrivals. In virtually every year the majority of these ships were American. A spot-check of ship arrivals during several years from 1821 and 1846 clearly shows the predominance of American commercial interests on the California coast.[28] For example, foreign trade for selected years was of the following extent: 1822, 17 ships, of which 7 were American;[29] 1825, approximately 47 ships, of which 20 were American, 8 British, 3 Spanish, 2 Russian, and 1 French;[30] 1826, 44 ships, of which 22 were American, 8 British, the rest distributed among half a dozen nationalities;[31] 1831-1835, 99 ships, including 13 American trading vessels, 22 whalers (most of American registry), and the rest distributed between Mexican, English, Italian, Hawaiian, and Russian;[32] 1836-1840, 68 ships, including 26 American traders, 17 British, and the rest distributed among half a dozen nationalities;[33] 1841-1845, 148 ships, including 45 American, 26 Mexican, 11 British, and the rest distributed.[34]

---

[26]Bancroft, *op. cit.*, vol. 4, p. 475.
[27]*Ibid.*
[28]*Ibid.* Vols. 2, 3, and 4 contain a marine list of ships compiled from official Mexican customhouse records from 1821 to 1845.
[29]*Ibid.*, vol. 2, p. 492.
[30]*Ibid.*, vol. 3, p. 116.
[31]*Ibid.*, vol. 3, p. 116.
[32]*Ibid.*, vol. 3, p. 381.
[33]*Ibid.*, vol. 4, p. 101.
[34]*Ibid.*, vol. 4, p. 566. The records are incomplete and are rather misleading. For example, Hawaiian and Mexican ships, during the later years, were often owned and commanded by Americans from Hawaii or California.

The extent of the hide and tallow trade, and American predominance in California commerce, is indicated in the record of ship arrivals for 1831. Of the nineteen ships that arrived on the coast, the majority were hide ships from Boston.[35] This form of trade was at its most profitable stage during the 1830's. In 1834 the Mexican government passed a secularization law, abolishing church properties and redistributing the lands held by the clergy.[36] The indiscriminate slaughter of cattle that followed this move caused a boom in the hide and tallow shipments by American vessels.

Monterey was the main port of entry through which legally entered goods were tabulated for payment of customs. In 1835, $50,000 in customs were collected.[37] A clearer indication of the volume of traffic carried by American ships is seen in the customs collections for the year 1842. A total of $74,000 was collected, of which $50,000 was derived from the cargoes of two Boston ships engaged in the hide and tallow trade.[38]

The Bryant and Sturgis *Pilgrim* arrived off Santa Barbara early in 1835. In the forecastle, as a foremast hand, was Richard Henry Dana, who later wrote of his experiences on the two vessels on which he served, the brigs *Pilgrim* and *Alert*—both Bryant and Sturgis vessels. His narrative, now an American classic, immortalized the activities of two Boston ships during the peak years of the hide trade and has come down as the only firsthand account of that trade written from the common seaman's point of view. He was an intelligent observer and his facts have stood up well when tested by later historical researches.

Boston ships by the time of the arrival of the *Pilgrim* were bringing in about two-thirds of the manufactured articles from New England.[39] Dana made some sarcastic remarks about the native Californians, who imported wine to a land that grew grapes, and shoes manufactured in New England to a land that

---

[35]*Ibid.*, vol. 3, p. 365.
[36]*Ibid.*, vol. 3, p. 366.
[37]*Ibid.*, vol. 3, p. 367.
[38]*Ibid.*, vol. 4, p. 340.
[39]Dana, *Two Years Before the Mast* (Boston, 1869), p. 85. Bryant and Sturgis ships almost monopolized the hide trade.

The Seaborne Frontier in California

supplied much of the leather.[40] Other manufactured goods brought in by American ships to be exchanged for hides and tallow were such prosaic items as canvas, American cotton, chintz, red flannel, hats, sacks, sugar, cocoa, lard, dried beef, rum, brandy, plow points, tobacco, candles, gunpowder, iron, and nails. The list could be extended but it is sufficient to demonstrate how the elements of American material culture were transplanted to the Pacific coast.

For the first fifty years after the American Revolution (until approximately 1835), American interest in California was stirred by these casual commercial contacts. Returning ships brought back wonderful tales glorifying this fabulous land in the minds of eastern Americans.[41] At the same time that trade promoted these forms of cultural diffusion, American seaborne visitors were gradually moving into influential positions in or near the sea ports of California.

EARLY SEAWARD MIGRATION OF AMERICANS

Just how many Americans filtered into California is unknown. In the course of years sick seamen were put ashore in every port —some to stay after recovery. A few others, to escape a brutal boatswain or to evade the long trip to Canton, jumped ship, settled down with a ranchero's daughter, and later became landed gentry. Many worked in the vineyards and ranches or just became indolent peasants. The Yankee seamen who settled California "left their New England consciences at the Horn,"[42] embraced the Catholic church, and became naturalized citizens of California.

---

[40]*Ibid.*, p. 86. The material in the shoes "doubled Cape Horn" twice.

[41]Written accounts of California before 1830 are scarce. The journals of Richard J. Cleveland and William Shaler, concerning their voyages in 1803 and 1804, must have had a limited reading public, as did the account of R. J. Reynolds, seaman on the *New Hazard* in 1810-1813. Knowledge from firsthand accounts were spread orally in the seaports of the Atlantic coast. After 1835 the account of Richard Henry Dana and the letters to eastern papers from T. O. Larkin helped arouse the interest of Americans prior to the gold rush.

[42]Morrison, *op. cit.*, p. 20.

The Spanish laws were no obstacle to immigration as they were to commerce. Foreign seamen were received hospitably if their connections with their ship had been sufficiently severed. The same policy was followed by the Mexican regime from 1821 until the outbreak of hostilities in 1848.[43] In the light of friendly immigration laws and the sharp contrast between shipboard life and the idyllic climate of California, it is not surprising that Americans of all types and stations in life were attracted to that coast. Very early in the history of American contacts, Americans, in a variety of occupations ranging from a grog-shop keeper in San Diego to a merchant prince in Monterey, had settled there.[44]

Early American Settlers. The early trickle of Americans into California is an obscure and poorly recorded movement. No American records were kept until the gold rush began and then only cabin passengers were recorded by the shipping companies. Hubert H. Bancroft's list of pioneers during the pre-American period, compiled from Spanish and Mexican records and also from personal interviews with survivors in the late 1880's, is the chief source for arrivals of seaborne Americans prior to 1848.[45] Some names and dates involved in the early migration may be illuminating in showing the subtle process whereby American interests became increasingly entrenched on the coast of California:

    1816   Archie Bean, sailmaker on the American ship *Lydia;* settled somewhere along the coast. Vol. 2.

            Thomas W. Dook, a sailor on the *Albatross;* reputed to be the first American arrival; married a native Californian; settled down as a carpenter on the coast. Vol. 2.

---

[43]Bancroft, *op. cit.*, vol. 4, pp. 604-605. Governor Castro went so far as to allow Americans to enter California from the Hawaiian Islands regardless of the legality of their passports.

[44]Dana, *op. cit.*, p. 131. A popular figure with the hide and tallow men was a one-eyed bartender who deserted from an American whaler. The merchant prince, of course, was T. O. Larkin.

[45]Bancroft, *op. cit.*, vols. 2, 3, 4, 5. An alphabetical list of people with all available data is appended to these volumes. Much of the information is incomplete. Often in the case of people arriving by sea only the name, date, and ship is mentioned. In other instances brief biographical sketches and accounts of activities after arriving in California are provided.

1822 A. Hary, arrived on the American vessel *Snipe*. Vol. 3.

Henry Gyzelaar, arrived on the vessel *Sachem*. Vol 3.

1829 Alfred Robinson, arrived as clerk on the Bryant and Sturgis ship *Brookline;* remained as an agent for the hide and tallow business, traveled up and down the coast; lived near Monterey. Vol. 5.

John Rainsford, an Irish sailor who arrived on an unknown American ship; settled in Monterey; in 1839 moved to San Francisco. Vol. 5.

1830 (Approximately) Charles Brown, a deserter from the American whaler *Helvetius;* became a prominent settler and Indian fighter. Vol 2.

U. S. Kinckley, a nephew of Captain William Sturgis, engaged in trade to California from Honolulu; married a native Californian; became a personal adviser to Governor Alvarado; lived in Monterey and engaged in the Hawaiian-California commerce. Vol. 3.

1833 Thomas Riddington, a former sailor on the *Avarucho;* settled in San Diego; became a shoemaker and in 1844 a justice of the peace. Vol. 5.

1836 William Hance, an American sailor deserted from the *Sarah and Caroline;* became a lumberman near Monterey. Vol. 3.

1840 Walter Adams, a Boston sailor arrested in Monterey; remained in maritime employment from that port. Vol. 2.

E. A. Farwell, a Boston printer who arrived on the American vessel *California*, probably as mate; settled on a ranch somewhere on the coast. Vol. 3.

1841 Josiah Belden, a Connecticut man who came with the first immigrant party overland; ran T. O. Larkin's store in Monterey. Vol. 2.

Robert Birnie, arrived from Honolulu as a supercargo; became a clerk in San Francisco and later a real estate agent in Oakland. Vol. 2.

1842 Henry Ford, a New England man who arrived by sea; participated in the "Bear Flag Revolt." Vol. 2.

1845 Alex Abell, a New York man, arrived from Honolulu; member of a commercial firm in San Francisco in 1847; later became a well-known business man and one of the first senators in the newly formed California legislature. Vol. 2.

1848 A. H. Gillespie, arrived originally in 1846 as Lt. A. H. Gillespie, U.S.M.C., to carry Larkin's instructions concerning California policy; returned to live in San Francisco; died in 1873. Vol. 3.[46]

Economic and Social Activities. The population of California increased by approximately one thousand between 1820 and 1830; about 350 of this number came from abroad.[47] Before 1826, according to Bancroft, "all . . . newcomers were, in this period, as a class law-abiding citizens of considerable influence."[48] Though few in number, Americans settled in strategic points along the coast and wielded considerable power both in shaping Californian affairs and in influencing official American policy in regard to annexation. Prominent in the commercial life of California were men such as Hartnell, Cooper, Spence, and Gale, each of whom was allied with influential Spanish-California families.[49] A business triumvirate made up of Messrs. Leese, Spear, and Hinckley set up a partnership in 1836 on Yerba Buena Island in San Francisco Bay. Later Mr. Leese broke off and established a store and warehouse at a different spot on the island.[50] By 1840 Americans were scattered from San Diego to San Francisco, working as traders, merchants, and ranchers. The foreign population at that time was reported to be approximately 380.[51] Not all of these were Americans, but it appears definite that the

---

[46]*See* n. 45 above.
[47]*Ibid.*, vol. 2, p. 633.
[48]*Ibid.*, vol. 3, p. 175.
[49]*Ibid.*, vol. 2, p. 633.
[50]*Ibid.*, vol. 3, pp. 709-710.
[51]*Ibid.*, vol. 4, p. 117.

The Seaborne Frontier in California 141

few who influenced Californian affairs were from the United States.[52]

Many Americans connected with the sea otter trade became naturalized Mexican citizens. After 1841 such names as Sparks, Thompson, Jones, and Fitch appeared. These men, under Mexican citizenship, largely controlled the trade to the Hawaiian Islands and to such points in Mexico as Matzalan.[53]

By 1841 American influence was becoming noticeable not only in commercial life but also in social affairs. California women seemed to prefer American husbands. Bancroft quotes a native Mexican who complained that "a Californian cavalier cannot woo a senorita if opposed in his suit by an American sailor."[54] The facts recorded in the *Pioneer Register* bear out the validity of this complaint. The commercial dominance of Americans and naturalization—often followed by intermarriage—both tended to make the activities of the foreign-born population more prominent than those of natives after 1840.[55]

Work of T. O. Larkin. The career of Thomas O. Larkin is most significant in the early American infiltration of California by sea. He was a New England merchant who saw the opportunities in California very early and soon entertained serious plans for annexation. In 1831 Larkin arrived in San Francisco on the bark *Newcastle*. He immediately moved to Monterey, where he built a store, a ship chandlery, and a warehouse.[56] His business enterprises seemed to have been honest and he soon became the dominant figure in the commercial and social life of the small port. Visiting ship captains always sought out Larkin or

---

[52]*Ibid.*, vol, 4, p. 121. Instances are recorded in which wealthy Americans financed the Californian provincial government for a time.

[53]Ogden *op. cit.*, pp. 132-139.

[54]Bancroft, *op. cit.*, vol. 4, p. 3. n. 1.

[55]*Ibid.*, vol. 4, pp. 38-39. American naval visits occurred in 1841 and 1842 as a result of violence stirred up by an American, Isaac Graham. His arrest and threatened deportation, along with that of several other Americans, caused the visits of Commodore J. H. Aulick in November, 1841, and Commodore T. A. C. Jones in November of the following year for the purpose of settling claims resulting from the arrests.

[56]Kelsey, *The United States Consulate in California* (Berkeley, 1910), p. 88.

one of his agents before transacting business. Publicity-minded, Larkin always entertained the American Pacific Squadron royally, holding balls and receptions for the officers and fandangos for the men. He became the go-between for the California rancheros as well as the Mexican government and American traders. In some of the letters of Larkin there are references to sailors and traders who succumbed to the charms of California.[57] Alfred Robinson, who married the daughter of one of Larkin's Mexican friends, even changed his name to "José Maria Alfredo."[58]

Just how many Americans came into California by sea between 1832 and 1849 is not known, but the movement was greatly speeded up both by the Mexican overthrow of Spain and Larkin's commercial activities. American settlement was still haphazard and rather casual prior to the gold rush, but Larkin had his eye on the future. He sensed the destiny of California and comprehended its strategic importance to American expansion. As a one-man chamber of commerce, by talking California to Americans on their way home and writing glowing letters of description back East, he did much to publicize and give true information about California. "His carefully planned publicity bureau of one hundred years ago scored a perfect bull's eye and at a very long range. He practically, if not entirely, won over the popular and widely circulated *New York Sun* to support the proposed acquisition of California."[59]

The first organized group to migrate by sea to California was a company of Mormons led by Samuel Brannock. A 450-ton vessel, the *Brooklyn,* was chartered to carry the party of 238 people. The group left New York and sailed around the Horn, arriving at San Francisco in July, 1846.[60] Most of this party proceeded eastward into Utah to meet the overland expedition led by Brigham Young. Brannock, however, returned to California after

---

[57]Cleland, "The Early Sentiment for the Annexation of California," p. 72.

[58]Reprinted with permission of the publisher from *From Cowhides to Golden Fleece* by Reuben L. Underhill (Stanford: Stanford University Press, 1946), p. 32.

[59]*Ibid.,* p. 32.

[60]Hafen and Rister, *Western America* (New York, 1941), p. 369.

disagreeing with the Mormon leader over a location for the settlements.

Seaward contacts helped to make California a familiar name to almost everyone in the United States by 1847. Its seizure during the Mexican War publicized it and revealed governmental recognition of its strategic and commercial importance. Thus the stage was set for the cataclysmic years known as the Gold Rush.

Gold Rush Migrations. When the startling news from Sutter's Fort reached the East in mid-September,[61] the small sea coast towns were just settling down after the minor boom caused by the Mexican War. Almost overnight America appeared to be preparing again for war, so extensive were the preparations for the trips to the gold fields. Foundries, sail lofts, rope walks, shipyards, and pawn shops began a booming business. Adventurous men, anxious to ship on a California-bound expedition, were willing to liquidate all their material assets to get in on the great adventure.[62]

It was only natural that men from New England should select the Cape Horn route. Their traditional contacts with the Pacific lay in that direction. The early China trade and California hide and tallow trade made this route familiar to them. Even the would-be miners who had never gone to sea considered it much safer than the long uncertain trip overland through deserts and hostile Indian lands. The largest influx of seaborne immigrants to California arrived during the spring and summer of 1849, beating the overland expeditions by two or three months.[63]

The largest group of Cape Horn immigrants were taken to California by organized companies or associations. The New England associations resembled old English trading companies. Every member was a "stock holder" or part owner. It was thought

---

[61]*Ibid.*, p. 354. T. O. Larkin dispatched the official news June 1, but it did not reach Washington until mid-September.

[62]Howe, *Argonauts of Forty Nine* (Cambridge, 1923), p. 4; Morison, *op. cit.*, p. 233. Nantucket was drained of one-quarter of her voting population in six months of 1849; 800 men left New Bedford in 1849, 150 ships departed from Boston in 1849, and 160 in 1850.

[63]Frost, *History of the State of California* (Auburn, N. Y., 1853), p. 175.

that their ships could be used to ply back and forth between New England and California, bringing gold back and taking needed supplies out, but the companies' aims were not limited to mere transportation to the gold fields; they were mining and trading companies as well.

As transportation companies these New England associations were a huge success, even though the California ports were not equipped for loading and unloading. Docks had not been built and expensive lightering was required to transfer cargo ashore. They failed completely, however, as trading companies in California. Experience proved that cooperation did not flourish in an atmosphere of exploitive and extractive opportunism. Most of the members, when gold was near, were not inclined to work for the common good. The general deterioration of seagoing morale when port was made also tended to break up these little ventures. For these reasons all associations broke up, the members going their several ways soon after the Gold Coast was reached.

The first company to be organized was the group of the ship *Edward Everettt*, which was characteristic of the pattern of all the rest. The association, organized in December of 1848, totaled 150 men and included one clergyman, four doctors, eight whaling captains, one mineralogist, fifteen professional men, various students, merchants, farmers, manufacturers, and mechanics.[64]

The enumeration of the New England companies does not indicate the exact number of Americans who sailed around the Horn to California, but it gives some idea of the extent of these ventures in 1849. The names are self-explanatory and reveal the dual purpose for which they were organized: California Mining and Trading Co., California Mining Association, Bunker Hill Mining and Trading Co., Bay State Trading and Mining Co., Suffolk Mutual Mining Co; Salem Mechanic Mining and Trading Co., and others for Plymouth, Bedford, Nantucket, etc. Most of these companies owned but one vessel and were dissolved after the initial trip. Sixty-five vessels were bought or chartered by these companies in 1849.[65]

---

[64]Howe, *op. cit.*, pp. 49-53.
[65]*Ibid.*, pp. 187-213.

The Seaborne Frontier in California

Migration to California by this route was not important as far as numbers were concerned, but the spirit of these trading companies and the philosophy on which they were organized had an important effect on California society. Most of the individual immigrants were young hardy men, usually single and out for adventure and riches. The men of the New England companies, often from the same town, were in large part sea-bred folk with common traditions. The ships' companies, infused with a common spirit of unity, adopted a democratic organization that tended to obscure class distinctions while at sea. They brought in Anglo-Saxon law, and their sense of morality and order helped stabilize California society.

The clipper ships were in their heyday between 1850 and 1852. The discovery of gold boomed their business by a demand for transportation of fast freight to California. It was practically a one-way carrying trade; in some cases the return trip was made in ballast and half-manned. Hardy men, who could stand the hardships and brutalities of a square-rigged ship of that day, shipped on as deck hands with the idea of deserting as soon as they got to the Gold Coast.[66]

The migration to California across the Isthmus of Panama and Nicaragua was in direct contrast to the Horn route. It included all types of people[67]—adventurers, crooks, white-collar men, prostitutes, families, and public officials. The Isthmus route was considered safer and quicker. The movement across this route can more truly be called a migration than the trip around South America.

Fortunately for the "forty-niners" and later immigrants, the United States government had long been conscious of the strategic importance of the Isthmus routes. Inspired by British interest in the Isthmus, the United States signed a treaty with New Granada in December, 1846 obtaining right of way and transit rights for a possible canal or railroad across the Isthmus of Panama.[68]

---

[66]Daniels, *The Clipper Ship* (New York, 1928), pp. 130-135.
[67]White, *The Forty-Niners* (New Haven, 1918), p. 96.
[68]Kemble, *The Panama Route, 1848-1869* (Berkeley, 1943), p. 3.

The demand for a quick route to the Gold Coast after 1848 furnished an incentive for developing the Isthmus route. Late in 1848 a stock company was formed under the laws of New York State by a group of New York City merchants. William Henry Aspinwall of the commercial firm of Howland and Aspinwall was the chief stockholder and George L. Stephens was elected president.[69] Early in 1849 a surveying party under Colonel John L. Hughes of the United States Army Topographical Engineers was sent to the Isthmus to begin the preliminary work of building the railroad. By 1851 the first section of the road had been completed from the Caribbean terminus at "Aspinwall" in Navy Bay to Gatun[70] (the first set of locks in the present canal). After overcoming almost unsurmountable geographical obstacles, the line was built across from opposite ends and completed in January, 1855. It began operation under a government mail subsidy during the height of the boom in California. Although the rail connections were established rather late in the gold rush period, early government interest and pressure from merchants, mainly from New York City, resulted in the establishment of steamship lines on either side of the Isthmus in time to carry the first gold seekers to California.

Original plans for steamship lines connecting the Atlantic and Pacific coast were stimulated by the annexation of Oregon. After 1846 bills were coming before Congress constantly for the establishment of subsidized mail lines to the Northwest Coast. In March, 1847, Congress passed the Mail Steamer Bill, which was to apply generally to all maritime activity of American merchants.[71] In May of the same year bids were let for the establishment of a line of steamers from Panama City to the Columbia River and Puget Sound region.[72] Arnold Harris, a New York merchant, made the lowest bid and won the contract, but, lacking the necessary capital, transferred the contracts in November, 1849, to William Henry Aspinwall. A few months later a New

---

[69]Otis, *Illustrated History of the Panama Railroad* (New York, 1861), p. 21.
[70]*Ibid.*, p. 31.
[71]Kemble, *op. cit.*, p. 12.
[72]*Ibid.*, p. 20.

The Seaborne Frontier in California

York corporation was formed by private means to establish a line of ships to operate on the Atlantic leg of the journey from New York to the mouth of the Chagres River on the Isthmus of Panama. The trustees of this organization were Messrs. George Law, Marshall O. Roberts and Bowes R. McIlvaine. By the end of 1848 both parts of the line were ready to operate under a government subsidy. The Pacific Mail Steamship Company, controlled by Aspinwall, was to receive a total yearly subsidy of $870,000.[73] The United States Mail Steamship Line, under George Law, received a somewhat smaller amount, which varied from $390,000 to $500,000 per year.[74] When news of the discovery of gold reached the East, Aspinwall of the Pacific Mail route got permission to change the terminus of his line from Puget Sound to San Francisco Bay. As the demand for rapid transportation to the gold fields began to be felt, cutthroat competition became the order of the day.

At first the two subsidized lines began competing with each other by sending their ships in each other's territory with cut-rate prices. Soon other individuals invaded the field and made it necessary for the Pacific Mail and the United States Mail to reach a working agreement. In the first year of operation J. Howard and Sons of New York began operating a ship or two on the Atlantic side of the Isthmus. This competition was quickly eliminated by Aspinwall, who bought the rival steamers. Late in 1848 the Empire City Line, financed and operated by Charles Morgan of New York, began running ships on both legs of the journey. For a year and a half Morgan was able to offer serious competition, but in 1850 he, too, was bought out by Aspinwall of the Pacific Mail Company.[75] The most serious competition was offered by Cornelius Vanderbilt, whose Independent Line began operating in 1851 between New York and the mouth of the San Juan River in Nicaragua—the entrance to a new route across the Isthmus that Vanderbilt had opened in 1850. Vanderbilt's ships operated between New York and Nicaragua until 1854, during which time

---
[73]*Ibid.*, p. 30.
[74]*Ibid.*, pp. 59-60.
[75]*Ibid.*, pp. 58-59.

the passengers on all lines enjoyed the benefits of the rate war and the ever increasing speed of the ships. His Independent Line offered such serious competition that the two subsidized lines were forced to combine resources and absorb the Vanderbilt ships into their own systems, at the same time buying off the "commodore" with a liberal sum. He remained, however, in a position of control in the corporate structure of the United States Mail Steamship Company. In 1859, when the government subsidy expired, the United States Mail Steamship Company withdrew and Vanderbilt again stepped in to run the Atlantic leg of the route. The Pacific Mail and the newly formed Panama Railway Company combined forces and made an unsuccessful attempt to oust Vanderbilt. A truce between Vanderbilt and Aspinwall was effected in 1860. From then on until the close of the line the two companies, working within a close operating agreement, formed a quiet, efficient monopoly.[76]

The history of the Panama routes is a continual story of improvement in service and ability to meet the demand of increasing traffic. At first a steamer left New York each month for Panama or Nicaragua to connect with a steamer that sailed on to San Francisco, after giving passengers time to make the difficult overland trip at the Isthmus. Later the sailings were increased to bimonthly departures, with connections on both ends. After the completion of the Panama railway, Atlantic steamers left New York on the first, eleventh, and twenty-first of each month, arriving in Aspinwall eight days later. Connections were possible at Panama on each sailing. This met the demand and kept at least two shiploads of passengers en route to California nearly every day for the last ten years of the life of the system.

The Isthmus routes, which operated from 1848 until 1869, were by far the most important sea routes to California. It is estimated that during the twenty years of operation 442,111 people were transported to the gold fields.[77] Between 1849 and 1859 one-fifth of the migration went to California by these routes. During the second decade nearly one-half of the total number

---

[76]*Ibid.*, p. 81.

[77]Kemble, *op. cit.*, Appendix II, p. 254.

The Seaborne Frontier in California

traveled this route. The completion of the transcontinental railway in the Unted States sounded the death knell for the steamer lines. By 1869 they were almost completely eclipsed and abandoned in favor of the land route.[78]

It is not hard to visualize the volume and importance of seaward migration to California from the descriptions of San Francisco Bay during the heyday of the gold rush. A contemporary writer in 1850 made the observation that he thought it possible to walk from Yerba Buena Island to San Francisco across the decks of anchored ships. He estimated that there were five hundred ships anchored abreast and abandoned by their officers and crews. He described the dismal sequel to the seaward rush to the gold fields. "Numberless vessels, mostly from the United States, filled the bay, in front of San Francisco, many of them deserted by their crews."[79] "Many of these, never to go to sea again, were beached and used as jails, hotels, and boarding houses."[80]

Just as the discovery of gold had a terrific impact on American society, the influx of people by sea and the increased shipping activities transformed the face of San Francisco and the society of California. Laborers, merchants, families, clergymen, thieves—men of all classes arrived by sea over the route described. Unconsciously they made their contribution to America by helping to make California American.

ANTECEDENTS OF ANNEXATION POLICY

The flow of Americans into California after 1816 was but one phase of American development on the coast. As an element in the formation of foreign policy, the American population on the coast was an important, but by no means the only, factor.

Fear of Foreign Aggression. After 1818 influential papers and periodicals, such as the *Niles Register* and the *Saint Louis Inquirer,* aroused by J. B. Prevost, special commissioner investigating the Northwest boundary question, directed attention

---

[78]*Ibid.,* p. 114.
[79]Frost, *op. cit.,* p. 88.
[80]Howe, *op. cit.,* p. 114.

to the Russian threat to San Francisco Bay. Prevost's letters, starting in November, 1818, helped to familiarize the American public with the problem of foreign competition in California.[81] The same theme was the subject of William A. Slacum's letters to Secretary of State Forsythe in 1836. On his mission to the Northwest Coast (see Chapter II), Slacum traveled through California. From his observation he concluded that the Russians were very much in earnest in their desire for a foothold in San Francisco Bay.[82] Concern about Russian policy was removed after 1824[83] and was replaced by fear of British or French annexation. This fear is reflected in the letters of Consul T. O. Larkin. In writing to Calhoun, secretary of state, in August, 1844, he described what he fancied to be French and English jealousy over California and the prospects of French commercial expansion from the Marquesaes Islands.[84] He rated England as the greater threat, due to her foothold in Oregon and the Hudson's Bay establishment in San Francisco.[85]

It is clear that official interest was aroused by the foreign threat, since Larkin was instructed to keep the State Department informed of the extent of foreign influence in California. In July of 1845 Larkin wrote a letter, published in the New York *Journal of Commerce*, reiterating the threat of a potential English or French annexation.[86] During his years as American consul (1844-1845) Larkin also corresponded heavily with other Americans in key points in California on the subject of foreign aggression.[87]

---

[81]*Ibid.*, p. 8.

[82]*Senate Documents*, No. 24, 25th Congress, 2nd session, p. 29. In a letter dated November, 1836, Slacum not only outlined the Russian threat but reported that "300 American riflemen in upper California were ready to throw off Mexican rule."

[83]Russian power was stabilized by the treaty resulting from the imperial ukase of 1821 (see Chapter II).

[84]Kelsey, ed., *op. cit.*, p. 46.

[85]*Ibid.*, p. 47.

[86]Kelsey, "Early Sentiments for the Annexation of California," pp. 50-51. Larkin went so far as to suggest splitting a part of California with England in return for a part of Oregon.

[87]Underhill, *op. cit.*, p. 97. Abel Stearns at San Diego and Jacob Leese at Sonoma are examples of his unofficial "agents."

The Seaborne Frontier in California

All information was faithfully relayed to the State Department. As R. W. Kelsey, who studied Larkin's activities as American consul, concluded: "such information from the Monterey consulate must have had no small influence on the policy of the United States government with respect to California."[88]

The fear of foreign threats will be seen reflected in later diplomatic moves. This phase of policy formation is important because preoccupation over foreign aggression was based mainly on the assumption that California was an indispensable area in the successful pursuit of American Pacific trade.

Publications About California. A less positive, but none the less important, force in the forming of a California policy was the influence of the writings of American visitors and residents. The earliest was the narrative of William Shaler, who traded along the coast in 1803 and 1804 (see pp. 133-34, 162). His journal, published in 1808, leaves the reader with the impression that he foresaw the day of American annexation and felt called upon to give a political and military evaluation of the situation with this event in mind. His significant conclusion was that "the conquest of this country would be absolutely nothing, it would fall without an effort to the most inconsiderable force."[89]

After 1832 the letters of Thomas Larkin were the main source of information contributing to the popularization of California. Alfred Robinson, who had come to California on a hide ship in 1829, wrote a standard work about his adopted country, entitled *Life in California, 1846*.[90] Colonel John C. Frémont's report of his exploring expedition came out in the same year.

President Jackson's Interest in California. Diplomatic negotiations of the United States in relation to California both preceded and paralled the development of American interest in California and the peopling of the coast by Americans. The official moves became involved in the larger question of Amer-

---

[88] Kelsey, "Early Sentiments for the Annexation of California," p. 48.

[89] Shaler, "A Journal of a Voyage Made Between China and the Northwest Coast of America, Made in 1804," *American Register*, pp. 137-175.

[90] This book was reviewed in the popular trade journal, *Hunt's Merchant Magazine*, vol. 14 (January-June, 1846), pp. 349-353.

ican-Mexican relations and clearly illustrate the point that maritime security was the principal consideration in the formation of policy toward California.

The interest of President Jackson in the San Francisco Bay area was, according to John Quincy Adams, stirred by the letters of William A. Slacum to Secretary of State Forsythe.[91] At any rate, in August of 1835, the same month in which Forsythe received the letter from Slacum, the secretary of state was directed to instruct the American minister in Mexico, Butler, to inject a new element into the Texas boundary negotiations. Butler was informed that since "it has been represented to the President that the port of St. Francisco, on the western coast of the United Mexican States, would be a most desirable place of resort for our numerous vessels engaged in the whaling business in the Pacific, far preferable to any to which they have access, he has directed that an addition should be made to your instructions relative to the negotiation for Texas. The main object is to secure within our limits the whole bay of St. Francisco."[92] The fate of the negotiations apparently hinged on the purchase of the San Francisco Bay, as Forsythe continued: "If, however, you cannot obtain a southern line which will include within our limits the whole bay of St. Francisco, . . . bring the negotiations to a close as directed from the Department on the second of July, 1835, No. 094."[93]

Nothing came of the efforts of Butler, but another attempt was made in January, 1837, when the Mexican general, Santa Anna, came to Washington to discuss the question of Texan independence and possible annexation to the United States. President Jackson is reported to have made the suggestion that, "if Mexico [would] extend the line of the United States to latitude 38 north and then to the Pacific including north California we might instruct our 'minister to give them three millions and a half dollars. . . .' "[94]

---

[91] Adams, C. F. *Memoirs of John Quincy Adams* (Philadelphia, 1876), vol. 11, p. 348.

[92] *House Executive Documents*, No. 42, 25th Congress, 1st session, p. 19.

[93] *Ibid.*

[94] Cleland, "Early Sentiment for the Annexation of California," p. 17.

The Seaborne Frontier in California 153

These unsuccessful negotiations are the last official mention of California for several years, yet government interest was not entirely submerged. Secretary of the Navy Upshur, in his annual report to the president in 1841, stressed the unstable conditions in California and offered the opinion that American commercial interests along the coast were no longer safe without increased naval power in the Pacific.[95]

President Tyler's Pacific Coast Policy. Renewed efforts to gain a foothold on the Pacific coast were made by the Tyler administration. Waddy Thompson was accredited Envoy Extraordinary and Minister Plenipotentiary to Mexico in April, 1842, and was dispatched to Vera Cruz to await instructions. A definite movement was set in motion to acquire California. In Thompson's first dispatch to the State Department, he said that he considered Mexico willing to sell California and Texas.[96] He went to great length in describing the advantages of American acquisition of California, pointing to the commodious harbor at San Francisco, the foreign threat of England and France, and the ease by which the Oriental trade could be controlled. Commercial ascendancy, he argued, would come to the United States in the Pacific as it had in the Atlantic. What he considered the prime objective of his mission is revealed in a sentence from the dispatch to Secretary Webster: "as to Texas, I regard it of little value compared with California."[97]

President Tyler and Secretary of State Webster considered the dispatches from Minister Thompson, and acted favorably upon his suggestions. In June, 1842, Thompson was issued instructions to push negotiations for the purchase of California.[98] He was to use a casual approach, presenting the offer as an alternative method of settling the long-standing claims of American citizens against the Mexican government; Mexico was not to perceive that the annexation of California was, as Secretary

---

[95]*Senate Documents*, No. 1, 27th Congress, 2nd session, p. 369; also cited in Bancroft, *op. cit.*, vol. 4, p. 258.

[96]Cleland, "Early Sentiments for the Annexation of California," p. 27.

[97]Rives, *op. cit.*, vol. 2, p. 45; Cleland, "Early Sentiments for the Annexation of California," p. 28.

[98]Rives, *op. cit.*, vol. 2, p. 46.

Webster said, "an object upon which we have set our hearts."[99] In the full instructions, however, Webster was clear in pointing out the main objective of the negotiation: "the benefits of the possession of a good harbor on the Pacific is so obvious . . . the President strongly inclines to favor the idea of a treaty with Mexico."[100] Negotiations broke down due to the unwillingness of the Mexican government and the immaturity of the situation.[101] The seizure of Monterey by Commodore T. A. C. Jones was the incident that preceded the breaking off of negotiations in Mexico City. This incident in itself is significant as it revealed future United States policy prematurely to the world.[102]

POLICY OF PRESIDENT POLK

Changing conditions in California—the increasing number of English-speaking people, political instability, agitation for home rule, destruction of the missions—all conspired to cause a disorganized situation that played into President Polk's hands, after 1844, in his efforts to detach California from Mexico. The tempo of the negotiation speeded up in the years immediately preceding the Mexican War. The policy in relation to California became increasingly a part of the total question or American relations with Mexico. Its development fits into a series of events: (1) in March, 1845, a joint resolution of Congress approved the annexation of Texas three days before Polk was inaugurated; (2) Mexico considered annexation a "casus belli," but no war was declared; (3) in August, 1845, General Taylor advanced to the Nueces River; (4) in October, 1845, the Larkin dispatches were written; and (5) in November, 1845, Polk issued instructions for the conciliatory Slidell mission.

---

[99]Webster, *Writing and Speeches* (Boston, 1903), vol. 13, p. 612.
[100]*Ibid.*, p. 611.
[101]Cleland, "Early Sentiment for the Annexation of California," p. 40.
[102]Bancroft, *op. cit.*, vol. 4, ch. 12. The incident of the seizure is discussed from an examination of the primary sources. Bancroft concluded that Jones's move was in keeping with United States policy of preventing foreign aggression in California. The French and English fleets had been maneuvering suspiciously before Jones's departure from Callao to Monterey.

The Seaborne Frontier in California

Instructions to Sloat and Larkin. It is well known that long before the outbreak of hostilities, President Polk was eager to annex California.[103] The orders issued to Commodore J. D. Sloat in June, 1845, clearly show that the Pacific coast was as much in the minds of government officials as was the disputed Texan boundary or the claims against Mexico: "The Mexican ports on the Pacific are said to be open and defenseless. If you ascertain with certainty that Mexico has declared war against the United States, you will at once possess yourself of the port of San Francisco and blockade or occupy such ports as your force will permit."[104]

With the American navy thus primed, the subsequent moves that revealed the clear-cut policy of the United States were the instructions to T. O. Larkin in Monterey and also the instructions to John Slidell, negotiating in Mexico City. During the summer of 1845 Larkin wrote a letter to the State Department stressing the incomparable value of California to the United States and detailing the activities of the Hudson's Bay Company and the official aid of the British in an attempted revolution in California against Mexican rule.[105] This dispatch from Consul Larkin was read carefully and taken seriously in official circles in Washington. A prompt reply was sent to California in the form of secret instructions to Larkin[106] from Secretary of State James Buchanan. The instructions were written on October 17, 1845. One copy was sent around Cape Horn on the United States frigate *Congress;* another was sent overland across Mexico by the hand of

---

[103]Rives, *op. cit.*, vol. 1, p. 719. George Bancroft at the age of ninety recalled a conversation with Polk early in his administration in which Polk sketched his four main objectives, one of which was the acquisition of California.

[104]*Ibid.*, vol. 2, p. 164.

[105]Kelsey, *op. cit.*, p. 51; Buchanan, *op. cit.*, vol. 6, p. 278; Underhill, *op. cit.*, p. 32. Larkin had held schemes of peaceful annexation since 1840. The value of California to the future maritime development of the United States and the constant foreign threat were his favorite themes.

[106]Buchanan, *The Works of James Buchanan* (New York, 1919), vol. 6, p. 278; Kelsey, *op. cit.*, p. 101. The conclusion of this author is that Larkin's letter of July, 1845, directly provoked the sending of official instructions.

Lt. A. H. Gillespie, U.S.M.C. This was the beginning of the famous Gillespie-Frémont intrigue that supposedly resulted in the political coup in California. The plot theory of the California revolt has never been satisfactorily supported or refuted, but the contents of Larkin's instructions are a clear statement of official policy in regard to California.[107]

Larkin's Instructions and Efforts. According to instructions delivered orally by Gillespie in April, 1846, Larkin was commissioned confidential agent and requested to furnish the government with important information regarding political conditions in California and the threats of foreign interference. The interests of the Pacific trade and the whale fisheries were given as the paramount drive for checking English designs on California. The hope was expressed that the people of California would want to join the United States if they could be freed from Mexico without causing complaint from that government. Larkin was to investigate the disposition of the population as to American annexation and supply the State Department with information concerning the population, financial and economic conditions, names and characters of principal people, types of judicial and administrative control, and the possibilities of maritime trade. Specific information was requested about the extent of the American population, places of settlement, origin, and routes used in traveling to California. The central theme of American policy is summarized in the following excerpt from Larkin's instructions: "The interests of our commerce and our whale fisheries on the Pacific Ocean demand that you should exert the greatest viligance in the discovery and defeating of any attempts which may be made by foreign governments to acquire control over that [California] country."[108] Larkin was cautioned that, while "this government, however, does not under existing circumstances intend to interfere between Mexico and California, they would vigorously interpose to prevent the latter from becoming

---

[107]Cleland, "Early Sentiments for the Annexation of California," pp. 72-73; Kelsey, *op. cit.*, appendix, pp. 100-103; Buchanan, *op. cit.*, vol. 6, pp. 275-278 were consulted for desired excerpts and facts from Larkin's instructions from Secretary of State Buchanan, dated October 17, 1845.

[108]Buchanan, *op. cit.*, vol. 6, p. 278.

a British or French colony."¹⁰⁹ The stated course of action hinged on two policies: (1) to work peaceably for detachment of California from Mexico, based on the goodwill of the Californians; and (2) to stop short of nothing, including war, in forestalling English or French seizure of the province.

Conveniently, Larkin received the instructions a few days before the outbreak of hostilities along the Rio Grande. Two days after the actual start of the war he began his campaign in earnest, in the spirit of his instructions. Letters were sent out to "Mexican Americans"—Abel Stearns of Los Angeles, John Warner of San Diego, and Jacob Leese of Sonoma.¹¹⁰ To these leading merchants, Larkin sketched the possibility of war with Mexico and the desirability of peaceful acquisition of California by the United States. Although Stearns replied favorably in regard to the influential people in the vicinity of Los Angeles, the general feeling was that most Californians were not yet ready to sever connections with Mexico, although the "leading ones" were.¹¹¹ Larkin's activities were cut short by the Bear Flag revolt in June of 1846 and the occupation of Monterey by Commodore J. D. Sloat in the following month.

Slidell's Mission. The secret mission of John Slidell was another aspect of American policy concerning California. Slidell's instructions, issued less than a month after the Larkin instructions were written, show that Polk was pursuing a double-barreled policy in an effort to seize California without war. While Larkin was feeling out the opinion of Californians on the possibility of peaceful annexation and keeping a wary eye on foreign activities, Slidell was to be in Mexico negotiating for the purchase of Upper California and New Mexico. Secretary of State Buchanan's secret instructions authorized the commissioner to settle all claims outstanding and pay five million dollars for an advantageous boundary settlement.¹¹² He was to negotiate for a cession of a portion of California; twenty-five million dollars could be

---

[109]Kelsey, *op. cit.*, appendix, p. 102.

[110]*Ibid.*, p. 66.

[111]*Ibid.*, p. 72. He meant American businessmen. Underhill, *op. cit.*, p. 97. Larkin relayed all this information to Washington.

[112]*Senate Documents*, No. 52, 30th Congress, 1st session, p. 78.

paid if Monterey was included, and twenty million if the boundary line was run north of that port. It is clear from Buchanan's instructions that the port of San Francisco was to be the major stake in the negotiation:

> The government of California is now but nominally dependent on Mexico, and it is more than doubtful whether her authority will ever be reinstated. Under these circumstances it is the desire of the President that you will use your best efforts to obtain a cession of that province from Mexico to the United States... money would be no object when compared to the value of the acquisition... You may in addition to the assumption of the claims offer twenty million for any boundary commencing on any point on the western line of New Mexico and running due west to the Pacific; so as to include the bay and the harbor of San Francisco.[113]

"The possession of the bay and harbor of San Francisco is all important to the United States.... If ... it should be turned against our country by the cession of California to Great Britain, our principal commercial rival, the consequences would be most disastrous."[114]

American officials thought the time propitious for detaching California. The fear of foreign annexation and commercial contacts along the coast were contributing factors to this belief. Slidell's failure, however, was to prove otherwise. The ruling class in Mexico was unwilling to alienate Mexican territory, no matter how tenuously held. Unstable political conditions, following a bloodless revolution, blocked the negotiations.[115]

War Aims. The role of California as a factor in precipitating the Mexican War cannot be ignored in this review of maritime antecedents of final annexation. It has been suggested that American maritime activities partially formed the economic basis for acquisition of California. Trade contacts helped to popularize it in the minds of easterners and brought the first New Englanders to the coast. The handful of Americans holding key positions

---
[113] Buchanan, *op. cit.*, vol. 6, pp. 304-305.
[114] *Senate Documents*, No. 52, 30th Congress, 1st session, p. 79.
[115] Rives, *op. cit.*, vol. 2, p. 80.

The Seaborne Frontier in California

quickly became prominent in Californian affairs after 1840. The California trade first drew the attention of officials in Washington to the importance of a seaport and to the ominous threat of foreign annexation.

Because of these factors, the United States was determined to have California in 1846 in the event of war, or to encourage peaceful annexation if events fell short of war.[116] It is not safe to say that if there had been no California there would have been no Mexican War, but at least the Californian policy coincided with and paralleled other developments and became a crucial aim in the prosecuting of the war.[117] On the other hand, it has been said that "if the question of Texas stood alone, affairs with Mexico might well have been left to settle themselves. But the Texan question by no means stood alone."[118]

This conclusion suggests that the question of the Texan boundary and the settlement of claims were minor aspects of the war policy. A cession of Mexican territory in payment for claims had long been the intention of the United States government, but "the fact remains that such payment by cession of territory belonging to the Mexican republic—was not Texas—it was New Mexico and California—especially California."[119] Yet it is impossible to wring from the documents an admission that a direct attack upon Mexico was intended.[120] It is equally impossible to see any other purpose in the diplomatic and military maneuvers that took place between May, 1845, and May, 1846. Polk was willing enough to buy California but, failing this, he was bent on finding a pretext for obtaining it otherwise. Regardless of the short-range motives of the President after 1845, the deciding factors in the formation of the annexation policy were the well-established maritime contacts, fear of foreign dominance on the Pacific coast, and the deteriorating political and economic ties between California and Mexico.

---

[116]Bancroft, *op. cit.*, vol. 5, p. 199.
[117]Cleland, "Early Sentiment for the Annexation of California," p. 81.
[118]Rives, *op. cit.*, vol. 1, p. 719.
[119]Rives, *op. cit.*, vol. 2, p. 657.
[120]Buchanan, *op. cit.*, vol. 6, pp. 471-472. In Polk's war message, May 11, 1846, California is not mentioned in reviewing the causes of war.

Statehood. Hostilities were ended by the Treaty of Guadalupe Hidalgo, signed early in 1848. California, as conquered territory, was held for a time under military rule. The native Californians and especially the American-born residents soon became restive under martial law. With the increased population resulting from the gold rush, popular desire for a more democratic form of government arose.[121] A constitutional convention met in Monterey in September, 1849. A state government was set up and senators were elected to represent the newly formed state in Washington. This was extralegal action that became involved directly in the slavery question then raging in the country. The debates in Congress over the annexation and statehood of California hinged around the remarks of the veteran statesmen—John C. Calhoun, Henry Clay, and Daniel Webster—arguing about the problems of the balance of power in Congress between the slave and free states and the nature of the Federal Union.[122]

California came into the Union under the constitution adopted the year before at Monterey. Its statehood was granted as a part of the Compromise of 1850. The overwhelming problem of slavery submerged all other arguments for its annexation and admission to the Union. The early arguments for the occupation of the Pacific coast needed no reiteration. Commerce and migration had done their work.

---

[121] Riegel, *America Moves West* (New York, 1947), p. 391.

[122] Goodwin, *The Trans-Mississippi West,* pp. 465-466; DeVoto, *Year of Decision* (Boston, 1943), pp. 476-477.

Chapter V

The Americanization of Hawaii

The accident of geographical location and the sailing limitations of square-rigged ships conspired to make the Sandwich, or Hawaiian, Islands the crossroads of the Pacific trade. They became a supply point and transshipment depot for the commerce with China and for the Northwest fur trade. The increase in American trade with California after 1821 and the continued interdependence of the Northwest Coast, the Hawaiian Islands, and the China trade, built up a community of interests in the northeastern area of the Pacific Ocean.

EARLY TRADE TO 1820

American contacts with the Hawaiian Islands were an outcome of the drive, inspired by economic necessity, that sent New England ships all over the world after the American Revolution. The same ships that were engaged in the Northwest Coast-Canton trade touched Hawaiian Island ports. Probably the first American vessels to call at the islands were the *Columbia* and *Lady Washington*, in 1789.[1] Casual though this contact was, it had far-reaching cnosequences. The *Lady Washington* left three men ashore on the island of Hawaii to gather sandalwood,[2] thus starting a trade that had a tremendous effect on the later political and economic life of the islands. The *Columbia*, on her way to Canton, picked up the Hawaiian boy, Attoo, whose presence in New England later was supposed to have stimulated the founding of the Mission school at Cornwall, Connecticut.[3]

---

[1]Morison, "Boston Traders in the Hawaiian Islands," *Massachusetts Historical Society Proceedings*, vol. 54 (1920-1921), p. 11.

[2]Carpenter, *America in Hawaii* (Boston, 1899), p. 16.

[3]Morison, "Boston Traders in the Hawaiian Islands," p. 11. It was from this school that the missionary band went to the Hawaiian Islands in 1820.

Other vessels followed the *Columbia* and *Lady Washington*. By 1791 five ships were regularly touching the Hawaiian Island ports. In 1801 fifteen American vessels were so engaged.[4]

Foreign Competition. From the beginning foreign competition was present to some degree. Captain Cook, on his third voyage, had discovered the islands in 1778. In 1792 Captain George Vancouver, who had been with Cook, revisited the islands and brought seeds, fruit trees, firearms, cows, and sheep. He went so far as to place the islands under an informal protectorate of England, although it was never officially established.[5] British vessels were never numerous in the early years, and after 1801 they all but disappeared until other incentives for trade developed later in the century.[6]

Several Russian vessels touched the islands between 1809 and 1815. Governor Baranov of the Russian-American Company desired a colony in the Hawaiian Islands as a way station on the route to China. A Russian blockhouse was built at Honolulu, and another on the island of Waimea.[7] Russian colonizing plans were near fulfillment when the Hawaiian king requested them to leave. The Russian government quickly disavowed the act of aggression.

The Sandalwood Trade. In spite of the efforts of foreign navigators to secure a monopoly in the Hawaiian Islands, American vessels were in the majority. Because of the location of the islands, the names of ships and men involved are practically the same as those engaged in the general Pacific trade between the East coast of America and Canton. Included were:[8] Captain Ingraham of the *Hope*, 1792; Captain Boit of the *Union*, 1792; Captain Richard J. Cleveland and William Shaler of the *Lelia Byrd*, 1803;[9] Captain Amasa Delano in 1806; and Captain Suter

---

[4]Reprinted with permission of the publisher from *The American Frontier in Hawaii: The Pioneers 1789-1843* by Harold Whitman Bradley (Stanford: Stanford University Press, 1942), p. 17.

[5]Carpenter, *op. cit.*, p. 16.

[6]Bradley, *op. cit.*, p. 17.

[7]Carpenter, *op. cit.*, p. 17.

[8]Morison, "Boston Traders in the Hawaiian Islands," p. 12.

[9]Cleveland, ed., *Voyages of a Merchant Navigator*, pp. 95-99. Shaler and Cleveland are credited with taking the first horses to the Hawaiian

The Americanization of Hawaii

of the *Pearl* in 1808. Such names indicate that, in the early years, the islands were used as a supply and fresh water stop for ships engaged in the larger Pacific trade.

When, about 1810, the islands began furnishing sandalwood for the China trade their importance increased. The sandalwood trade grew up as an adjunct to the fur trade and soon became as important to the Hawaiian Islands as furs had been to the Northwest Coast.[10] Partial loads of sandalwood taken to Canton in the early 1790's netted no profit,[11] but T. H. Perkins and Company of Boston suggested to their Canton agent, in 1807, that vessels be sent to the Hawaiian Islands for this article of exchange.[12] Captain Edmund Fanning, about the same time, 1806-1808, was active in the sandalwood trade in the Fiji Islands, where he had entered into formal contracts with the native king for the cutting of sandalwood logs.[13] His cargoes arrived in Canton simultaneously with the first imports of the T. H. Perkins agents. The Winship brothers, Jonathan and Nathan, in the ships *O'Cain* and *Albatross*, headed from the Northwest Coast in 1809, eager to fill out their cargo with sandalwood for Canton as an experiment.[14] The first venture was profitable, and they returned to Honolulu to effect a contract with the king for a monopoly of the sandalwood supply. This was one of the earliest examples of the use of the contract system in the sandalwood trade.[15]

Islands. The indifference of the natives to the strange animals is shown by Cleveland's remarks: "This want of appreciation of the value of the present, which they had taken so much pains to procure, was naturally a disappointment to the donors, who could only hope that time and experience would serve to convince the stolid chieftain that an important element in the work of civilization was comprised in their possible services."

[10]Porter, "John Jacob Astor and the Sandalwood Trade of the Hawaiian Islands," *Journal of Economic and Business History*, vol. 2 (November, 1929 to August, 1930), p. 496.

[11]Howay, "Outline Sketch of Maritime Fur Trade," *Canadian Historical Association, Report of Annual Meeting*, 1932, p. 13.

[12]Bradley, *op. cit.*, p. 29.

[13]Fanning, *Voyages*, pp. 61-63.

[14]Bradley, *op. cit.*, p. 29.

[15]*Ibid.*, p. 30. One-fourth of the profits were to go to the king.

Gradually, after 1810, as Northwest furs declined more and more ships stopped at the Hawaiian Islands to swell scanty cargoes with sandalwood.[16] After 1817 the value of the wood in Canton rose, and practically every ship sailing from America to Canton by way of the islands took on at least a few piculs (133½ lbs.) of sandalwood.

The supply of native wood was a royal monopoly. Because of this, the nature of the trade after the War of 1812 necessitated rather intimate and involved relations between the American traders and the Hawaiian government. The contract system used by the Winship brothers came into general use. Merchants negotiated contracts with the king on Oahu or with local chieftains on the other islands. The lesser chiefs acted as agents, supplying native labor to cut the logs and transport them to spots along the coast, designated in the contracts.[17] The Hawaiian chieftains drove notoriously hard bargains, sometimes demanding seagoing vessels in payment for wood.[18] One contract shows that the king, in return for 850 piculs of sandalwood, obtained sixteen kegs of rum, a box of tea, and $8,000 worth of small arms and ammunition.[19]

Coinciding with the new era in the Hawaiian trade was the growing scarcity of specie, due partly to the depression of 1819 in the United States. The result was that sandalwood temporarily

---

[16]Porter, "John Jacob Astor and the Sandalwood Trade," pp. 503-505. The activities of Astor's Pacific Fur Company is typical. He had at least six ships operating systematically in the sandalwood trade between 1810 and 1826—one collecting wood in the islands; one taking off furs on the Northwest Coast; one en route from New York to Hawaii with manufactured goods; and another sailing among the Spanish ports of the Pacific selling China goods for silver specie.

[17]Bradley, *op. cit.*, p. 55.

[18]Porter, "John Jacob Astor and the Sandalwood Trade," p. 511. The firm of John Jacob Astor, for example, sold the old fur ship *Forester* to the Hawaiian king for a cargo of sandalwood. Bradley, *op. cit.*, p. 62. Bryant and Sturgis, in 1819, sold the famous "Cleopatra Barge" for 8,000 piculs of wood. This vessel had belonged to Elias Hasket Derby of Salem, and had been a successful privateer during both Anglo-American wars.

[19]Bradley, *op. cit.*, p. 56.

The Americanization of Hawaii

became the chief medium of trade. Local Hawaiian chieftains began exploiting the native wood to supply the increased demands of the China traders. The year 1821 marked the flood of this exploitive trade,[20] though even then signs of decline could be seen. On the islands of Hawaii and Oahu the source of supply was already exhausted. The market in Canton had become glutted; the price per unit had been cut nearly in half.[21] Local chiefs, who had been supplying the American ships, began to find themselves increasingly in debt to merchants. American merchants began to realize the impasse facing the Hawaiian ruling class. As debts increased, the means for liquidating them decreased.[22] Americans began to look around for means of claiming payment. This resulted, as will be noticed later, in the first American pressure of an official nature upon the Hawaiian government.

The sandalwood trade, due to its exploitive and extractive nature, had no permanent effect on the economy of the islands. It did form, for a time (approximately 1810-1825), the chief economic incentive for American trade in Hawaii. The islands became more than a refreshment stop along the route to the Chinese market. As far as the islands were concerned, the ruling class became wealthy for a time, then found itself in debt to American merchants. By 1820 the economy of Hawaii was increasingly tied to that of the entire Pacific area.

COMMERCIAL TRENDS AFTER 1820

The revolution in Mexico and South America in the early 1820's had a marked effect on the status of Hawaii in the general Pacific trade. With the removal of Spanish restrictions in California in 1821 and the development of the hide and tallow trade, Yankee ships increasingly began to bring in American manufactured goods and Chinese products to the newly opened ports.[23]

---

[20]*Ibid.*, p. 64. Thirty thousand piculs of wood entered Canton in that year.

[21]*Ibid.*, p. 66. The price per picul had declined from $10 to $6.50 by 1824.

[22]Porter, "John Jacob Astor and the Sandalwood Trade," p. 501.

[23]Ogden, *The California Sea Otter Trade* (Berkeley, 1941), p. 90.

Since the ships, after rounding the Horn, called at Hawaii on their way to California, the islands became the center of a lively commercial activity that was dominated by American merchants. Hawaii became important as a transshipment point. By 1831 a profitable trade between California and Hawaii had developed. California received manufactured goods from the United States; Hawaii received horses, beef, hides, specie, and furs from California. This trade was nearly all in the hands of American merchants in both places.[24]

Hawaiian Islands as a Whaling Center. Coincident with the rising California trade was the development of the Pacific whaling industry. It overlapped the booming sandalwood trade that, for a time, overshadowed it. From the visit of the whaler *Argo* of Nantucket, in 1820, which first fished the Japanese whaling grounds, the volume of traffic rapidly grew. By 1822 there were at times from forty to sixty whaling vessels lying in Honolulu harbor at once.[25] So great was the economic impact of the whale fishery on the islands that the seasonal ebb and flow of traffic set the pace for Hawaiian economic life. The whaling vessels usually set out for the northern whaling grounds at the beginning of the summer season, returned to Hawaii in the fall to refit and repair, and spent the winter cruising the coast of California or along the equator and among the South Sea Islands.[26] When spring came the cycle was repeated. This system, by 1841, resulted in semiannual visits of between 200 and 250 vessels to the ports in the Hawaiian Islands. It was estimated that each ship spent approximately $700 during each call.[27] Whaling

---

[24]Bradley, *op. cit.*, p. 76. Carlton Aberdeen, British consul in Honolulu, was quoted by Bradley as estimating the extent of American control in 1831.

[25]Carpenter, *op. cit.*, p. 36; Morison, "Boston Traders in the Hawaiian Islands," p. 41. J. C. Jones, agent of the Boston trading firm of Marshall and Wilde, said in a letter in 1822: "During the summer the harbor has been crowded with whaling ships, not less, say than sixty. This has consequently made provisions scarce and dear . . . we are now obliged to pay money for everything we use. . . ."

[26]Bradley *op. cit.*, p. 80.

[27]Carpenter, *op. cit.*, p. 36.

The Americanization of Hawaii

was the basis of the economic life of the islands until 1860, when plantation economy supplanted commerce.[28]

The effect of early commerce on the social life of the islands has been nearly summed up by an eminent maritime historian:

> A new era began in 1820 with the arrival of the first missionaries, the first whalers, and the opening of a new reign. It was the missionaries who brought Hawaii in touch with a better side of New England civilization than that presented by the trading vessels and their crews. But without the trade, the missionary would not have come. The commercial relations between Massachusetts and Hawaii form the solid background of American expansion in the Pacific, the fundamental influence that worked steadily for annexation in 1898.[29]

American Establishments Ashore. Another influential aspect of American contacts with Hawaii contributing to the background of annexation was the development of commercial establishments ashore. Originally, retail stores developed from efforts to dispose of individual ships' cargoes. In 1817 James Hunnewell and a man named Dorr, who came to Honolulu in the vessel *Bourdeaux Packet,* set themselves up ashore long enough to sell their cargo of mixed goods and moved on to Canton.[30] Some obscure and transient traders briefly carried on business ashore between 1818 and 1820. After 1821 the demand for American and European goods, stimulated by the influx of whalers to the islands, caused increased competition among the larger commercial houses, such as Bryant and Sturgis, T. H. Perkins and Company, and Marshall and Wilde.[31] As a result, semipermanent establishments to supply the retail trade were set up ashore. After 1825 the large firms abandoned the Hawaiian market, and small retail establishments became the rule. Among the most important were those of James Hunnewell and Henry A. Pierce (a partnership), John C. Jones, William Reynolds, William

---

[28]Bradley, *op. cit.,* p. 80.
[29]Morison, "Boston Traders in Hawaiian Islands," vol. LIV (1920-1921), p. 19. Courtesy of the Massachusetts Historical Society.
[30]*Ibid.,* p. 84.
[31]*Ibid.,* p. 85.

French, and Elias Grimes. All of these merchants, except Pierce, were from the United States. The ties between the United States and Hawaii were strengthened by the activities of American traders and men ashore engaged in distributing imports. The invoices of James Hunnewell from 1826 to 1832 include such articles as cotton goods, fancy goods, stationery, shoes, umbrellas, table covers, towels, cutlery, hatchets, fish hooks, pocket pistols, scissors, files, jack-knives, razors, finger rings, Calcutta twine, tea, sugar, chocolate, salt pork, champagne, rum, perfume, chairs, pantaloons, etc.[32] A letter, in 1823, from J. C. Jones to his firm in Boston listed similar articles: cloth, readymade clothes, sea coal, lumber, copper paint, rigging, wheel barrows, hand carts, light wagons, ox carts, writing desks, etc.[33]

Increasingly after 1820 Americans dominated all phases of commercial life ashore. Honolulu, which was nothing but a collection of thatched-roof shacks when the first Americans saw the islands, by 1826 had taken on the characteristics of a modern city. Wooden houses, well laid-out streets, fenced-in houses, and seventeen grog shops marked the change.[34] Statistical data illustrating American commercial dominance are incomplete, but Bradley has pieced together a few figures that show a general picture.[35] From 1832 to 1836 the total value of foreign-owned property in Honolulu amounted to $500,000, four-fifths of which was owned by Americans. In 1841 it was estimated that the total value of property held by Americans, not including ships, amounted to about one million dollars. A tabulation of such property held in 1840 includes twenty retail houses, four wholesale houses, two hotels, twelve boardinghouses, two taverns, two billiard rooms, seven bowling alleys, one copper foundry, one paint oil factory, one lumber yard, four blacksmith shops, and fourteen carpenter shops.[36]

During the year 1843 a total of 129 whaling ships touched Honolulu, as did 40 merchant vessels, of which 25 were Amer-

---

[32]*Ibid.*, p. 87.
[33]*Ibid.*, p. 45.
[34]Bradley, *op. cit.*, p. 87.
[35]*Ibid.*, p. 266, citing *Niles Register*, October, 1836.
[36]*Ibid.*, p. 231.

ican. The merchant vessels brought in goods valued at $150,000 and whaling vessels spent $31,000 ashore for supplies. Customhouse receipts and tonnage dues for the year amounted to $50,000. Hawaiian products, taken from the islands, amounted to $91,000 in value and included such articles as sugar, kukui oil, bullock hides, goat skins, arrowroot, and mustard.[37]

Records of imports for 1844 list a wide variety of manufactured goods from the eastern United States and England; hides, tallow, otter skins, wine, and horses from California; lumber, spars, and salmon from the Northwest Coast; specie and bullion from Mexico; tea, nankeens, silk, rice, and British manufactures from China; and cigars, rope, and coffee from Manila.[38]

Such details of Hawaiian trade for characteristic years show that as early as 1820 the islands were no longer merely an emporium or place of resort for transient vessels in the China trade. From that year the process continued whereby the elements in European and American material culture were transplanted to this Pacific outpost, and its economic life was tied more and more closely to that of the United States.

FOREIGN IMPACT

Ships, cargoes, and commercial firms constituted the only means by which Anglo-Saxon institutions were carried to the islands. The process of Americanization was simultaneously one of cultural diffusion and cultural deterioration. The first signs of cultural change were evident from the arrival of American missionaries and the boom in the sandalwood trade. To carry on business with the traders, the natives had to conform to European and American standards of work. Whiskey and disease brought in by the ships, and clothes introduced by the missionaries, contributed to the sudden decline in the native population. Business exploitation, supported by an influx of Oriental laborers after 1850, turned a majority of the remaining Hawaiian natives into a wage-earning proletariat.

---

[37]Hines, *An Exploratory Expedition to Oregon* (Buffalo, 1851), p. 230.
[38]Bradley, *op. cit.*, p. 230.

Foreigners in the Islands. Foreigners began filtering into the islands immediately after the first trade contacts. According to Bradley's estimates, there were three living on the island in 1790, eleven in 1794, and twenty-three by 1800. By 1817 it was estimated that the total number of Americans and Europeans was between one and two hundred.[39] As in the case of the early foreign population in California, most of them were deserters from vessels or traders living temporarily ashore. In some cases seamen who desired to leave their vessels were discharged in Hawaii. Captain Metcalf, skipper of a Yankee vessel in the China trade, dropped two sailors ashore in 1790. As it happened, one of them adopted native life completely, rose in Hawaiian politics, and served as co-regent during the interval of the king's absences.[40] Contacts such as these contributed to the change in the temporal affairs of the islands long before the influence of New England religion was felt.[41]

The first missionaries arrived in 1820 aboard the brig *Thaddeus* of Boston.[42] The small band of Congregational ministers made but little headway at first. Their arrival was significant, however, in that it coincided with the beginning of the Pacific whaling industry and the height of the sandalwood trade.

The career of Stephen Reynolds is another example of an American engaged in the Pacific trade.[43] In 1810, as a common seaman aboard the *New Hazard* of Boston, he made the usual stop at the Hawaiian Islands. Sailing again in 1822 as an officer aboard another vessel, he was discharged during the stopover at the islands and went into business in Honolulu, married an American girl there, and became a prosperous dealer in sandalwood and diversified manufactured products. As a self-made lawyer and harbor pilot, he was a useful and well-liked figure around Honolulu until 1855.

---

[39] Bradley, *op. cit.*, p. 34.
[40] *Ibid.*
[41] Delano, *Voyages*, p. 397. In 1806 Delano found several Americans, who had previously commanded ships in the China trade, living on Oahu.
[42] Morison, *A Maritime History of Massachusetts*, p. 261.
[43] Reynolds, *The Voyage of the New Hazard*, edited by Howay, introduction, pp. vi-vii.

The Americanization of Hawaii

In 1823 the *Paragon* of Boston brought to Hawaii a group of Americans who later were to have some effect on the politics and economy of the Islands.[44] Thomas Crocker, first American consul, and his clerk, Robert Elwell, were two of the group. The second mate of the *Paragon*, John Dominis, remained in Honolulu. The name Dominis gained some political importance later when his son married a native princess who later became Queen Liliuokolani.[45] Another of the *Paragon's* company who became a permanent resident of Hawaii was Charles Brewer, who soon owned several New England vessels in the Pacific trade and later formed a partnership with Henry A. Pierce and John Hunnewell. Under the name of Brewer and Company, the organization was still active at the time of annexation in 1898.[46]

Influence of American Civilization. After 1820 missionaries and men of commerce continued to arrive in increasing numbers. Although small in total numbers, they had a significant effect. Since the interests of most of the traders were exploitive and they usually considered themselves temporary residents,[47] the welfare of the islanders was not their chief concern. Their principal contribution, as indicated previously, was the introduction of all the items considered essential for civilized life in countries of Western Europe and America.[48]

Missionary influence and its relationship to maritime trade was indicated by the remarks of the Rev. Gustavus Hines, who visited the islands in 1840: "So extensive is their intercourse with other nations, and so complicated the business to be transacted, that the king finds it indispensably necessary to put the helm of government into capable hands of enlightened foreigners."[49]

---

[44]Carpenter, *op. cit.*, p. 37.

[45]*Ibid.*

[46]*Ibid.*, Brewer became an American minister to the Hawaiian government.

[47]Bradley, *op. cit.*, p. 82, cited from the report of J. C. Jones, agent for the Boston firm of Marshall and Wildes. Between 150 and 200 foreigners were reported by him in 1826.

[48]Reynolds, *op. cit.*, p. 401. Reynolds reported that horses, introduced by Richard J. Cleveland in 1803, had multiplied and were present in great numbers.

[49]Hines, *op. cit.*, p. 226.

That this meant mainly missionaries is clear when the personnel of the king's cabinet in 1840 is considered: minister of the interior: Dr. G. P. Judd, medical missionary; privy councillor: Rev. Mr. Richards, Congregational missionary; supreme judge: Rev. Mr. Andrews, Congregational missionary; and attorney general: Robert Crichton Wyllie, merchant. Hines concluded that "everything goes according to their direction."[50]

Growing complexities, observed by Hines, resulted in the inevitable shift in power from the native king and local chieftains to a small group of powerful foreigners. Constitutional government was adopted in 1840. During its period of development from 1839 to 1842 it showed superficial resemblance to British forms, as in the titles of officials. Fundamentally, however, the structure of the written constitution, its provisions for universal suffrage and town meetings, and land tenure laws showed American influence.[51] A New England theocratic flavor is unmistakable in one provision of the constitution: "No law shall be enacted which is at variance with the word of the Lord Jehovah."[52]

The American frontier, both commercial and social, was established in Hawaii by 1839.[53] By the time the American communities along the Columbia River and in the ports of California began needing cultural items, such as printing presses, books, missionaries, and school teachers, the Americans in the Hawaiian Islands were in a position to furnish them.[54] Nor was it unusual for Americans on the coast, who could afford it, to send their children to Honolulu to be educated.[55]

From 1840, while an increasing number of foreigners in the islands became permanent residents, the total native population declined because of death and emigration. In 1842 it was esti-

---

[50] *Ibid.*, p. 225.

[51] Bradley, *op. cit.*, p. 326.

[52] Morison, *op. cit.*, p. 264.

[53] Bennett, "Early Relations of the Sandwich Islands to the Old Oregon Territory," *The Washington Historical Quarterly*, vol. 4, no. 2, p. 124.

[54] *Ibid.*, p. 125. All of the seaborne mail from the States to the West Coast came in via the islands.

[55] Underhill, *From Cowhides to Golden Fleece* (Stanford, 1946), pp. 65-67.

mated that a thousand natives were leaving the islands each year, attracted by the possibilities of travel and adventure aboard foreign ships. In 1844 between three thousand and four thousand of these natives were thought to be in Oregon working for the Hudson's Bay Company.[56] The total foreign population, however, approximately doubled every decade after 1840:[57] In 1850 there were fifteen hundred foreigners; in 1854, two thousand foreigners; in 1861, at the beginning of Chinese immigration three thousand foreigners.

More specific figures on the foreign population of Honolulu were estimated by *The Friend*, a Honolulu paper, for the year 1847.[58] Of the total number of six hundred foreigners, there were seven missionaries, five lawyers, twenty merchants, and one hundred fifty mechanics. One-half of the total number of foreigners were said to be Americans.[59] In 1855 the collector of general customs, Goodale, estimated that American investments in the islands amounted to approximately five million dollars.[60]

Statistics such as those cited are indications of the economic base upon which American control of the islands was to rest. The emergence of a wealthy and aggressive merchant class, followed by a planter aristocracy, necessitated the adoption of Anglo-Saxon law to protect private property and to uphold the rights of each party under the business contract. No longer could the complexities of modern business be subjected to the whims of the king and his local chieftains. The Rev. Richard Armstrong, writing in 1847, indicated the signs of the time: "The idea that this floating, restless, money-making go-ahead white population can be governed by natives alone is out of the question."[61] He

---

[56]Bradley, *op. cit.*, p. 227.
[57]Stevens, *American Expansion in Hawaii* (Harrisburg, 1945), p. 37.
[58]*The Friend*, January 15, 1857, cited by Stevens, *op. cit.*, p. 37.
[59]Stevens, *op. cit.*, p. 40. The peak of the whaling industry from 1845 to 1857 coincided with the trend toward numerical superiority of Americans after 1847. In the twelve years, 4,402 American vessels visited the islands as compared to 405 of all other nations. Cited from "Dispatches," VII, October 7, 1857 from Commissioner Gregg to Secretary of State Cass.
[60]*Ibid.*
[61]*Ibid.*, p. 37.

feared that the Texas game was about to be played in Hawaii.

The link between the gradual Americanization of the islands and the first statement of policy by the United States government is easy to see. As Bradley has said:

> The forces represented by American missionaries, American whalers, American merchants, and American planters had so firmly established their position in Hawaiian life that nothing short of the use of force could have deprived them of their preeminence in the islands. Nor were they without influence in Washington, for the government there could not permit the most important archipelago in the mid-Pacific to fall prey to some power whose rule might be inimical either to American investments in the islands or to a possible extension of the territory of the United States to the Pacific.[62]

UNITED STATES POLICY, 1842-1867

Though annexation was long deferred, the United States, as early as 1842, made clear both to Hawaiians and to the rest of the world its special interest in the islands and a special responsibility for their welfare. The thread of commercial and other economic interests runs through all American policy statements, crossing strands of European imperialism, Hawaiian political conditions, and domestic issues in the United States.

Whaling Deserters and Sandalwood Debts. The interest of the United States government was first aroused by conditions resulting from the whaling industry and the sandalwood trade. In 1824 a petition was sent to President Monroe, signed by over one hundred residents of New Bedford, Massachusetts, who were engaged in the Pacific whaling industry.[63] The memorial called attention to the dangerous number of deserters roaming among the Hawaiian Islands and to the possibility that a pirates' stronghold might develop there, and requested that a naval station be established in the islands to prevent mutinies of whaling crews and to keep the growing number of deserters in check.[64] This

---
[62]Bradley, *op. cit.*, p. 333.
[63]*Ibid.*, p. 105.
[64]*Ibid.*

The Americanization of Hawaii 175

petition was passed on to Secretary of the Navy Southard, who, in turn, passed it on to the commander of the Pacific squadron stationed in Callao, Peru.

Debts growing out of the sandalwood trade had been accumulating since approximately 1820. J. C. Jones was appointed "agent of the United States for commerce and seamen" in that year by President Monroe.[65] His periodic reports to the State Department showed that American merchants were owed between $40,000 and $50,000 by the king and local chiefs for unfulfilled sandalwood contracts.[66]

The debts to American merchants and the disturbance resulting from the whale fishery led, in 1826, to the first significant visit to the islands.[67] Captain T. A. C. Jones, in the U. S. S. *Peacock*, was dispatched from Callao to Honolulu with instructions to deal with the deserters from whaling vessels, and also to investigate the sandalwood claims. His mission was to be a friendly visit of inspection.

Captain Jones, after substantiating the statements of the New Bedford memorial, rounded up a large group of transients and gave them a choice of vessels to ship out on. To the Hawaiian government he suggested more stringent rules to check desertions, such as fines for whaling captains who failed to report missing men. A thorough investigation of the sandalwood debts was made, and the findings presented in the form of a claim to the king. Jones did not press the issue of payment but very tactfully suggested that it be considered by the Hawaiian government.[68] A short seven-article treaty that went far beyond the original purposes of the naval visit was actually signed. It declared peace and friendship between Hawaii and the United States. The Hawaiian king agreed to protect the ships and citizens of the United States in time of war as well as Americans ashore,

---

[65]Carpenter, *op. cit.*, p. 53.

[66]Bradley, *op. cit.*, p. 107.

[67]*Ibid.*, p. 89. Lt. Percival, in the U.S.S. *Dolphin,* had been sent to the islands in 1819 to apprehend some mutineers and apply some pressure on the chieftains for payment of the sandalwood debts. The results were doubtful.

[68]Bradley, *op. cit.*, p. 107.

who were engaged in lawful pursuits.[69] The treaty was never ratified, but it laid the groundwork for subsequent negotiations.

A real effort was made by the Hawaiian government, for a short time, to liquidate the debts. Chiefs began cutting more wood and increased taxes, but in 1828 they were still short of their contract commitments. In 1829 Captain Finch of the U. S. S. *Vincennes* paid another visit to the islands to put on more pressure for settlement. He met with the governor of Oahu (King Boki) and several of his chiefs. Notes were signed and the remaining debts acknowledged, but without permanent results. King Boki soon died and the chiefs who had been present at the meeting with Captain Finch disappeared one by one. The debts remained on the books of the American merchants long after the sandalwood had become worthless in the Canton market.[70]

The Tyler Doctrine. The first official statements of policy grew directly out of the insecure position of the Hawaiian government. In December, 1842 two Hawaiian envoys, the Rev. William Richards and Timoteo Haalilio, arrived in Washington to obtain United States recognition of Hawaiian sovereignty. In a letter to Secretary of State Webster, dated December 14, 1842, they supported their plea for formal recognition as an independent country by enumerating the gains made in the last twenty-five years under American and European influence—adoption of a written language and the Christian religion, and the establishment of property rights, schools, libraries, and a constitutional monarchy.[71] The amount of American property under the protection of the island government was listed annually for recent years, showing ninety to one hundred whalers, twelve to fifteen merchant vessels, and fourteen hundred American citizens owning approximately three to four million of dollars worth of property.[72] The strategic value of the islands and their indispensability to

---

[69]Carpenter, *op. cit.*, p. 56.

[70]Bradley, *op. cit.*, p. 107.

[71]Carpenter, *op. cit.*, p. 74; *House Executive Document*, No. 35, 27th Congress, 3rd session, p. 4.

[72]*House Executive Document*, No. 35, 27th Congress, 3rd session, p. 6.

The Americanization of Hawaii

American commerce was emphasized in detail:

> They are on the principal line of communication between the continent of America and the eastern continent of Asia; and such are the prevailing winds upon that ocean that all vessels requiring repairs or supplies, either of provisions or of water, naturally touch at those islands, whether the vessels sail from the Columbia river on the north, or from the far distant ports of Mexico, Central America, or Peru upon the south and it should be further added, that there is no other place in all that part of the Pacific ocean where repairs of vessels can be made to so good an advantage, or supplies obtained in such abundance, and on so favorable terms.[73]

Less than a week later, December 19, 1842, Secretary of State Webster wrote an answer to the Hawaiian envoys assuring them that the United States appreciated the importance of the islands; that although a formal treaty was not needed at that time, the United States wanted to see an independent Hawaii and that no other country should take aggressive steps.[74] A copy of all the correspondence was sent to all other nations. This was scant comfort to Messrs. Richards and Haalilio, who had come seeking the protection from foreign aggression that an unequivocal recognition of Hawaiian sovereignty by the United States would have afforded.

President Tyler's annual message on December 31, 1842 was partially inspired by the visit of the Hawaiian representatives. He recommended the desirability of a sovereign Hawaii and restated in clearer terms the assurance of Webster to Richards and Haalilio in the letter of December 19:

> While its nearer approach to this continent and the intercourse which the American vessels have with it—such vessels constituting five-sixths of all which annually visit it—could not but create dissatisfaction on the part of the United States at any attempt, by another power . . . to take possession of the islands. . . . The United States government seeks . . . no peculiar advantage, no exclusive control over the Hawaiian government, but is content

---
[73]*Ibid.*
[74]*Ibid.*

with its independent existence, and anxiously wishes for its security and prosperity. Its forebearance in this respect under the circumstances of the very large intercourse of their citizens with the islands, would justify this government, should events hereafter arise to require it, in making a decided remonstrance against the adoption of an opposite policy by any other government.[75]

President Tyler, in the same message, also requested an appropriation for an official consul to reside at Honolulu.[76] In March, 1843 Secretary of State Webster appointed George Brown to the post and reasserted the policy stated in the Tyler message of December 31st. Brown was to impress upon the islanders the peaceful intent of American policy and to make clear to foreigners the strong desire of the American government that the islands remain independent. He was also to watch carefully the agents of foreign governments in the islands and visit the Marquesas Islands for the same purpose.[77]

Maintaining Hawaiian Independence. The "Tyler Doctrine" was put to an early test within a few months. A British naval ship H. M. S. *Carysfort*, Captain Paulet commanding, anchored in Honolulu harbor in February, 1843. This visit was precipitated by a dispute between the British consul and the Hawaiian government about land titles. Paulet threatened Honolulu with bombardment and sent the king an ultimatum. The king had no choice but to give in. Paulet proceeded to set up a British colony on Oahu, to raise troops, and to establish a commission to rule the island. A protest was made to President Tyler, who in turn sent a formal commission to England to protest against the act of Paulet. An English vessel was quickly sent to the islands to repudiate Paulet and undo what he had done. In July of 1843 the Union Jack was hauled down and King Kamehameha III was restored to the throne.[78]

---

[75]*Ibid.*, p. 2. Much of this was written by Webster.
[76]*Ibid.*
[77]Webster, *Writings and Speeches* (Boston, 1903), vol. 12, pp. 434-435.
[78]Alden, *Lawrence Kearny, Sailor Diplomat* (Princeton, 1930), pp. 187-198; Carpenter, *op. cit.*, pp. 74-79; Bradley, *op. cit.*, pp. 451-456; *Senate Documents*, No. 139, 29th Congress, 1st session, pp. 39-47. The Paulet incident is treated in detail in all of these works.

In 1851 French aggression of a similar kind, involving a dispute over court procedure and jury personnel, put the "Tyler Doctrine" to another test.[79] Webster, again secretary of state, in his instructions to the American consul, William C. Rives,[80] reiterated Tyler's doctrine of special interest by pointing out that "the Hawaiian Islands are ten times nearer the United States than to any powers of Europe. Five-sixths of all their commercial intercourse is with the United States, and these considerations, together with others of a more general nature, have fixed the course which the government of the United States will pursue in regard to them." Rives was instructed specifically not to interfere by force but not to accept the French seizure of Oahu. The American desire for the independence of the islands was to be the main guide of his policy.[81]

Webster wrote in much stronger terms to the French consul in Hawaii, the French minister in Washington, and the American minister in Paris. France was bluntly accused of aggression. The commercial predominance of the United States in the islands was emphasized and a thinly veiled threat of force was stated in these words: "The Navy Department will receive instructions to keep the naval armament of the United States in the Pacific Ocean in such a state of strength and preparation as shall be requisite for the preservation of the honor and dignity of the United States and the safety of the government of the Hawaiian Islands."[82] The French, surprised by the attitude of Webster, disclaimed any aggressive intent in the incident and withdrew from the island.

Hawaiian policy, as stated in the Tyler doctrine of special interest, had been strengthened by two tests. By 1850 the spread of American people to the West Coast and the annexation of Oregon and California made the islands even more vital to the American nation. Growing interest in the Caribbean and the

---

[79]Carpenter, *op. cit.*, p. 87. Two French war vessels made up the force.
[80]Webster, *op. cit.*, vol. 14, p. 437.
[81]Bemis, ed., *American Secretaries of State and Their Diplomacy,* vol. 6, p. 109.
[82]Webster, *op. cit.*, vol. 14, p. 437.

treaties for canal rights across New Granada and Nicaragua became part of the Pacific advance during the boom years of whaling and gold mining in California. The progress of steam navigation was also expanding American commerce.

The annual message of President Fillmore in December, 1851 recognized the increased importance of Hawaii to American security and commerce, and reasserted the original policy of 1842:

> Long before the events which have of late imported so much importance to the possessions of the United States on the Pacific we acknowledged the independence of the Hawaiian government. This government was first in taking the step, and several leading powers of Europe immediately followed. We were influenced in this measure by the existing and prospective importance of the islands as a place of refuge and refreshment for our vessels engaged in the whale fishery, and by the consideration that they lie in the course of the great trade which must, at no distant day, be carried on between the western coast of North America and Eastern Asia. We were also influenced by a desire that those islands should not pass under the control of any other great maritime state, but should remain in an independent condition, and so be accessible and useful to the commerce of all nations. I need not say that the importance of these considerations has been greatly enhanced by the sudden and vast development which the interests of the United States have attained in California and Oregon, and the policy heretofore adopted in regard to those islands will be steadily pursued.[83]

Pierce's Interest in Annexation. Annexation of Hawaii was talked of in official circles before the Civil War. The settlement of the Oregon dispute and the annexation of California tied the islands closer to the mainland. Growing jealousy of England and France in relation to the islands reinforced a desire in Washington to annex Hawaii to forestall any possible aggression.[84] In 1853 Secretary of State Marcy, in instructing John Mason, minister in Paris, to feel out the possible attitude of France on the

---

[83]*Congressional Globe,* vol. 21, 32nd Congress, 1st session, appendix, pp. 2-3.

[84]Carpenter, *op. cit.,* p. 108.

The Americanization of Hawaii

subject of American annexation, showed the official feeling at the time: "It seems inevitable that they must come under the control of this government and it would be but reasonable and fair that these powers [England and France] should acquiesce in such a disposition of them, provided transfer was effected by fair means."[85]

President Pierce, in his inaugural address in March, 1853, made a general statement of policy in respect to annexation of overseas areas: "Our attitude as a nation and our position on the globe render the acquisition of certain possessions not within our jurisdiction eminently important for our protection if not in the future essential for the preservation of the rights of commerce and the peace of the world."[86] This statement reflected the general emotion of manifest destiny that was sweeping the country at the time, but it also had a direct bearing on the Hawaiian Islands.

In February of the following year, David L. Gregg, commissioner in the Hawaiian Islands, sent a dispatch to Secretary of State Marcy describing the weakened condition of the Hawaiian government. Annexation was probable, he thought, due to the conviction of the king that foreign threats made the continued independent status of the islands impractical.[87] Secretary Marcy's reply to Gregg in April 1854 empowered him to proceed with negotiations that would establish a protectorate but in no way would affect the sovereignty of the islands.[88] This was, in effect, a plan of annexation in answer to the proposal of the king for conditional annexation in the event of sudden foreign aggression.

Britain and France naturally objected strongly. The fleets of both nations left Callao for Honolulu to discourage the king from any move toward American annexation. American negotiations for annexation nevertheless went on in desultory fashion until late in 1854. Two obstacles were then encountered that held up

---
[85]*Ibid.*
[86]Bemis, *op. cit.*, vol. 6, p. 147.
[87]Carpenter, *op. cit.*, p. 113.
[88]Bartlett, ed., *The Record of American Diplomacy*, pp. 357-358.

proceedings. First, the king demanded larger annuities for himself and his chiefs, in the event of being deposed by annexation, than Commissioner Gregg saw fit to pay; and second, the king insisted upon writing a stipulation in the treaty providing for full statehood for the islands if annexed to the United States. This provision, which was actually written, threw the annexation negotiations squarely into the heart of the slavery controversy then raging in the United States. At this point Secretary of State Marcy notified Gregg that any treaty admitting Hawaii as a state would probably fail to receive Congressional approval.

The Hawaiian king, Kamehameha III, died in December, 1854 and his son, with an English-trained wife, proved more reluctant to relinquish sovereignty to the United States.[89] At the same time the threats of foreign invasion were fading into the background. Negotiations were broken off due to this combination of circumstances. A decade passed before the subject was reopened.

President Johnson's Policy. The Civil War was partly responsible for driving Hawaiian policy temporarily into the background. Whaling, already on the decline, was partially destroyed during the war. Gradually, as the sugar industry replaced general trade and whaling as the chief economic base of Hawaii, reciprocity negotiations were opened. One attempt was made in 1855, and another during the Civil War, in 1864. Both ended in failure.

American attempts to establish trade reciprocity again raised the question of annexation. Edward McCook, minister to Hawaii in 1867 under President Johnson and Secretary of State William E. Seward, after an unsuccessful meeting with Hawaiian representatives in San Francisco, wrote Seward that:

> I feel that I have accomplished all I can accomplish in my present position, and shall probably wish to return to my home in Colorado, unless you favor the absolute acquisition of the Hawaiian Islands in which event I would like to conduct the negotiations. I think their sovereignty could be purchased from the present

---

[89]Hooley, "Hawaiian Negotiations for Reciprocity," *Pacific Historical Review*, vol. 7 (March, 1938), p. 140.

The Americanization of Hawaii

king (Kamehameha V) and I feel sure that the people of the United States would receive such a purchase with universal acclaim.

Seward's answer to McCook stated official State Department policy clearly:

... It is proper that you should know for your own information that a lawful and peaceful annexation of the islands to the United States, with the consent of the people of the Sandwich Islands, is deemed by this government, and that, if the policy of annexation should really conflict with the policy of reciprocity, annexation is in every case to be preferred.[90]

In the annual message of December, 1867, President Johnson recommended reciprocity as an intermediate step toward annexation:

The attention of the Senate of Congress is again respectfully invited to the treaty for the establishment of commercial reciprocity with the Hawaiian kingdom entered into last year and already ratified by that government. The attitude of the United States toward these islands is not very different from that in which they stand toward the West Indies. It is known and felt by the Hawaiian government and people that their government and institutions are feeble and precarious, that the United States, being so near a neighbor, would be unwilling to see the islands pass under foreign control. The prosperity is continually disturbed by expectations and alarms of unfriendly political proceedings as well as from the United States as from other foreign powers. A reciprocity treaty, while it could not materially diminish the revenues of the United States, would be a guarantee of the good will and forebearance of all nations until the people of the islands shall of themselves, at no distant day, voluntarily apply for admission to the Union.[91]

The Tyler doctrine, recognizing American interests in Hawaiian trade and reflecting fear of foreign occupation of the islands, did not lead directly and smoothly to annexation of the

---

[90]Carpenter, *op. cit.*, pp. 43-44.
[91]*Ibid.*, pp. 44-45.

islands. There was no broad public support for such a move even in 1860.[92] But the statement of American special interest was the first step toward anexation. It reflected the dominant interest of the United States and pledged support of the security and independence of the islands, though without treaty commitments.[93] It was important in that it drew Hawaii within the American orbit and became the basic doctrine that governed American relations with Hawaii until its final annexation.[94]

---

[92]Stevens, *op. cit.*, p. 43. Exceptions were opinions reflected in West Coast papers such as *Oregon Statesman,* November 3, 1852, *DeBow's Review,* January, 1855, and *Hunt's Merchants Magazine,* 1853-1854.

[93]Malloy, *Treaties, Conventions, International Acts, Protocols, and Agreements, 1776-1909* (Washington, 1910), vol. 1, pp. 909-915. Even in the first treaty of commerce and amity between the United States and the Hawaiian government, signed in December, 1849, no recognition of Hawaiian sovereignty or commitments of protection are found.

[94]Stevens, *op. cit.*, p. 5.

Chapter VI

Expansion to Japan

It has been said that Japan, as it emerged from the nineteenth century, was a "child of American diplomacy."[1] This is one clue in the search for antecedents of modern Japanese-American relations; but, to go even farther back, the background of this diplomacy is found to originate in maritime contacts during the period of Pacific expansion before the American Civil War.

The ten years from 1843 to 1853 were a busy decade in American Pacific development. It saw the tightening of political and commercial ties with China, the extension of United States paramount interest in Hawaii, and the annexation of Oregon and California. According to Foster Rhea Dulles, during this period "it was then only natural that final acquisition of Oregon and California should even further emphasize our interest in Asia."[2]

EARLY SEA CONTACTS

The opening of Japan, at this point, became a part of the extension of American interest in the Pacific Ocean—a part of the same maritime and overland advance that occupied the Pacific coast—the historic urge toward the East that historians relate to the westward march of European civilization. Manifest destiny, expressed by the "national mission" concept, was a part of the drive toward the East.[3] The new era in the Pacific after Wanghai, which opened the ports of northern China, involved the waters of the North Pacific in which the Japanese Islands lay.[4]

---

[1]Bailey, *Diplomatic History of the American People* (New York, 1947), p. 336.
[2]Dulles, *China and America*, p. 34.
[3]Cole, *Dynamics of American Expansion Toward Japan* (Chicago, 1943), p. 2.
[4]*Ibid.*, p. 8.

The famous *Lady Washington* and a small vessel, the *Grace*, called at a southern port in Japan as early as 1791, but their efforts at trade were repulsed and no permanent ties resulted. It was through the contacts of foreign rivals that American vessels began calling, to any extent, at Japanese ports. For centuries the Dutch had held the only trade concession in Japan. It was through employment by the Dutch East India Company in Batavia, Java, that a few Americans saw the islands in the early years.[5] In 1799 the American vessel *Franklin* was engaged by the Dutch to freight a cargo to Nagasaki. The Salem vessel *Margaret*, Samuel Derby, captain, was chartered in 1801 for the Batavia-Nagasaki trade. She made additional voyages for the Dutch between Batavia and Nagasaki in 1803, 1806, 1807, and 1809. Another Boston ship, the *Eclipse*, under charter of the Russian-American Company, called at Nagasaki in 1807 en route from the Northwest Coast of America to Kamchatka. American interest in Japan was not aroused to any appreciable extent by these contacts.

Porter's Pacific Cruise. British whaling activities during the War of 1812 resulted indirectly in the first official American notice of the importance of Japan in the Pacific trade. Captain David Porter, in command of the U. S. S. *Essex*, was detached from the South Atlantic squadron in the fall of 1812 and given orders to proceed around Cape Horn. He was to operate against British unarmed vessels and armed whalers bearing letters of marque. In the *Essex* he ranged far and wide up the Spanish main studying the extent of English whaling in that sea. In operating between the South American coast, Galapagos Islands, and Marquesas Islands, the *Essex* captured six British whaling vessels.[6] Some he rearmed and renamed to augment his squadron; others were sent to the neutral port of Valparaiso; still others he burned at sea.

The main purpose of his voyage is shown by his own words: "If only I could succeed in driving the British from the ocean, leaving it free for our own vessels, I conceive that I shall have

---

[5]Dennett, *Americans in Eastern Asia* (New York, 1941), p. 243.
[6]Dulles, *Lowered Boats* (New York, 1933), p. 50.

Expansion to Japan

rendered an essential service to my country."[7] To facilitate his aim, he searched among the islands of the Marquesas group for an operating base. An island, originally called Nukahina, suited his purposes so well that he enlarged the scope of his original orders and annexed it in the name of the United States, naming it Madison Island. A fort was built and formal possession was proclaimed in November, 1813. Porter's proclamation to the natives reflects the dual purpose of future trade protection and strategic use in pursuing the war: "They have given assurances that such of their brethren [Americans] as may hereafter visit them from the United States, shall enjoy a welcome and hospitable reception among them, and be furnished with whatever refreshments and supplies the island may afford . . . and prevent the subjects of Great Britain from coming among them until peace shall take place between the two nations.[8]

Porter's act was never acknowledged in Congress but it is illustrative of the effect of whaling on Pacific geopolitics. The rest of Porter's operations in the Pacific need not be described here. The significant result was his interest in the possibilities of the whale fishery for American vessels. When he got back to the United States in 1815, he wrote a letter to President Madison suggesting that a world exploring expedition be fitted out to explore and survey all legendary islands and lands. The type of expedition he suggested was similar to the one commanded by Lt. Wilkes some years later. His ideas embraced the whole Pacific and expressed the need for opening the unknown kingdom of Japan "to beat down their rooted prejudices, secure to ourselves a valuable trade and make that people known to the world."[9]

Porters' suggestion had no immediate results. Before official interest was aroused sufficiently to conceive of an exploring expedition or a scheme to open Japan to world trade, much more maritime activity of a broader geographic scope was necessary

---

[7] Porter, *Journal of a Cruise Made to the Pacific, 1812-1814* (New York, 1822), vol. 1, p. 118.

[8] *Ibid.*, vol. 2, p. 79.

[9] Cole, ed., "Documents," *Pacific Historical Review*, vol. 9, pp. 61-65.

than was provided by the Northwest fur trade or the China trade. The whale fishery provided, in large part, the incentive to official action.

American Whalers in the Pacific. The activity of the whale ships in relation to the ebb and flow of the economic life of Hawaii has already been mentioned. In 1791, the same year the first American vessel touched a Japanese port, the *Beaver* of Nantucket, rounded the Horn and cruised the whaling grounds off the southern coast of South America.[10] Six other vessels followed in the same year.

Whaling was virtually destroyed by the sea warfare between 1812 and 1814. It gradually recovered with the discovery of the "off shore" whaling grounds north of the equator to the 12th latitude and between longitude 90 degrees west and 120 degrees west.[11] Nantucket led the recovery by sending out twenty-three vessels in 1815, sixty-one in 1819, and eighty-four in 1821.[12] At least twenty seaports in southern New England sent out whaling vessels, but Nantucket and New Bedford led, followed by Fairhaven, New London, Sag Harbor, and Westport.

Hawaii was first contacted by a Nantucket whaler, the *Equator,* in 1820. The whaling grounds off the coast of Japan were discovered in the same year by another Nantucket vessel, the *Maro,* Captain Allan in command.[13] Thirty ships followed in the next year. In the next few years following the discovery of the Japanese whaling grounds, American whaling ships began cruising to nearly every conceivable spot in the Pacific and Indian Oceans.[14] The first whale was caught off the Northwest Coast of

---

[10]Dulles, *Lowered Boats,* p. 46.

[11]Tower, *A History of American Whale Fishery* (Philadelphia, 1907), p. 48; Hohmann, *The American Whaleman* (New York, 1928), appendix, p. 310. The American consul in Paita, Fayette M. Ringgold, wrote to Assistant Secretary of State John Appleton in September, 1858, describing the status of whaling in that year. His opinion was that American whaling in the Pacific was due to the action of Captain Porter in destroying the British industry during the War of 1812.

[12]Tower, *op. cit.,* p. 49.
[13]Dulles, *Lowered Boats,* p. 55.
[14]*Ibid.,* p. 56.

Expansion to Japan 189

America in 1835. By 1845 whalers were working off the Kamchatka peninsula. Soon they were venturing through the Bering Straits to more northerly latitudes than either Cook or Vancouver had reached.

Geographic Scope and Extent. The scope of the whaling industry is indicated by an enumeration of the principal whaling grounds, routes traveled, and lands sighted.[15] Many of these areas were later explored by American naval expeditions. There were six major whaling grounds in the Pacific: (1) Onshore grounds—along the coast of Peru and Chile; (2) Offshore grounds—latitude 5 degrees, 10 degrees north; latitude 90 degrees, 120 degrees west; (3) Middle grounds—between New Zealand and New Holland; (4) Japan grounds—the Japanese and Bonin Islands (5) Northwest coast of America; and (6) Indian Ocean. In addition, four miscellaneous traverses east and west in the Pacific should be mentioned: (a) along the equator from South America to the Kingsmill Islands, (b) in the South Pacific, an area between latitude 21 degrees and 27 degrees south; (c) between latitude 27 degrees and 35 degrees north; and (d) the vicinity of the Hawaiian Islands, Society Islands, Fiji Islands, Samoan Islands, and New Zealand.

The Cape Horn route was most often used, in which case the vessels sailed from the onshore to the offshore grounds to the Society Islands, Hawaii, and often to the whale grounds off the cosat of Oregon. When the northern grounds became popular, Hawaii was in the center of the route between the Arctic Sea and the equatorial grounds to the south. Vessels rounding the Cape of Good Hope usually passed south of New Holland and up through the South Seas to Hawaii on their way to the Japanese or Arctic whaling grounds.

Lands sighted and often contacted were Zanzibar, the Red Sea, New Zealand, Tasmania, Java, the Moluccas, the Solomon Islands, Lombok, Bali, Kergulen Island, the Bonin Islands, Samoa, the Philippines, the Friendly Islands, the Admiralty Islands, and the Fiji Islands. On the eastern side of the Pacific the Galapagos Islands were a rendezvous point. Farther west, Tahiti,

---

[15]Hohmann, *op. cit.*, pp. 149-152; Dulles, *Lowered Boats*, p. 56.

the Society Islands, the Tonga Islands, and the Marquesas lay in the track of the whaling vessels.

Whaling was an extensive business, not only geographically, but in terms of ships and national income. A steady growth is recorded after 1818. In 1835, 434 vessels were engaged.[16] Of the 94,075 tons involved, 56,352 tons came from New Bedford and 26,472 tons from Nantucket.[17] For an average year between 1835 and 1860 it is recorded that approximately 620 ships were engaged, representing a total investment of eight million dollars.[18] In 1847, five-sixths of the 600 vessels engaged in whaling were operating in the Pacific.[19] The rest were in the Atlantic, Davis Strait, or the Indian Ocean. In 1858 approximately 661 vessels were active.[20] One indication of the extent of operations in the northern waters in the vicinity of Japan is the number of vessels calling at Hawaii in any particular year. Of the 661 active in 1858, approximately 400 were recorded in the islands.[21]

SYSTEMATIC EXPLORATION

Most of the ships using Hawaii as a base were occupied in both the northern and southern whaling grounds. The fact that two-thirds of all the whale vessels were active in these areas aroused official interest and resulted in the systematic gathering of information about the Pacific area and in exploration to extend such information.

Reynolds's Report. By 1828 Pacific whaling had developed sufficiently to attract official attention, J. N. Reynolds, a civilian employee of the navy who later served as Commodore Downes's secretary on the *Potomac*, was ordered by the secretary of the navy, Samuel Southard, to compile all available information

---

[16]Pitkin, *A Statistical View of Commerce*, 1835, p. 42.
[17]*Ibid.*
[18]Tower, *op. cit.*, p. 51.
[19]*Ibid.*
[20]Hohmann, *op. cit.*, p. 313, cited from Table A of a letter from the consul at Paita, Ringgold, to the assistant secretary of state in September, 1858.
[21]Stevens, *American Expansion in Hawaii* (Harrisburg, 1945), p. 31, citing the *Pacific Coast Commercial Advertiser,* January 20, 1859.

Expansion to Japan 191

about the Pacific whaling industry. Accordingly, Reynolds went to New England, visited the principal whaling centers,[22] and interviewed as many whaling skippers and navigators as were found at home with their log books and sea journals. Information of a hydrographical and logistical nature was compiled from bits of conversation and excerpts from the records of these navigators.[23] Reynolds discovered that the voyages were getting longer and were being extended into the less-known seas of the high latitudes, both north and south. He brought back records of discoveries made by whaling captains such as the one of Captain Coffin in the Bonin Islands.[24] One whaling captain, Edmund Gardner of New Bedford, suggested that an exploring trip be sent out to follow the track of whalers northwest from the Hawaiian Islands, north from Ladrone Islands to Japan, and the chain of islands south of Japan.[25]

So impressive was the amount and nature of the information collected, Reynolds remarked in his report, that "the Navy Department is in possession of more information of those seas than the admiralty of any other nation, however commercial, for those seas are truly our field of fame. Too much credit cannot be given our whalers, sealers, and traffickers in those seas for the information they have acquired, and the liberalty, generally speaking, with which they have imparted it."[26] The report was submitted to the secretary of the navy in September, 1828. It made no recommendations or suggestions concerning future policy. It was an objective report containing only factual information.

Fanning's Agitation for an Expedition. Edmund Fanning, a Stonington whaling captain who knew the South Seas before the War of 1812, persuaded President Madison to authorize a small expedition to explore the South Sea Islands. The expedition was on the verge of sailing when the outbreak of war put an end to it. Fanning called himself the originator of the idea of

---

[22]*Executive Documents*, No. 135, 23rd Congress, 2nd session, p. 1.
[23]*Ibid.*, p. 2.
[24]*Ibid.*, p. 18. Coffin discovered a cluster of islands in the Bonin group.
[25]*Ibid.*, p. 17.
[26]*Executive Documents*, No. 135, 23rd Congress, 2nd session, p. 28.

Pacific exploration—and probably with good reason. Between 1831 and 1837 Fanning petitioned Congress and wrote letters to Secretary of State Woodbury and Presidents Jackson and Van Buren,[27] urging an expedition very similar to the one carried out later under Lt. Wilkes. Fanning was ignored during the preparation for the expedition and his advice, so freely given, was never acknowledged.[28]

Wilkes's Expedition. It is difficult to establish the fact that the Wilkes expedition grew directly out of the recommendation of David Porter, the report of J. N. Reynolds, and the agitation of Edmund Fanning. The sequence of events is of some significance, however. The Reynolds report of whaling was referred to the Senate Committee on Commerce in January, 1838. In August, 1838, Secretary of the Navy J. K. Paulding issued instructions for the Wilkes expedition.[29] A squadron of six vessels was to depart from Norfolk, round Cape Horn, and sail to the Navigator, Society, and Fiji Islands for exploration. The expedition was to examine the Antarctic continent, if possible, touch the Hawaiian group, and proceed to the Northwest Coast of America for extensive surveys of the coast and river valleys.[30] The coast he was to "examine in particular, with the view to the selection of a safe harbour, easy of access, and in every respect adapted to the reception of vessels of the United States in the whale fishery, and the general commerce of the seas; it being the intention of the government to keep one of the squadron of the Pacific cruising near these islands in the future."[31]

The ships were equipped with both natural scientists and experts in navigation and surveying. A shorter route to Canton by way of the Sulu Sea was to be explored. Information and sailing directions were to be compiled for later use by whalers and

---

[27]Fanning, *Voyages* (New York, 1938), p. 103.

[28]*Ibid.* In his letters to Jackson and Van Buren, a feeling of injured pride and martyrdom is noticeable, as well as a tendency to go to extremes for the sake of supporting his arguments.

[29]*Senate Documents*, No. 105, 23rd Congress, 2nd session, p. 1.

[30]Bancroft, *Works*, vol. 31, p. 668.

[31]Wilkes, *Narratives* (Philadelphia, 1849), vol. 1, introduction, p. xxvi.

merchants engaged in the China trade.[32] The Northwest Coast of America was to be surveyed with special reference to the bay of San Francisco.[33]

In the four years that the expedition was in the Pacific the ships of the squadron operated in different areas in accomplishing the overall aims of the voyage. While part of the squadron was exploring the fringe of the Antarctic continent, another part was sailing among the Kingsmill and Ellice Island groups. A vast amount of information about the Pacific was brought back to the country and added to the haphazard and spotty knowledge already acquired by the whalemen. It contributed to a growing knowledge of the Pacific Ocean at a time when the Pacific coast and the Hawaiian Islands were being drawn closer within the sphere of American commercial activity.[34]

BACKGROUNDS OF THE PERRY MISSION

The growth of Pacific commerce after the signing of the Treaty of Wanghai in 1844 extended American interest in the Northern Pacific. With the opening of northern Chinese ports, vessels increasingly passed through the island chain south of Japan. At the same time, as whaling along the equator and in the South Seas declined, more and more whalers cruised the waters around the Kamchatka peninsula, the Japanese main islands, and the Bering Straits. Direct contacts with Japanese ports resulted.

As early as 1837 an Olyphant and Company vessel, the *Morison*, had been sent from Canton into Yedo Bay to look over the prospects of trade and missionary work. She was fired upon and departed in failure.[35] In 1845 the whaler *Manhattan*, of Sag

---

[32]*Ibid.*

[33]*Ibid.*

[34]*Ibid.*, vol. 5. Whole chapters of Wilkes's narrative were devoted to different aspects of commerce. The last chapter of volume 5 describes whaling in great detail, and gives sailing directions for the best cruising grounds. The scientists wrote up their findings concerning the plant and animal life on lands explored, in separate volumes.

[35]Dennett, *op. cit.*, p. 246.

Harbor, sailed into Yedo Bay to return some shipwrecked Japanese fishermen. The American vessel was received hospitably but was watched carefully. No contacts were allowed with the natives. After an ultimatum, the *Manhattan* was forceably towed to sea by small boats and cast adrift.[36] A year later, the *Lawrence*, another whaler of Poughkeepsie, New York, went ashore in a gale on one of the main islands of Japan. Seven survivors were captured and imprisoned as spies. Eventually they were freed through the efforts of Dutch traders who held a concession on Deshima, in Yedo Bay.[37] A group of deserters from the whale vessel *Ladoga* received similar treatment when captured in 1848. Word of their captivity leaked out through Deshima.[38] News of the mistreatment of American seamen gradually reached Canton and the United States, where responsible officials began planning counter measures.

Official interest in a treaty with Japan was first expressed in the instructions to Edmund Roberts,[39] sent in 1832 to Muscat and Cochin-China to negotiate a treaty of commerce. Part of his instructions authorized him to go on to Japan and effect a similar treaty. Nothing came of it, but in his letters back to Secretary of State McLane in 1834 he recommended sending an unarmed merchant ship to Japan for the purpose. In his opinion the Japanese were willing but the Dutch were apprehensive.[40]

Some interest was aroused by Roberts. On his second visit to Muscat and Cohin-China he had definite instructions to go to Japan. His sudden death in Macao in 1836 caused the matter to drop.[41] Another attempt to open Japan to trade was made through the Caleb Cushing mission to China in 1844. Orders giving him full powers to negotiate a treaty arrived from Washington after Cushing had departed for home.[42]

---

[36]Dulles, *Lowered Boats,* p. 246.
[37]*Ibid.,* p. 249.
[38]*Ibid.;* Griffin, *Clippers and Consuls,* p. 304.
[39]Nitobe, *The Intercourse Between the United States and Japan* (Baltimore, 1891), p. 31.
[40]Dennett, *op. cit.,* pp. 244-245.
[41]*Ibid.,* p. 246.
[42]*Ibid.,* p. 249.

Expansion to Japan

These two desultory attempts to encourage Japanese trade show that interest in this area in these years was still secondary to that in the China trade. After the publication of the documents of Cushing, however, talk of a similar treaty with Japan was not allowed to drop from official circles. Representative Pratt of New York submitted a bill in February, 1845, proposing a mission to Japan and Korea to open trade and protect American commerce in those seas.[43]

Pressure from Merchants. The growing pressure for commercial protection in and around Japan is seen in the next year, 1846. A group of New Yorkers made up of bankers, merchants, marine-insurance men, shipbuilders, mechanics, and steam engine manufacturers submitted a memorial to the Senate through Senator Dix of New York citing their grievances resulting from the lack of a commercial treaty with Japan.[44] Senator Dix presented the memorial to the Senate and it was referred to the Foreign Affairs Committee, June 1, 1846. No action was taken.

At this point in the development of a Japanese policy the work of Aaron H. Palmer exerted considerable influence. He was a prominent New Yorker and director of the American and Foreign Agency—a commission agency for foreign trade in machinery for steam vessels.[45] Between 1842 and 1847 Palmer made extensive studies of the markets of Asia, compiled vast amounts of information, and distributed pamphlets in both America and Asia. Between 1846 and 1849 he prepared numerous reports for the State Department. They contained information of a technical nature needed in planning an expedition to Japan.[46]

Secretary of State Buchanan submitted a report in February, 1847 on the state of trade with nontreaty countries.[47] Most of the information concerning Japan had been written by Palmer.

---

[43] *Executive Documents*, No. 138, 28th Congress, 2nd session, p. 2.
[44] *Executive Documents*, No. 96, 29th Congress, 2nd session, p. 33.
[45] Dennett, *op. cit.*, p. 352.
[46] Bemis, ed. *American Secretaries of State and Their Diplomacy*, vol. 6, p. 15. In 1849 Secretary Clayton approved of Palmer's plan for an expedition. Though not in use then it later became part of Perry's operation plan.
[47] *Executive Documents*, No. 96, 29th Congress, 2nd session, pp. 1-39.

In it was sketched the early American contacts and the relations of California and Oregon to the Oriental trade.[48] Background material was also included covering the geographic structure of Japan as well as language, religion, and local customs.[49] It was a rather full treatise on the potentiality of Japan as a market. About two years later President Polk received a memorial from Palmer of a similar nature.[50] He advocated a general Pacific advance in the vicinity of Japan. Further elaborating his ideas, as in Buchanan's report in 1847, he pointed out that Siberia, Manchuria, and the Aleutians were joined interdependently by commerce with the new states on the Pacific. They were soon to be joined, he thought, with the Atlantic ports by a canal across the isthmus.[51] Sakalin Island was described as being important to American whaling vessels. The abundance of whales in the seas around the Japanese islands was described and the need was indicated for some working arrangements with local authorities to provide provisions for vessels.[52] The description of the wreck of the *Lawrence* and the mistreatment of the crew was cited to support his arguments.

Grievances of Whalemen. In 1849 Commodore David Geisinger, stationed at Whampoa, sent a report to the Secretary of Navy William Graham about specific grievances of American seamen in Japan. Geisinger had ordered Commander Glynn, in the U.S.S. *Preble,* to go to Japan in 1847 to demand the release of the captives from the whaler *Ladoga.* His report was presented to the House of Representatives August 28, 1850.[53] It was a damning bit of evidence against the Japanese. Reproductions of the interviews between Glynn and the Japanese were given word for word. It demonstrated to Congress the extreme caution and suspicion with which the Japanese dealt with foreigners. It was shown in the report that Commander Glynn was forced to

---

[48]*Ibid.,* 36-37.
[49]*Ibid.,* p. 17.
[50]*Senate Miscellaneous Documents,* No. 80, 30th Congress (March 8, 1848), pp. 1-77.
[51]*Ibid.,* pp. 1-43.
[52]*Ibid.,* p. 43.
[53]*Executive Documents,* No. 84, 31st Congress, 1st session, pp. 1-44.

take an adamant and threatening stand to force the surrender of the seamen.[54] Excerpts of the narratives of two of the captives were included as part of the report.[55] This furnished concrete evidence of Japanese cruelty. It was an emotional appeal for establishing civilized relations with Japan.

Commander Glynn returned to New York in the spring of 1851 and immediately went to Washington where he "doubtless laid before the government the details of his cruise."[56] At any rate he wrote a letter tto President Fillmore, dated June 10, 1851, in which he stressed the importance of the Japanese islands along the China trade route.[57] He urged that a letter be written to the Japanese Emperor asking for protection of American seamen and American commerce.[58] Glynn was convinced that the time was propitious to take a firm and dignified stand at the risk of using force to advance American interest in Japanese waters.

Plans and Instructions. Immediate action resulted. On the same day, June 10, 1851, that President Fillmore received Commander Glynn's report, Secretary of State Webster wrote instructions to Commodore John H. Aulick ordering him to proceed to Japan and negotiate a treaty of amity and commerce.[59] The grievances growing out of the whaling industry were not mentioned directly in Webster's letter. The need for supply bases for steamships was emphasized more strongly: ". . . it is the President's opinion that steps should be taken at once to enable our enterprising merchants to supply the last link in that great chain which united all nations of the world. In order to facilitate this enterprise, it is desirable that we should obtain, from the Emperor of Japan, permission to purchase from his subjects the necessary supplies of coal, which our steamers on their outward

---

[54]*Ibid.*, pp. 28-44.
[55]*Ibid.*, pp. 8-17.
[56]Paullin, *Diplomatic Negotiations of American Naval Officers*, p. 246.
[57]*Senate Documents*, No. 59, 32nd Congress, 1st session, pp. 57-62. Glynn had written to Howland and Aspinwall, steamship owners of New York, about the same topic in February, 1851.
[58]*Ibid.*, pp. 74-78.
[59]*Senate Documents*, No. 59, 32nd Congress, 1st session, pp. 80-81.

and inward voyages may require."⁶⁰ Shortly after receiving the instructions from Webster, Commodore Aulick became too ill to carry them out. The proposed trip was delayed for a few weeks. When it became apparent that no suitable naval officer was available, it was cancelled.

The idea of a naval mission to Japan was not abandoned by any means. Officials had become convinced of its desirability. Past experience with the Japanese had likewise convinced them that the expedition, in contrast to the Cushing mission, should be reinforced by a powerful fleet.⁶¹

Development of Perry's Mission. Nothing was done for nearly a year after Aulick's voyage failed to materialize, but early in 1852 pressure increased. In April the Senate asked President Fillmore for a compilation of all information concerning American relations with Japan.⁶² In July Senator Gwinn moved that a bill be passed authorizing "an exploration and reconnaissance of the courses of navigation used by whaling vessels in the regions of Bering Straits, and also of such parts of the China Seas, Straits of Gaspar, and Java Sea, as lie directly in the route of vessels to and from China."⁶³

This motion suggested an expedition of much broader scope than was planned the year before under Commodore Aulick. Following Senator Gwinn's motion, William H. Seward rose and made extended remarks in support of Gwinn's proposal. He painted an eloquent word picture of the history of whaling from Phoenician times down to 1852. He described the perils of the unknown Pacific whale grounds and paid tribute to the achievements of American seamen there. His whole speech was a ringing call for commercial expansion and imperialism. He saw the

---

⁶⁰*Ibid.*, p. 80.

⁶¹Paullin, *op. cit.*, p. 246. A. H. Palmer had written to President Fillmore in 1851 recommending a mission to Japan and suggesting that it be made up of an imposing array of naval might.

⁶²*Senate Documents*, No. 59, 32nd Congress, 1st session, pp. 1-59. All of the reports, correspondence, and instructions, from Edmund Roberts' proposed trip to Japan to Commander Glynn's visit, was provided by this document.

⁶³*Congressional Globe*, appendix, 32nd Congress, 1st session, p. 1973.

Expansion to Japan 199

extent of the whaling industry and the need for closer ties with Japan as a part of the westward orientation of America. His concluding remarks held the famous oratorical question that revealed his belief in manifest destiny: "Who does not see that ... the Pacific, its shores, its islands and vast regions beyond will become the chief theater of events in the world's great hereafter?"[64]

The final steps of authorization, with opinion in Congress strongly formed in favoring a mission to the Pacific, were taken in November, 1852. Secretary of the Navy John P. Kennedy wrote a letter to Commodore Matthew C. Perry outlining the broad purposes of the expedition.[65] Commodore Aulick's general instructions of 1851 were to apply to the present mission. More specifically, Perry was instructed to negotiate a treaty with Japan to provide protection for shipwrecked sailors, supply points and coal depots for vessels, and limited trade or barter in Japanese ports.[66] As a secondary objective the Japanese were to be impressed with the fact that the United States was the only mighty power bordering the Pacific and that there was a distinct difference between Europeans and Americans. The use of force was authorized if needed, but the friendly disposition of the United States was to be emphasized. Exploration and reconnaissance was authorized in Perry's orders but it was to be done only if it did not interfere with the primary objective of the expedition.[67]

President Fillmore's letter to the Japanese emperor, which Perry was to deliver, reiterated the main points in Perry's instructions but developed further the ideal of American friendship. Any missionary efforts were disclaimed. The letter was designed to impress the emperor with the extensive wealth and power of the United States and the ease with which steamers

---

[64]*Congressional Globe*, appendix, 32nd Congress, 1st session, p. 1775.

[65]*Senate Executive Document*, No. 34, 33rd Congress, 2nd session, pp. 2-9. Compiled in 1855 with all correspondence relative to the Japanese expedition.

[66]*Ibid.*, pp. 5-6.

[67]*Ibid.*, p. 9.

could complete the twenty-day trip between the two countries. It was a combination of expressions of friendship and veiled threats. "These are the only objects for which I have sent Commodore Perry with a powerful squadron to pay a visit to your Imperial Majesty's renowned city of Yedo: friendship, commerce, a supply of coal and provisions, and protection for our shipwrecked people."[68]

THE EXPEDITIONS TO JAPAN, 1853-1855

Commodore Perry's expedition to Japan was a dramatic incident that had far-reaching effects on American Pacific Ocean development. The mechanical and superficial aspects of the expedition, the size of the squadron, its movements, Perry's diplomatic skill, the impressive military display in Yedo Bay, and the actual negotiations and provisions of the treaty need not be described here.[69] Not only is this narrative familar material but it adds little if anything to the understanding of the significance of the expedition.

Perry's Purpose. In getting a real perspective on the Japan mission certain obstacles are encountered. In contrast to the Cushing mission to China, Perry had to operate in a vacuum. No trade precedents were established and there were no Americans on the scene. All the evidence that remains concerning the fundamental aims of the expedition are Perry's instructions and his later statements. The instructions were innocuous and weakly worded and have little relationship to the actual plan pursued

---

[68]*Senate Executive Documents,* No. 34, 33rd Congress, 2nd session, p. 10.

[69]Hawks, *Narrative of the Expedition of an American Squadron to the China Seas and Japan Under Commodore M. C. Perry, U.S.N.* This is the principal source compiled from logs and journals of the officers by F. L. Hawks. They were published as *Senate Documents,* No. 97, 33rd Congress, 2nd session, Serial 802. Serial volumes 803 and 804 contain technical accounts of the scientists and navigators; *Senate Executive Documents,* No. 34, 33rd Congress, 2nd session, pp. 1-195, contains the correspondence relating to the Perry mission; Cole, ed, *With Perry in Japan: The Diary of Edward Yorke McCauley* is a brief account of an irresponsible young officer who later attained flag rank.

Expansion to Japan 201

by Perry. Likewise there was apparently little connection between the letters to the Japanese emperor from Fillmore and Perry and the actual purpose of the expedition.

Ostensibly the opening of Japan to American friendship and trade was the main theme. Yet in December, 1852, Perry was writing to Secretary of the Navy Kennedy about the advisability of occupying Great Lew Chew for use in case of hostilities with Japan.[70] The secretary approved the proposed occupation but warned against precipitous action and urged Perry to cultivate friendship with the natives and to encourage them to grow vegetables and fresh supplies for the supplying of ships;[71] this was done. Before Perry made his first visit to Japan he wrote to Secretary of the Navy again concerning annexation. He saw the importance of Peel Island in the Bonin group as a link in the route to China and a resort for whale vessels in Japanese seas.[72] After his first visit to Japan he wrote again to Secretary of the Navy Dobbin, in August, 1853, concerning the importance of an island base in the area. "Everyday of observation strengthens the opinion, so often expressed in my communications . . . that the large and increasing commerce of the United States with this part of the world makes it not only desirable but indispensable that ports of refuge should be established at which vessels in distress may find shelter."[73] Before Perry returned to Japan for his final treaty negotiation in March, 1854, he bought some land along the waterfront at Port Lloyd on Peel Island and took formal possession of the island.[74] His superiors in Wash-

---

[70]*Senate Executive Documents*, No. 34, 33rd Congress, 2nd session, p. 12.

[71]*Ibid.*, p. 15.

[72]Hawks, *Narrative of the Expedition* (see n. 69), pp. 211-214.

[73]*Senate Executive Documents*, No. 34, 33rd Congress, 2nd session, p. 44; Paullin, *op. cit.*, p. 254. Perry had collected information from New Bedford shipmasters and owners about cruising grounds and the usual places of resort for their vessels in the North Pacific.

[74]Hawks, *Narrative of the Expedition*, pp. 283-285. A group of foreigners, led by a Nathaniel Savery, had established a small community on Peel Island. Savery declared the island free and applied to Perry for "protection." Formal possession was taken and a constitution for the "colony of Peel Island" was written.

ington advised him against such a move before they knew it was actually accomplished.[75] The annexation, however, was never recognized.

To support his plan of annexation of island bases, Perry continually warned of foreign threats in the North Pacific area. England, he reminded the government, "was already in possession of the most important points in the East India and China Seas . . . the route of commerce which is destined to become of great importance to the United States."[76] In warning of threats from France and Russia, his statement to the Secretary of the Navy was entirely foreign to any wording or connotations of his orders: "I assume the responsibility of urging the expediency of establishing a foothold in this quarter of the globe, as a measure of positive necessity to sustainment of our maritime rights in the East. . . . for it is not impossible that some other power, less scrupulous, may slip in and seize upon the advantage which would justly belong to us."[77]

The opening of Japan to American trade, which, according to the instructions, was the prime objective of the voyage, seemed to be secondary to efforts at obtaining naval bases, coaling stations, agricultural colonies and perhaps holdings in China. Perry's plan for controlling the Northern Pacific involved Kelung (Formosa), Lew Chew (Okinawa), and the Bonin Islands—particularly Peel Island.[78] Perry considered Lew Chew indispensable as a base to eliminate the Dutch and English along the Shanhai-San Francisco trade route. Formosa, he thought, was needed as a base and coaling station. Accordingly, two ships of

---

[75] *Senate Executive Documents,* No. 34, 33rd Congress, 2nd session, p. 113.

[76] Swisher, "Commander Perry's Imperialism in Relation to American Present Day Position in the Pacific," *Pacific Historical Review,* February, 1947, p. 33, citing Perry's official report in Washington, 1857.

[77] *Senate Executive Documents,* No. 34, 33rd Congress, 2nd session, p. 81.

[78] Swisher, Carl. "Commodore Perry's Imperialism in Relation to America's Present Day Position in the Pacific." February 1947, *Pacific Historical Review,* p. 33.

Expansion to Japan

the squadron were dispatched to that island to chart the coasts and search for coal.[79]

Surveying Expedition. The objections raised in Washington to Perry's grandiose plans for colonies and island bases show that territorial expansion was not a part of official policy behind the Japanese expedition. Another aspect of the opening of Japan, however, indicated that the United States had more than a narrow interest in negotiating a simple treaty of commerce and friendship. This was the Ringgold expedition that was planned to parallel and supplement the expedition of Commodore Perry.[80]

Preparations for the Ringgold expedition were going on in the spring of 1852. In April Secretary of the Navy William A. Graham sent a letter to the president of the Senate stating the need for an exploring expedition to survey the waters and coast line around China and Japan.[81] The House Appropriations Committee was informed of the same need in August, 1852. The response was an appropriation of $125,000 "for prosecuting a survey and reconnaissance for naval and commercial purposes, of such parts of Behring's Straits of the North Pacific Ocean and the China Seas, as are frequented by American whaleships and by trading vessels in their routes between the United States and China."[82]

Five ships were fitted out, the flag ship being the old *Vincennes* of the Wilkes expedition. Commander Ringgold, in charge of the squadron, was supplied with the documentary background of the Perry expedition—such as A. H. Palmer's treatise on commercial and scientific aspects of the Far East and Commander

---

[79] *Ibid.*

[80] Cole, ed., *Yankee Surveyors in the Shogun's Seas* (Princeton, 1947), 161 pp. Cole maintains that the exploring expedition under Commander Ringgold and Lt. Rodgers from 1853 to 1856 has been neglected and undeservedly forgotten in the part of the opening of Japan, commonly known as the Perry Expedition. His compilation and editing of the chief primary sources of the voyage, in addition to his own introductory narrative based on them, throw light on this aspect of Pacific Ocean policy.

[81] *Ibid.*, pp. 4-5.

[82] *Ibid.*

Glynn's report of the cruise of the *Preble*. The squadron departed from Hampton Roads on June 11, 1853. In the Indian Ocean the squadron split up, on ship sailing south of Australia, the others through Sunda Straits to survey trade routes in the East Indies. A rendezvous was effected in Hong Kong in September, 1854. From this point the squadron, now under command of Lt. John Rodgers, sailed into the North Pacific area and surveyed Formosa, the Bonin Islands, and single islands between Lew Chew and the Japanese island of Kyushu.[83] Early in 1855 the main surveying of the Japanese Islands began. Coast lines were plotted, sounded, and charted.

Rodgers' squadron touched Yedo Bay about a year after Perry had negotiated his treaty. During its stay two American merchant vessels appeared in the harbor to trade.[84] The Americans lodged a protest with Rodgers against the reluctance of the Japanese to deal with them.[85] The two owners of one of the American merchant vessels, William C. Reed and T. T. Dougherty, sent a memorandum back to Secretary of State William L. Marcy in which they pointed to the need for an outright commercial treaty with Japan, a consular agent in the ports, and plenty of naval force to back it up.[86] The mission of Townsend Harris accomplished most of these suggestions in 1858 but without the direct presence of naval power.

Exploratory work was continued after the delay in Japan. Ships of the squadron, working in company and alone, charted the Kurile Islands of Petropavlovsk, the coast of Siberia to the Bering Strait, the Sea of Okhotsk, and the Arctic Ocean as far as latitude 72 degrees 5 minutes.[87] The return route to San Francisco, made along the Aleutian chain, was also surveyed and charted. A search for coal ashore was carried out in many of the places mentioned.

Due to the fact that the exploring expedition was planned at

---

[83] *Ibid.*, p. 11.
[84] The *Lady Pierce* and the *Caroline E. Foots*.
[85] *Ibid.*, p. 4.
[86] *Ibid.*, p. 17.
[87] *Ibid.*, p. 18.

Expansion to Japan 205

the same time that the Perry mission was under discussion and was sent out in time to be in Japan when Perry's treaty was being tested, it must be considered an almost equal part of the same national effort that opened Japan and extended national interest into the North Pacific area.

Results of Perry's Mission. The immediate result of the Perry mission was the signing of the Treaty of Kinagawa on March 31, 1854. The ports of Simoda and Hakodade were open to American vessels for procurement of supplies. The protection of shipwrecked Americans was guaranteed.[88] No specific provisions were made to establish trade.[89] It was essentially a shipwreck convention. Four years later a treaty of broader scope was negotiated by Townsend Harris on July 29, 1858, which provided for trade and residence of American merchants. Three new ports were to be opened gradually for commerce: Kanagawa, 1859; Nee-e-gato, 1860; and Hiogo, 1863 (Nagasaki had been opened in 1857).[90]

Another direct and concrete result of Perry's treaty of 1854 was the rush of other foreign countries—Britain in October, 1854, and Russia in January, 1855—to Japan to negotiate similar treaties. After the Townsend Harris treaty of July, 1858, foreign treaties increased; Netherlands in October, 1858; Russia in August, 1858; Britain in August, 1858; France in October, 1858; Portugal in August, 1860; German Customs Union in January, 1861; and Italy, Spain, Denmark, Belgium, Sweden, and Norway followed in quick succession.[91]

Economic returns of the newly tapped Japanese trade were naturally meager in the short period between the opening of the country and the drastic decline in American maritime activity after 1861. In November, 1858, an American whaling vessel, the *Tempest* of New London, arrived at Hakodade with a cargo of

---

[88] Malloy, *Treaties, Conventions, International Acts, Protocols, Agreements, 1776-1909*, vol. 1, p. 996.

[89] *Senate Executive Documents*, No. 107, 34th Congress, 1st session, pp. 500-509.

[90] Malloy, *op. cit.*, vol. 1, pp. 1000-1006.

[91] Nitobe, *op. cit.*, p. 60; Dennett, *op. cit.*, p. 304.

ship chandlery supplies.[92] The first commercial establishment, Walsh-Hall and Company, was established in Yokohama in 1859. Another merchant, R. B. Smith, set up business in 1860.[93]

Table 7 gives a statistical view of Japanese commerce following the Perry mission.[94] It not only shows that the volume was small but that the United States' share in the total was not impressive or by any means dominant.

Table 7
STATISTICAL VIEW OF JAPANESE COMMERCE
FOLLOWING THE PERRY MISSION

United States–Japanese Trade

Year	Imports from Japan	Exports to Japan
1855	$6,527	Nil (specie)
1856	$16,821	$4,000
1860	$155,000	$138,774

General Foreign Trade

Year	Imports from Yokahama	Exports to Yokahama
1859	$400,000	$150,000
1860	$3,954,000	$945,200

In retrospect it can be seen that the long-range results of the opening of Japan fell far short of what appeared to Perry at the time to be the beginning of an American commercial and political empire in the North Pacific. His schemes of annexation, designed for strategic control of the seas and as bulwarks against similar moves by foreign nations, were repudiated by the Pierce administration. It had been demonstrated both in the Japanese Islands and in China by 1860[95] that there was a point to which

---
[92] Griffin, *op. cit.*, p. 322.
[93] *Ibid.*
[94] *Ibid.*, p. 322.
[95] See Ambassador Reed's instructions, ch. III.

Expansion to Japan

American policy would not go—this was the extension of political control over Asiatic lands. In spite of the grandiose vision of many, after the annexation of the Pacific coast and the initiation of the "Tyler Doctrine" in relation to Hawaii, the imperialistic urge was temporarily checked until, as Dennett says, "President McKinley cabled to the American Commissioners at Paris to demand the cession of the Philippine Islands to the United States."[96]

Although American manifest destiny never reached Japan nor was the American commercial empire seen by Perry very impressive, the significant results of the maritime advance in the North Pacific were the developments of counter measures in Japan itself to outside pressure. Lt. John Rodgers, commanding the surveying expedition, noted the early beginning of the rearmament policy in a letter to Secretary of the Navy Dobbins in June, 1855: "the emperor had ordered all the bells but two in each city to be sent to Jedo [sic] to be run into cannon. It is said that he has established the manufacture of arms in the capital, and made thousands after American models . . . the basic feeling was a compound of perilous exposure, fear, and a determination to hold off the westerners until protection could be devised."[97]

For a time, Japan did adjust to American policy. She acted as the focal point of American interests in the North Pacific and was a rather congenial partner in Far Eastern affairs until approximately the turn of the century. Her status changed noticeably after 1900 from that of a partner to one of a rival.[98] Japan, in pursuing her own program of expansion after 1895, put the United States on the defensive diplomatically and militarily until late in the Solomon Island campaign in 1942.

---

[96]Dennett, *op. cit.*, p. 291.

[97]Cole, Allan B. *Yankee Surveyors in the Shogun's Seas.* (Copyright 1947 by Princeton University Press) p. 102. Reprinted by permission of Princeton University Press.

[98]Dennett, *op. cit.*, p. 596.

Epilogue

In the preceding discussion of Pacific Ocean influences on American policies of westward and overseas expansion and on policies toward China, certain developments have appeared to be most significant. It has been shown that it was the quest for a medium of exchange in Canton after 1785 that sent American ships into the Pacific. Their wandering took Americans to the Northwest Coast for furs, to the Mexican province of California for cowhides and Spanish silver specie, to many of the South Sea islands for bêches de mer and edible birds' nests, and to the Hawaiian Islands for sandalwood logs and supplies. As whaling vessels began cruising the Pacific after 1820, American contacts were reinforced in many areas—particularly in Hawaii, California, and in the Japanese Islands of the Northwestern Pacific.

As a result of exploration and commercial contacts, a maritime frontier was established on the Pacific coast and in the Hawaiian Islands that aroused official interest in placing American claims upon the area that eventually became the Oregon Territory. The seaward advance to the Pacific coast and Hawaii preceded and encouraged the overland migration. Both aspects of American expansion can be considered complementary parts of the same process.

Increased activities of American whalemen after 1850 focused official American attention upon the isolated kingdom of Japan. Due, in part, to American commercial and diplomatic pressure before 1860, Japan shook off her medieval lethargy and soon emerged as a world power to challenge the position of America in the Pacific.

While the United States vessels were making important contacts along the Pacific coast of America, in Hawaii, in Alaska, and among South Sea Islands, a long enduring and fairly consistent policy was developing in regard to China. As early as the

Epilogue

1840's the desire for commercial gain in the face of foreign rivalry, particularly of England and France, convinced a limited number of merchants and State Department officials that the United States should insist upon equal commercial opportunities in China and should work cooperatively with other nations to maintain some semblance of Chinese sovereignty. This was thought by American officials to be advantageous to the commercial interests of all nations engaged in the China trade. This policy, later known as the Open Door policy, was the key to American diplomacy in Asia to 1949 and in an expanded and active form to the present.

Bibliography

PRIMARY SOURCES

Adams, Charles F., editor. *Memoirs of John Quincy Adams.* 12 vols. Philadelphia: Lippincott, 1876. 546 pp.

"Annual Report on Commerce and Navigation." *Senate Executive Documents* for 1840, 1845, 1850, 1855, and 1860.

Bartlett, Ruhl J. *The Records of American Diplomacy, Documents and Reading.* New York: Knopf, 1947. 723 pp.

Buchanan, James. *The Works of James Buchanan.* Edited by John Moore. 12 vols. New York: Lippincott, 1919.

Cleveland, H. W. S., editor. *Voyages of a Merchant Navigator.* New York: Harper, 1886. 245 pp.

Clyde, Paul H., editor. *United States Policy Toward China, Diplomatic and Public Documents 1839-1939.* Durham: Duke University Press, 1940. 321 pp.

Coffin, George. *A Pioneer Voyage to California and Around the World.* Chicago: Gorham B. Coffin, 1908. 255 pp.

Cole, Allan B., editor. *With Perry in Japan, The Diary of Edward Yorke McCauley.* Princeton: Princeton University Press, 1942. 126 pp.

―――, editor, *Yankee Surveyors in The Shogun's Seas.* Princeton: Princeton University Press, 1947. 161 pp.

Congressional Globe, 26th Congress, 1st session, January 7, 1840.

Congressional Globe, vol. 12, 27th Congress, 3rd session, 1842-1843.

Congressional Globe vol. 15, 29th Congress, 1st session, 1845-1846. Appendix.

Congressional Globe, vol. 21, 32nd Congress, 1st session, December 2, 1851. Appendix.

Bibliography 211

Congressional Globe, 32nd Congress, 1st session, July 29, 1852. Appendix.

Congressional Globe, 32nd Congress, 2nd session, December 6, 1852. Appendix.

Dana, Richard H. *Two Years Before the Mast*. Boston: Field, Osgood, 1869. 470 pp.

Delano, Amasa. *Narrative of Voyages and Travels*. Boston: E. G. House, 1817. 598 pp.

Executive Documents, No. 105, 23rd Congress, 2nd session, pp. 1-28.

Executive Documents, No. 71, 26th Congress, 2nd session, pp. 1-83.

Executive Documents, No. 170, 26th Congress, 1st session, pp. 1-4.

Executive Documents, No. 119, 26th Congress, 1st session, pp. 1-85.

Executive Documents, No. 57, 26th Congress, 1st session, pp. 1-15.

Executive Documents, No. 34, 26th Congress, 2nd session, pp. 1-4.

Executive Documents, No. 35, 27th Congress, 1st session, pp. 1-7.

Executive Documents, No. 96, 29th Congress, 2nd session, pp. 1-39.

Executive Documents, No. 84, 31st Congress, 1st session, pp. 1-44.

Executive Documents, No. 97, 33rd Congress, 2nd session, serials 802, 803, and 804.

Fanning, Edmund. *Voyages to the South Seas, Indian and Pacific Ocean*. New York: William H. Vermilye, 1938. 324 pp.

Forbes, Richard B. *Notes on Ships of the Past*. Boston, 1887. 93 pp. (Publisher unknown).

Hacker, Louis M., editor. *The Shaping of the American Tradition*. New York: Columbia University Press, 1947. 1240 pp.

Hines, Gustavus. *An Exploring Expedition to Oregon*. Buffalo: Derby, 1851. 437 pp.

House Executive Documents, No. 42, 25th Congress, 1st session, pp. 1-94.

House Executive Documents, No. 35, 27th Congress, 3rd session, pp. 1-11.

Howay, Fred W., editor. *The Dixon-Meares Controversy: Canadian Historical Studies.* Toronto: Ryerson Press, 1929. 150 pp.

―――――, editor. *Voyages of the Columbia to the North West Coast, 1787-1790* (Collections, Massachusetts Historical Society, vol. 79). Boston: 1941. 518 pp.

Kelley, J. Hall. "A Circular to All Persons of Good Character Who Wish to Emigrate to Oregon," 25 pp. *Magazine of History,* vol. 16, no. 36. Tarrytown, New York, 1918.

Malloy, William M., compiler. *Treaties, Conventions, International Acts, Protocols and Agreements between the United States of America and Others, 1776-1909.* 2 vols. Washington: Government Printing Office, 1910.

Miller, Hunter, editor. *Treaties and Other International Acts of the United States 1783-1855.* 6 vols. Washington: Department of State, Government Printing Office.

Polk, James K. *Polk, The Diary of a President, 1845-1849.* Edited by Allan Nevins. New York: Longmans Green, 1929. 404 pp.

Porter, Captain David. *Journal of a Cruise Made to the Pacific, 1812-1814.* 2 vols. New York: Wiley and Halsted, 1822.

Quincy, Josiah. *Journals of Major Samuel Shaw.* Boston: Crosby and Nicols, 1847. 360 pp.

Report of Committee of House of Representatives, No. 31, vol. 1, 27th Congress, 3rd session, pp. 1-77.

Report of Committees, No. 466, 29th Congress, 1st session, pp. 1-51.

"Report of the Committee of Both Houses of Congress," pp. 3-15, from *DeBow's Southern Review.* New Orleans, December, 1850.

Reynolds, Stephen. *The Voyages of the New Hazard.* Edited by Fred W. Howay. Salem: Peabody Museum; Portland: Southworth Anthoensen Press, 1938. 158 pp.

Senate Executive Documents. No. 135, 23rd Congress, 2nd session. pp. 1-20.

Senate Documents, No. 24, vol. 1, 25th Congress, 2nd session, pp. 1-31.

Bibliography

Senate Documents, No. 470, 25th Congress, 2nd session, pp. 1-35.
Senate Documents, No. 1, 27th Congress, 2nd session, pp. 1-369.
Senate Executive Documents, No. 58, vol. 2, 28th Congress, 2nd session, pp. 1-4.
Senate Executive Documents, No. 67, 28th Congress, 2nd session, pp. 1-104.
Senate Executive Documents, No. 138, 28th Congress, 1st session, pp. 1-9.
Executive Documents, No. 138, 28th Congress, 2nd session, pp. 1-33.
Senate Documents, No. 139, 29th Congress, 1st session, pp. 1-47.
Senate Executive Documents, No. 52, 30th Congress, 1st session, pp. 1-384.
Senate Miscellaneous Documents, No. 80, 30th Congress, 1st session, pp. 1-7.
Senate Documents, No. 59, 32nd Congress, 1st session, pp. 1-59.
Senate Documents, No. 49, 32nd Congress, 2nd session, pp. 1-3.
Senate Executive Documents, No. 34, 33rd Congress, 2nd session, pp. 1-195.
Senate Executive Documents, No. 107, 34th Congress, 1st session, vol. 19, part 1.
Senate Executive Documents, No. 22, 35th Congress, 2nd session, pp. 1-624.
Senate Executive Documents, No. 30, 36th Congress, 1st session, pp. 1-16.
Shaler, William. "A Journal of a Voyage Made Between China and the Northwest Coast of America, Made in 1808." *American Register*, vol. 3, 1808, pp. 137-175.
Thorp, Willard; Merle Curti; and Carlos Baker, editors. *American Issues*. 2 vols., Philadelphia: Lippincott, 1941.
Webster, Daniel. *Writings and Speeches*. National Edition, 18 vols. Boston: Little Brown, 1903.
Wilkes, Charles. *Narrative of the United States Exploring Expedition*. 5 vols. Philadelphia: Sherman, 1849.
Whitney, Asa. *A Project for a Railroad to the Pacific*. New York: Wood, 1849. 112 pp.

SECONDARY WORKS

Abend, Hallett. *Treaty Ports.* New York: Doubleday, Doran, 1944. 258 pp.

Adams, James T. *Revolutionary New England, 1691-1776.* Boston: Atlantic Monthly Press, 1923. 451 pp.

Albion, Robert G. *The Rise of the Port of New York, 1815-1860.* New York: Scribners, 1939. 386 pp.

Alden, Carroll S. *Lawrence Kearny, Sailor Diplomat.* Princeton: University Press, 1936. 233 pp.

Bailey, Thomas A. *A Diplomatic History of the American People.* 3rd edition. New York: Crofts, 1947. 900 pp.

Bancroft, Hubert H. *History of the Northwest Coast.* 4 vols. San Francisco: A. L. Bancroft, 1884.

―――, *History of California.* 7 vols. San Francisco: A. L. Bancroft, 1885.

―――. *Works,* vol. 31. San Francisco: A. G. Bancroft, 1890.

Beard, Charles A., and Beard, Mary R. *The Rise of American Civilization.* 2 vols. New York: Macmillan, 1935.

Bell, James C. *Opening a Highway to the Pacific: 1838-1846.* New York: Columbia University Press, 1921. 202 pp.

Bemis, Samuel F., ed., *American Secretaries of State and Their Diplomacy.* 10 vols. New York: Knopf, 1928.

―――, *A Diplomatic History of the United States.* New York: Holt, 1942. 882 pp.

Benns, F. Lee. *The American Struggle for the British West India Carrying Trade, 1815-1830.* Indiana Study, No. 56, vol. 10, 1923.

Benton, Thomas H. *Thirty Years View.* 2 vols. New York: D. Appleton, 1854.

Bernstein, Harry. *Origins of Inter-American Interest, 1700-1812.* Philadelphia: University of Pennsylvania Press, 1945. 101 pp.

Bowen, Frank C. *America Sails the Seas.* New York: McBride, 1938. 400 pp.

Bradley, Harold W. *The American Frontier in Hawaii, 1789-1843.* Stanford: Stanford University Press, 1942. 466 pp.

Carpenter, Edmund J. *America in Hawaii.* Boston: Small, Maynard, 1899. 275 pp.

Bibliography

Chevigny, Hector. *Lord of Alaska.* New York: Viking Press, 1942. 306 pp.

Christy, Arthur. *The Orient in American Transcendentalism.* New York: Columbia University Press, 1932. 367 pp.

Cleland, Robert G. *From Wilderness to Empire.* New York: Knopf, 1944. 388 pp.

Clyde, Paul H. *The Far East: A History of the Impact of the West on Eastern Asia.* New York: Prentice-Hall, 1948. 836 pp.

Cole, Allan. *The Dynamics of American Expansion Toward Japan, 1791-1860.* Summary of Ph.D. thesis. Chicago: University of Chicago Press, 1943. 14 pp.

Curti, Merle. *The Growth of American Thought.* New York: Harper, 1943. 753 pp.

Daniels, Hawthorne. *The Clipper Ship.* New York: Dodd, Mead, 1928. 277 pp.

Dennett, Tyler. *Americans in Eastern Asia.* New York: Barnes and Noble, 1941 (reprint). 694 pp.

DeVoto, Bernard. *Year of Decision, 1846.* Boston: Little, Brown, 1943. 484 pp.

Downes, Joseph. *The China Trade and Its Influences.* New York: Metropolitan Museum of Art, 1941. 17 pp.

Dulles, Foster R. *The Old China Trade.* Boston: Houghton Mifflin, 1930. 228 pp.

———. *Lowered Boats.* New York: Harcourt Brace, 1933. 280 pp.

———. *China and America.* Princeton: Princeton Universty Press, 1946. 261 pp.

Fish, Carl R. *The Rise of the Common Man, 1830-1850.* Arthur Schlesinger and Dixon R. Fox, editors, *A History of American Life,* vol. 6. New York: Macmillan, 1927. 338 pp.

Foster, John W. *American Diplomacy in the Orient.* Boston: Houghton Mifflin, 1926. 476 pp.

Fox, Dixon R., and Krout, John A. *The Completion of Independence.* Arthur M. Schlesinger and Dixon R. Fox, editors, *A History of American Life,* vol. 5. New York: Macmillan, 1944. 429 pp.

Frost, John. *History of the State of California.* Auburn, New York: Derby and Miller, 1853. 509 pp.

Fuess, Claude. *The Life of Caleb Cushing*. 2 vols. New York: Harcourt Brace, 1923.

Fuller, George W. *A History of the Pacific Northwest*. New York: Knopf, 1931. 333 pp.

Greene, Evarts B. *The Foundations of American Nationality. A Short History of the American People*, vol. 1. New York: American Book, 1922. 613 pp.

Griffin, Eldon. *Clippers and Consuls, 1845-1860*. Ann Arbor: Edward, 1938. 502 pp.

Griswold, A. Whitney. *The Far Eastern Policy of the United States*. New York: Harcourt, Brace, 1938. 473 pp.

Hart, Albert B. *The Foundation of American Foreign Policy*. New York: Macmillan, 1901. 240 pp.

Hafen, LeRoy R., and Rister, Carl C. *Western America*. New York: Prentice Hall, 1941. 666 pp.

Hohmann, Elmo P. *The American Whaleman*. New York: Longmans, Green, 1928. 347 pp.

Howe, Octavius T. *Argonauts of Forty-Nine*. Cambridge: Harvard University Press, 1923. 217 pp.

Irving, Washington. *Astoria*. Putnams (Hudson Edition), 1893. 676 pp.

Kelsey, Rayner W. *The United States Consulate in California*. Academy of Pacific Coast History, vol. I, No. 5. Berkeley: University of California, 1910. 103 pp.

Kemble, John H. *The Panama Route, 1848-1868*. University of California Publications in History, vol. 29. Berkeley: University of California, 1943. 289 pp.

Kimble, Gertrude S. *The East India Trade of Providence, 1787-1807*. Papers from the Historical Seminary of Brown University, J. F. Jameson, editor. Preston: Preston and Rounds, 1896. 34 pp.

Kirkland, Edward. *A History of American Economic Life*. New York: Harper, 1946. 174 pp.

Latourette, Kenneth S. *The United States Moves Across the Pacific*. New York: Harper & Row, Publishers, Inc., 1946.

Matthiessen, Francis O. *American Rennaissance*. London: Oxford University, 1941. 656 pp.

Bibliography

Marshall, William J. *Acquisition of Oregon.* 2 vols. Seattle: Lowan and Hanford, 1911.

Marvin, Winthrop. *The American Merchant Marine.* New York: Scribners, 1900. 444 pp.

Moore, John B. *American Diplomacy.* New York: Harpers, 1905. 266 pp.

Morison, Samuel Elliot. *The Maritime History of Massachusetts, 1783-1860.* Boston: Houghton Mifflin, 1923. 373 pp.

Munford, Kenneth. *John Ledyard: An American Marco Polo.* Portland: Bunfords and Mort, 1939. 302 pp.

Myers, Gustavus. *History of Great American Fortunes.* New York: Random House, 1936 edition. 712 pp.

Nitobe, Inazo. *The Intercourse Between the United States and Japan.* Baltimore: Johns Hopkins, 1891. 191 pp.

Ogden, Adele. *The California Sea Otter Trade 1784-1848* (University of California Publications in History, vol. 26). Berkeley: University of California, 1941. 251 pp.

Otis, Fessenden N. *History of the Panama Railroad.* New York: Harpers, 1861. 264 pp.

Paullin, Charles O. *Diplomatic Negotiations of American Naval Officers, 1778-1883.* Baltimore: Johns Hopkins, 1912. 363 pp.

Peabody, Robert E. *Merchant Ventures of Old Salem.* Boston: Houghton Mifflin, 1912. 168 pp.

Perkins, Dexter. *The Monroe Doctrine, 1823-1826.* Harvard Historical Studies, vol. 29. Boston: Harvard University Press, 1927. 260 pp.

_____. *Hands Off: A History of the Monroe Doctrine.* Boston: Little, Brown, 1944. 392 pp.

Phillips, James D. *Salem and the Indies.* Boston: Houghton Mifflin, 1947. 426 pp.

Phipps, John. *China and the Eastern Trade.* Calcutta: Baptist Mission, 1835. 338 pp.

Pitkin, Timothy. *A Statistical View of Commerce.* New York: Eastburn, 1817. 445 pp.

_____. *A Statistical View of Commerce.* New Haven: Durril and Peck, 1835. 596 pp.

Reynolds, John N. *Voyage of the United States Frigate Potomac.* New York: Harper, 1835. 560 pp.

Rives, George L. *The United States and Mexico.* 2 vols. New York: Scribner, 1913.

Schafer, Joseph. *A History of the Pacific Northwest.* New York: Macmillan, 1918 (revised edition). 307 pp.

Schlesinger, Arthur M. *Colonial Merchants and the American Revolution.* New York: Facsimile Library, 1939 edition. 606 pp.

Sparks, Jared. *Life of John Ledyard.* The Library of American Biography, Jared Sparks, editor. Boston: Little, Brown, 1855. 418 pp.

Stephens, H. Morse; and Bolton, Herbert E., editors. *The Pacific Ocean in History.* Pacific Historical Congress, July 19-23, 1915. New York: Macmillan, 1917. 501 pp.

Stevens, Sylvester K. *American Expansion in Hawaii, 1842-1898.* Harrisburg: Archives, 1945, 299 pp.

Thompson, Waddy. *Recollections of Mexico.* New York: Wiley and Putnam, 1846. 304 pp.

Tower, Walter S. *A History of the American Whale Fishery.* University of Pennsylvania Press Publicaton, No. 20. Philadephia: University of Pennsylvania, 1907. 115 pp.

Treat, Payson J., *The Early Diplomatic Relations Between the United States and Japan, 1853-1895.* 2 vols. Stanford: Stanford University, 1932.

Underhill, Reuben L. *From Cowhides to Golden Fleece.* 2nd edition. Stanford: Stanford University, 1946. 282 pp.

Van Alstyne, Richard W. *American Diplomacy in Action.* Stanford: Stanford University, 1944. 702 pp.

Weinburg, Albert K. *Manifest Destiny.* Baltimore: Johns Hopkins University, 1935. 485 pp.

White, Stewart E. *The Forty-Niners.* Chronicles of America, vol. 25, edited by Allen Johnson. New Haven: Yale University, 1918. 273 pp.

Winthur, Oscar O. *The Great Northwest.* New York: Knopf, 1947. 345 pp.

ARTICLES IN PERIODICALS

Bennett, Guy V. "Early Relations of the Sandwich Islands to the Old Oregon Territory." *The Washington Historical Quarterly,* vol. 4, no. 2 (April, 1913), pp. 116-126.

Brown, Margaret L. "Asa Whitney and the History of the Pacific Railroad Publicity Campaign." Reprint from *Mississippi Valley Historical Review,* vol. 20, no. 2 (September, 1933), pp. 209-224.

Bradley, Harold W. "California and the Hawaiian Islands, 1846-1852."*Pacific Historical Review* (February, 1947), pp. 18-29.

———. "Hawaii and the American Penetration of the Northeastern Pacific, 1800-1845." *The Pacific Historical Review,* vol. 12 (September, 1943), pp. 277-286.

Cleland, Robert G. "Asiatic Trade and the American Occupation of the Pacific Coast." *American Historical Society, Annual Report,* vol. 1 (1914), pp. 283-289.

———. "The Early Sentiment for the Annexation of California: An Account of the Growth of American Interest in California from 1835 to 1846." Reprint from *The Southwestern Historical Quarterly,* (Texas Historical Association, Austin, Texas, vol. 18, nos. 1, 2, 3), 1914, pp. 1-111.

Cole, Allan B. "Documents." *Pacific Historical Review,* vol. 9 (1940), pp. 61-65.

Cotterill, Robert S. "Pacific Railroad Agitation," *Mississippi Valley Historical Review,* vol. 5, no. 4 (March, 1919), pp. 396-414.

Hooley, Osborne. "Hawaiian Negotiations for Reciprocity." *Pacific Historical Review,* vol. 7 (March 1938), pp. 128-146.

Howay, Fred W. "An Outline Sketch of the Maritime Fur Trade." *The Canadian Historical Association, Report of Annual Meeting* (Ottawa, 1932), pp. 5-14.

Kuo, Ping Chia. "Caleb Cushing and the Treaty of Wanghai, 1844." *Journal of Modern History,* vol. 5 (March, 1933), pp. 24-57.

Latourette, Kenneth S. "The History of the Early Relations Between the United States and China, 1784-1844." *Connecticut's*

Academy of Arts and Science, vol. 22 (August, 1917), pp. 1-145.

Mazour, Anatole G. "The Russian-American and Anglo-Russian Conventions of 1824-1825: An Interpretation." *Pacific Historical Review*, vol. 14 (September, 1945), pp. 303-310.

Morison, Samuel E. "Boston Traders in the Hawaiian Islands." *Massachusetts Historical Society Proceedings*, vol. 54 (1920-1921), pp. 9-47.

North American Review, vol. 14 (1837), pp. 200-237.

North American Review, October, 1828; October, 1837; October, 1840.

North American Review, vol. 47, January, 1839.

Porter, Kenneth. "John Jacob Astor and the Sandalwood Trade of the Hawaiian Islands, 1816-1828." *Journal of Economic and Business History*, vol. 2 (November, 1929; August, 1930), pp. 495-519.

Powell, Fred W. "Hall Jackson Kelley." Reprint from *Oregon Historical Quarterly*, vol. 18, nos. 1, 2, 3, 4 (1917). 185 pp.

Pratt, Julius W. "James K. Polk and John Bull." *Canadian Historical Review*, vol. 24 (December, 1943), pp. 341-349.

Sage, Walter. "The Oregon Treaty of 1846." *The Canadian Historical Review*, vol. 27 (December, 1946), pp. 349-367.

Sherman, Henry. "Oregon Territory." *Hunt's Merchant Magazine*, vol. 6 (April, 1842), pp. 306-319.

Steele, Charles C. "American Trade in Opium to China Prior to 1820." *Pacific Historical Review*, vol. 9 (March, 1940), pp. 429-44.

Swisher, Carl. "Commodore Perry's Imperialism in Relation to America's Present Day Position in the Pacific." *Pacific Historical Review* (unbound), February, 1947 pp. 30-40.

PAMPHLET

Report of the Committee Appointed to Inquire into the Practicability and Expediency of Establishing Manufactures in Salem. Salem, Massachusetts Pamphlets. Salem: Warwick Palfrey, 1826. 31 pp.

Index

Adams, John, 8, 9. *See also* Federalist administration
Adams, John Quincy: China Policy, 105; Expansionist advocate, 29; Monroe Doctrine author, 57, 61, 62; Northwest Coast negotiations, 43; Pacific Ocean policy, 36; Treaty of 1819, 38-40
Alaska: China trade routes, 73; Ledyard and approach to Northwest Coast, 33; purchase of, 63
Alcott, Bronson, 17
Aleut Indians, 25
Alfredo, José Maria, 142. *See also* Robinson, Alfred
Allan, Captain, 188
American colonies, 3
American Northwest fur trade, early profits and decline, 24-29
Ames, Fisher, 9
Andrews, Reverend, 172
Armstrong, Richard, 173
Asia Minor, 87
Ascension Island, 74. *See also* Saint Helena Island
Aspinwall, William Henry, 86, 146-48
Astor Harbor, 52
Astor, John Jacob: Astoria, founding of, 26; California trade, 131; employees in politics, 42; Perkins, T. H., rivalry with, in China, 88; Russian contacts of his ships, 60, 64
Astoria: founded by Astor, 26; Ghent, Treaty of, restores, 23, 27, 39; official interest and, 42; 43; Pendleton report, significance of in, 52
Astoria (Irving), 48
Aulick, John H., 197, 198, 199
Australia, 67

Baltimore, 13
Bancroft, Hubert H., 47, 138, 141
Baranov, Alexander, Hawaiian contacts, 162; Yankees, agreement with, 26, 59, 60
Barrell, Joseph, 21
Baylies (Massachusetts representative), 41
Bay State Trading and Mining Company, 144
Bear Flag revolt, 157
Belle Isle Strait, 4
Benton, Thomas Hart, editor, 42; Oregon: boundary settlement, 58; interest in, 46, 47; pleas for, 44; railroad route, opposition to, 67; Whitney plan, 68
Bering, Vitus, 60
Boit, John, Jr., 80, 82, 162
Boki, 176
Borneo, 74
Boston, 84-87: colonial seaport, 5; *Columbia*, voyage of, 22; Ledyard visit, 32; money for industry, 11; trade, 80-88: China, 73-77, 84; West Indies, 13
Boston Manufacturing Company, 11
Bowditch, Nathaniel, 78, 79
Bradley, Harold W., 170, 174. *See also* Hawaii
Brannock, Samuel, 142

221

Brewer, Charles, 171
Brewer and Company, 171
British East India Company, 19, 97
British South Seas Company, 19
Brown, George, 178
Brown, Moses, 11
Brown, Samuel, 21
Bryant and Sturgis: California trade, 131, 135; established, 81; Hawaiian establishment, 167; *Pilgrim* and Dana, 136
Buchanan, James: Arrow War, neutrality in, 121; secretary of state, 155; Slidell, instructions to, 157; trade report on, 195
Bulfinch, Charles: Kelley, use of information by, 46; Linn report, part in, 51; Madison, information to, 23; Northwest Coast, financing of trip to, 21
Bunker Hill Mining and Trading Company, 144
Burlingame, Anson, 123
Butler, Anthony, 152

Cabot, George, 9
Cadiz, 33
Calhoun, John C.: Cushing, letter from, 113; Larkin, letter from, 150; secretary of state on Northwest boundary, 56-58; statesman, 160
California: contacts: early 128, 129, sea, 27; Gold Rush, 144, 149; Hawaii: relation to, 27-28, settlements, 172, 179, 180; Larkin, 142; Northern boundary, 38; Polk, policy of, 154-60; purchase attempt, 152; trade: Canton, 116, China, 89, Oriental, 196, postrevolutionary, 137, Salem, 80
California Mining Association, 144
California Mining and Trading Company, 144
Canning (foreign minister), 40, 44

Canton: American consuls in, 15; *Astoria* (Irving), 48; Cushing mission, 11; Downes sent, 96; economic returns, 24, 25; furs: Northwest Coast, 20-22, 28, Russian, 60; Hawaiian contacts, 161; Ledyard's interest, 31; Lewis and Clark expedition, 36; Opium War, disturbance, and, 98, 102; Pendleton report, 53; sandalwood, 162-65; trade: Boston, 73-82, 84-87, California, early, 133, 134, statistics, basis of, 89, supremacy, 116; Tientsin, Treaty of, 122
Cape Adams, 23
Cape Cod, 74, 81, 82
Cape Hancock, 23
Cape Horn: California approach, 129; *Columbia*, 22; *Essex*, 146; Gold Rush voyages, 143, 144; Ledyard's plans, 31; *Lelia Byrd*, 133; Lewis and Clark instructions, 36; Mormons' voyage, 142; *Potomac*, 95; routes: early, 73-75, Hawaii, 166, whaling, 189, sandalwood, 84; Wilkes expedition, 192
Cape of Good Hope, 43, 74, 80, 95
Capetown, 73-75, 89
Cape Verde Islands, 73
Capitol Hill, 8
Caribbean, 7, 43; colonies, 12
Carrington, Edward, 15, 105
Castlereagh, Lord, 39
Catherine II, 63
Ceylon, 73
Charles River, 11
China: American culture, influence of, 15, 17; *Columbia*, 22; congressional interest, 43, 55; Cook, Captain, 19; Cushing mission, 98-112; *Lady Washington*, 22; Lewis and Clark instructions, 36; McLane, development of policy, 208, 209; Open Door, 125-27; Perry mission, 198; *Potomac*, 97;

Index

railroads, influence on, 64-68; Ringgold surveying mission, 203; trade: Boston, 80-84; obstacles, 93; opium, 86; Russian fur, 60; Salem, 79, 80; U.S., early, 71, 87; Wanghai, after, 116-24; whaling and scope of China trade, 188; Wilkes expedition, 193
China clipper, 86
Chinook Harbor, 52
Chinook Indians, 26
Ching (acting viceroy), 111
Civil War: Hawaiian annexation, effect on, 86, 182; Japanese contacts prior to, 184; railroad development, blocking of, 69
Clark, George Rogers, 29
Clay, Henry, 160
Cleveland, Richard J., 80, 133, 134, 162
Clipper ships, 145
Coffin, Captain, 191
Cohoes (New York), 11
Colonial trade: Belle Isle Strait, 4; British regulation of, 3-5; Continental Association, 6; Gulf of St. Lawrence, 4; Nonimportation, 6; Parliamentary acts, 5; whaling, American, 4
Columbia River: American frontier, 172; British-American negotiations, 43; British claims, 39; California, routes to, 146; House of Representatives discussion (1820), 41, 43; Kelley, 45; Lewis and Clark instructions, 36; Pendleton report, 53; official policy, 56; Polk's message, 58; Slacum, 49
Columbia: captains and crew, 21, 81; Mexico, interest in, 129; voyage, significance of, 24
Compromise of 1850, 160
Continental Association, 6. *See also* Colonial trade
Contrabandista, 132

Cook, Captain: fur trade possibilities, discovery of, 21; Hawaiian Islands, discovery of, 162; Ledyard and the third voyage, 30, 32; Linn report, 50; Vancouver Island, 37; whalers, American, 189
Crocker, Thomas, 171
Crooks, Ramsey, 42
Crowell, Samuel, 24
Crowninshield, John, 78
Cushing, Caleb: Burlingame mission, precedent for, 123; Calhoun, letter to, 113; China mission, 97, 108, 110, 111, 114, 115, 194, 198; House of Representatives, report to, 49, 54; Japan expedition, precedent for, 195
Cushing, J. N., 109
Cushing, John Perkins, 84

Dalton, Tristam, 9
Dana, Richard Henry, 136
Declaration of Independence, 127
Deism, 16
Delano, Amasa, 162
Delano, William, Jr., 99
Denby, Charles, 124, 125
Dennett, Tyler, 125, 207
Derby, Elias Hasket, 10, 78
Derby, John, 21
Derby, Samuel, 186
Dewey, Admiral, 125
Dix, Senator, 195
Dobbin (secretary of navy), 201, 207
Dominis, John, 171
Dorr, Ebenezer, 130, 167
Dougherty, 204
Douglas, Stephen A., 68
Downes, Commodore: Downes's instructions compared to Kearney's, 100; Reynolds's report, 190; Sumatran coast, 95; Tyler's message to Congress, 107
Drake, Sir Francis, 23, 50

Dulles, Foster Rhea: Asia, interest in, 185; China, seaborne contacts with, 71; Wanghai, Treaty of, view of, 114
Dutch East India Company, 186

East India Company: monopoly, 20; Northwest Coast furs, 27; opium trade, 87
East India Society, 17
East Indies: China trade routes, 71; New York and Boston trade, 86; Salem trade, 78
Economic nationalism, 10
Elliott, Charles, 98
Elwell, Robert, 171
Emerson, Ralph Waldo, 17
Empire City Line, 147
England, 3, 5: Canton disturbances, 98; Northwest Coast boundary negotiations, 65; Open Door note, 126
Essex Junto, 9
European-Oriental trade, 75
Everett, Edward, 108, 114, 144

Falkland Islands, 74
Fanning, Edmund: sandalwood trade, 163; Wilkes expedition, 191, 192
Farnham, Russell, 42
Federalists, 72
Federalist administration, 8, 9
Federal Constitution, 9
Fernandez, Juan, 74
Fiji Islands: Salem trade, 79; sandalwood trade, 163; Wilkes expedition, 192
Fillmore, Millard: annual message (1851), 180; Glynn, letter from, 197; Japanese Emperor, letter to, 199
Finch, Captain, 176
Fiske, John, 78
Fitch, 141
Florida, 38

Floyd, on Oregon question, 41, 42, 44, 46
Forbes, R. B.: American consul in China, 110; China policy, pressure for, 99; Cushing, letter from, 112
Formosa, 73
Forrester, John, 78
Forsyth, John: Jackson, Andrew, influence on, 152; Linn report, 49; Slacum's letters, 150
Fort George, 38. *See also* Astoria
Forty-niners, 145
Foster, 60
Franklin, Benjamin, 30
Frémont, John C., 151
French, William, 168
Friend, The (periodical), 173
Fur trade, 208. *See also* Canton; China; Hawaiian Islands

Gale, William, 135, 140
Gardnew, Edmund, 191
Geisinger, David, 196
Geographical Sketch, A (Kelley), 45
Gideon Nye and Company, 116
Gillespie, A. H., 156
Gillespie-Frémont intrigue, 156
Glynn, Commander: Japanese whalemen, 196, 197; *Preble's* cruise, 204; Ringgold expedition, 204
Gold Coast, migrations, 145
Gold rush, 143
Graham, William, 196, 203
Gray, Robert: Adams, J. Q., 61; China trade, 77; *Columbia*, 22; *Hunt's Merchant Magazine*, 21; *Lady Washington*, 21; Linn report, 51; Pendleton report, 52; "River of the West," 23, 43, 44
Great Northern Railroad, 70
Green, Captain, 76
Gregg, David, L., 181, 182
Grimes, Elias, 168
Griswold, N. L. and G., 85

Index

Gulf of St. Lawrence, 4
Gwinn, Senator, 198

Haalilio, Timoteo, 176, 177
Hallet, Captain, 75
Hamilton, Alexander, 10
Hancock, John, 24
Hanna, James, 19
Harris, Arnold, 146
Harris, Townsend, 204, 205
Hartford (Connecticut), 30
Hartmell, 140
Hatch, Crowell, 21
Havana, 13
Hawaiian Islands: American influence, 174; annexation, 181; Bradley, Harold W. 170; establishments ashore, 167, 168, 169; foreigners, 170, 171, 172; Hendrick, Captain, in *Lady Washington*, 22; Johnson, Andrew, policy of, 182, 183; Kearney's mission, 102; naval station, request for, 174; Pierce, Franklin, 181; sea contacts, early, 27, 28; trade: Boston, 82, California, 131, 134, 141; early, 161, 164, fur, Northwest, 25, 51, 53; Tyler doctrine, 102, 176-78, 207; whalers haven, 166, 188-90; Wilkes expedition, 193
Hay, John, 70, 96, 125. *See also* Open Door policy
Heard, Augustine, 87
Heard and Company, 116
Heceta, 23
Hickey, Captain, 52
Hide and tallow trade, 134
Hill, J. J., 70
History of the Pacific Northwest, A (Fuller), 64
Honduras, 37
Hong merchant, 78
Hoppo, 77
Hooper, Stephen, 9
House of Amboy, 33

Howard, J. and Sons, 147
Howay, F. W., 20
Howland, 86
Howland and Aspinwall, 146
Hudson's Bay Company: American policy, 56; California, threat in, 150, 155; Canning's claims, 44; fur monopoly, 27, 28, 40; Kelley, 46; Hawaiian employees, 173; Northwest Coast rivalry, 19, 21; Pendleton report, 53, 54; Slacum, 50
Hughes, John L., 146
Hunnewell, James, 167, 168
Hunnewell, John, 171
Hunt's Merchant Magazine, 48

Independent Line, 147, 148
India trade: Boston, 86, 89; China routes, early, 73; Northwest Coast, 67; Salem, 78, 80; sea trade, influence of, 17
Indian Ocean, 15
Ingraham, Captain, 162
Irkutsk, 60
Irving, Washington, 48
Isle of France, 73, 78, 84, 89. *See also* Mauritius
Island of Sumatra, 75

Jackson, Andrew: California, 151, 152; Caribbean ports, 13; Fanning, 192; Pacific Ocean policy, 36, 152; Slacum's mission, 49
Jackson, Jonathan, 9
Japan: Closer ties sought, 199; Glynn in U.S.S. *Preble*, 196, 197; merchants favor mission, 195; Porter, 180, 187; Surveying expedition, 204; U.S. contacts, early, 184; whalers, American, 188
Java, Anjur, 74
Java Head, 74
Jedo, Japan, 207
Jefferson, Thomas: Kelley, 45, 47;

Ledyard, 29; Lewis and Clark, 35, 36; Whitney and Hill, 109

Johnson, Andrew, 182, 183

Jones, John: consul at Honolulu, 97; Honolulu business, 167; Hunnewell letter, 168; Monroe, report to, 175

Jones, T. A. C.: captured Monterey, 154; U.S.S. *Peacock*, 175

Journal of Captain Cook's Voyage (Ledyard), 31

Juan de Fuca Straits, 45

Judd, G. P., 172

Kamehameha III, 178, 187

Kanaka laborers, 25

Kearny, Commodore: Burlingame mission, 123; China mission, 103; Macao (1842), 100; Open Door prelude, 126

Ke, 101, 102

Kelley, Jackson Hall: Cushing report, 51, 52; Jefferson, theories of, 36; Linn report, 50; Northwest Coast agitation, 45, 46

Kelsey, R. W., 151

Kendrick, John: *Columbia*, 21; *Lady Washington*, 22; Ledyard, 32

Kennedy, John P., 199, 201

Kerr, 79

Kiakhta, 60

King, Edward, 99

Kiying, 111

Kowtow, 110

Kock, J. J., 16

Kuo, P. C., 110, 113

La Guaira, 13

Larkin, Thomas O.: California, 141, 151; consul, 150; Polk, 154, 155, 157

Latourette, K. S., 70, 114

Law, George, 147

Ledyard, John: Benton, 42, 47; Cook voyage, 19; Jefferson's vision, 36; plans, 31; Sparks's biography, 48; Whitney and Hill, 70

Leese, Jacob, 157

Leese, Spear and Hinckley, 140

Lewis and Clark: boundary settlement, 57; diplomatic negotiations, 43; forty-ninth parallel, claims to, 61; Jefferson, 29; joint occupation, 40; journals, 47; Ledyard, 34, 35; railroad routes, 67

Life in California, 1846 (Robinson), 151

Linn report, 49-52

Louis XVI, court of, 30

Louisiana, 34

Lowell, Cabot, 11, 12

Lowell, John, 9

Low, A. A., 99

Low, Seth, 86

McCook, Edward, 182, 183

McIlvaine, Bowes R., 147

McKinley, William, 207

McLane, Robert, 118, 119, 58, 194

Macao, 73, 77

Madagascar, 74

Madison, James: Astoria, claims on, 23; China, consul in requested, 105; Fanning, 191; Porter's war cruise, 187

Mahan, A. T., 29

Malay pirates, 78

Manchu dynasty, 116, 119

Mandarins, 79

Marcy, William L.: Gregg, 182; Marshall, 116; Japanese commercial treaty urged, 204; McLane, 118; Mason, 180, 181; Parker, 120

Mariner's Home, 17

Marine Bible Society, 17

Massa Fuero Island, 74

Marquesas Island, 74

Marshall, Humphrey, 116-19

Marshall and Wildes, 131, 167

Mason, John, 180

Index

Massachusetts Bay, 2
Mauritius, 73, 75, 80. *See also* Isle of France, 73
Mears (British captain), 48
Mediterranean Sea, 15
Merriweather Bay, 52
Metcalf, Captain, 170
Mexican revolution, 133, 165
Mexican War: California, seizure of, 143; Polk, 154-59
Middleton, Henry, 61, 62
Missionaries, 170, 171, 172
Mississippi River, 35, 36
Missouri River: Jefferson's interest, 29; Ledyard, 33; Lewis and Clark, 36
Monroe, James: Linn report, 50; Louisiana purchase, 34; Monroe Doctrine, 12, 15, 57, 62; Oregon, joint occupation of, 40; sandalwood debts, 175; Spanish claims on Northwest Coast, 39; whalemen petition, 174
Morehead, Senator, 55
Morgan, Charles, 147
Mormons, 142
Morris, Robert, 31, 32

Nankeens, 89
Napier, Lord, 97, 98
Napoleonic wars, 7
National Intelligencer, 65
Newburyport, 5
New England associations, names of, 144
New York: capital provided, 11; China trade, 84, 86; *Empress of China,* 76, 77; Ledyard, 51; seaport, 5; West Indies trade, 13
New York Commercial Advertiser, 65
New York Journal of Commerce, 150
New York Sun, 142
Niles Register, 149
Noncolonization principle, 15
Nonimportation agreements, 6

Nootka Sound: British traders, 37; Canning, 44; Ledyard, 33; *North American Review,* 48; Northwest Fur Company, 20; Spanish claims, 37, 38
Norris, John, 78
North American Review, 47, 48
Northwest Coast: boundary settled, 56; trade, 33
Northwest Fur Company, 20, 26-28, 32
"Notes on Virginia" (Jefferson), 29

O'Cain, Captain, 26, 59, 163
Olyphant, O. W. C., 86
Olyphant and Company, 87, 193
Open Door policy, 71, 96, 124-27: antecedents, 70; Cushing, 109; diplomacy, American, 209; Hay, 70, 96, 125
Opium, 87, 110, 115, 121
Opium War: American concern, 98-101; Cushing mission, 109; Tientsin, treaty of, 122; trade obstacle, 106
Oregon: Adams, J. Q. 38, 61; bills, 41, 42; boundary question, 27, 36, 37, 39; California annexation, 150; Great Britain, dispute with, 40-46; Ghent, treaty of, 27; Hawaiian interest, 173, 179, 180; Jefferson, 36; Oriental trade and California, 196; Pacific steamship lines, 146; trade and annexation, 71; whaling grounds, 189
Pacific Fur Company, 26, 60
Pacific Mail Steamship Company, 147, 148
Pakenkam, 57
Palmer, Aaron H., 195, 196, 203
Palmerston, Lord, 105
Panama Canal, 145
Panama Railway Company, 148
Parker, Peter, 120
Parsons, Theophilus, 9
Paulet, Captain, 178

Pauling, J. K., 192
Pauling (secretary of navy), 100
Pawtucket, 11
Pearl River, 73
Pendleton, 54
Pendleton report, 52, 55
Pérez, 23
Perkins, Thomas H., 9, 24, 27, 28, 81, 83, 87, 88, 131, 163
Perkins and Company, 84, 85, 167
Perry, Matthew C.: China policy antecedent, 102; Japan expedition sent, 199-203; results of mission, 205-7
Philadelphia, 5, 11, 13
Philippines, 67, 78, 73
Phillips, Wendell, 114
Phipps and Pitkin, 89
Pickens, 103
Pickering, Timothy, 9
Pierce, Franklin, 181
Pierce, Henry: Boston merchant, 53; British threat, 54; Hawaii: annexation, 180, 181; business, 167, 171; Parker, 120
Pintard, John, 21
Pioneer Register, 141
Polk, James K.: California policy, 154-59; elected, 57; Japan policy, 196; Northwest Coast policy, 58; Oriental trade, 36
Porter, David, 186, 187, 192
Powell, Fred, W., 45
Practical Navigator, 79
Pratt, Representative, 195
Prince, Captain, 78, 79
Prevost, J. B., 43, 149, 150
Providence, 5, 11, 13
Public Lands Committee, 67
Puget Sound: British-American negotiations, 43; California trade, 133; Congressional action, 54-56; Pacific steamship lines, 146, 147
Reed, William B., 121, 123, 204

Reynolds, J. N., 97, 190-92
Reynolds, Stephen, 170
Reynolds, William, 167
Revolutionary War: California interest, 137; Colonial merchants, 67; commerce, 2; Ledyard, 30, 31; postwar change, 15
Richards, William, 172, 176, 177
Ringgold, Commander, 203
Ringgold expedition, 203
Rio de Janeiro, 13
Rio de la Plata, 13
River of the West, 23, 35, 43
Rives, William C., 179
Roberts, Edmund, 194
Roberts, Issacker, 116
Roberts, Marshall O., 147
Robinet, W. M., 120
Robinson, Alfred, 142, 151. *See also* Alfredo, José Maria
Rockhill, W. W., 125, 126
Rodgers, John, 207
Rush, Richard, 43
Russell and Company, 115
Russia, 29, 126; American contacts, 59-63; Imperial ukase, 47; Northwest Coast, claims on, 38
Russian-American Company, 130, 162, 186
Russian-American Fur Company, 59, 60, 63
Russian Ukase of 1821: Monroe's message, 62; *North American Review*, 47; text, 61; United States-Russian treaty of 1824, 38
Russell and Company, 85, 86
Ryan, James, 99

Saint Helena Island, 74. *See also* Ascension
Saint Louis, 35, 41, 65
Saint Louis Inquirer, 42, 149
Saint Louis Intelligencer, 47
Salem: China, voyages to, 72, 73, 78-80, 84; industry, 11, 12; merchant class, 5, 78, 94

Index

Salem Mechanic Mining and Trading Company, 144
Salem Mill-Dam Corporation, 12
Sandalwood trade, 163-75. *See also* Canton; Cape Horn
San Diego, Battle of, 134n
Santa Anna, 152
San Roque, 23
Santa Marta, 13
Sealing voyages, 74
Seamen's Bethels, 17
Sea otter trade, 130, 141
Seward, William H.: Gwinn, and Perry's mission, 198; Hawaiian trade, 182, 183; Jeffersonian policy, 29
Shaler, William: California, 151; Cleveland and California trade, 133; *Lelia Byrd* and San Diego, 134; sandalwood trade, 162
Shaw, Major Samuel, 83, 105
Shaw and Randall Company, 83
Sherman, Henry, 48
Sherman, John, 124, 125
Silsbee, Nathaniel, 80
Singapore, 65
Sitka, 59, 63
Slacum, William A.: Forsythe, 150; Jackson, 152; Linn report, 55; navy purser, 49; Oriental trade, 8; report of, 18, 38, 50, 53
Slater, Samuel, 11
Slidell, John, 155, 158
Slidell mission, 154, 157
Sloat, J. D., 155, 157
Smith, Jedediah, 132
Smith, Thomas, H., 85
Society Islands, 74
South America, 14, 73
South Seas Company, 20
Southard, Samuel, 175, 190
Sparks, Jared: Ledyard, 32, 34; *North American Review*, 48
Spain, 29: California contacts, 128; Columbia River, discovery of, 23; Nootka Sound dispute, 37

Spaulding, Captain, 53
Spence, 140
Stearns, Abel, 157
Stevens (minister to England), 66, 105
Stevens, George L., 146
Stoekl, Baron, 63
Sturgis and Russell, 99
Sturgis, William: captain, 82; *Eliza* 81; Federalist merchant, 9; Kelley, 47; *North American Review*, 47, 48
Sue Aman, 112, 113
Suffolk Mutual Mining Company, 144
Sumatra, 94, 95
Sunda Straits, 74, 78
Suter, Captain, 162
Suter, John, 81, 82
Sutter's fort, 143

Taiping rebellion, Parker, 120; trade effect on, 116, 121; Wanghai, 115
Tariff Act of 1816, 89
Tasmania, 74
Taylor, General, 154
Terranova Affair, 106
Texas: Adams, J. Q., and 1819 treaty, 38; annexation, 154; war issues, 159
Thompson, Waddy, 141, 153
Thorndike, Israel, 9
Thoreau, Henry David, 17
transcendentalism, 17
Treaties: Ghent: Astoria returned, 23, 38; Oregon dispute, 27, 40; Pendleton report, 52; Guadalupe Hidalgo, 160; Kinagawa, 205; Nanking: British military cooperation, 121; Cushing mission, 109; Kearny, 101, 102; Paris (1783), 75, Seward-Burlingame, 115, 123; Tientsin, 115, 121-24; Tordesilla, 36; Wanghai: Cushing, 108; Marshall, 117, 119; negotiated,

111; Parker, 120; Perry mission, 193; provisions, 112; significance, 185; treaty of Tientsin, 121-23; Whitney, 65
Turkey, 87
Tyler, John: annual message (1842), 106; China, 107; Hawaii, 177; Thompson, 153; Wanghai treaty, 113
Tyler Doctrine, 176, 179, 183, 206

Unitarianism, 16
United States Mail Steamship Company, 148
Upshur (secretary of navy), 153

Vancouver, George: British naval explorer, 48, 49; Hawaiian contact, 162; journal cited, 52; Linn report, 50; whalers, American, 189
Vancouver Island: *Columbia*, 22; Kelley, 46; traders, British, 27
Valparaiso, 13
Van Braam, 16
Van Buren, Martin, 105, 192
Vanderbilt, Cornelius, 147, 148
Vessels: *Alert*, 81, 136; *Albatross*, 26, 59, 163; *Argo*, 166; *Ariel*, 101; *Astrea*, 78, 79; *Beaver*, 188; *Betsy*, 133; *Bourdeaux Packet*, 167; *Brooklyn*, 142; *Caroline*, 81; *Columbia*, 161, 162; *Congress* (U.S. frigate), 155; *Constellation*, 100; *Constitution*, 21; *Garysfort*, H. M. S., 178; *Clyde*, 112; *Eagle*, 131; *Eclipse*, 186; *Equator*, 188; *Eliza*, 81; *Empress of China*, 76, 77, 83; *Enterprise*, 60; *Essex*, 186; *Franklin*, 186; *Friendship*, 94, 95; *Grace*, 186; *Greenhow*, 53; *Harriet*, 75; *Hope*, 162; *Ladago*, 194, 196; *Lady Washington*, 21, 22, 77, 161, 162, 186; *Lawrence*, 194, 196; *Lelia Byrd*, 133, 134, 162; *Levant*, 87, 113; *L' Orient*, 33; *Louisanne*, 53; *Manhattan*, 193, 194; *Margaret*, 24, 186; *Maro*, 188; *Morison*, 193; *Newcastle*, 141; *New Archangel*, 59, 63; *New Hazard*, 170; *New Holland*, 74; *O'Cain*, 59; *Paragon*, 171, *Pearl*, 81, 163; *Peacock*, 95, 175; *Pedler*, 60; *Pilgrim*, 136; *Potomac*, 95, 97, 190; *Preble*, 196, 204; *Rowe*, 99; *Sachem*, 135; *Spanish Main*, 73; *Stonington*, 74; *Thaddeus*, 170; *Tempest*, 205; *Tonquin*, 26; *Union*, 81, 162; *Vincennes*, 176, 203

Wash-Hall and Company, 206
Waltham, 11
War of 1812: British patrols, 82; *Essex*, 186; opium trade, effect on, 88; Pacific trade, 27
Warner, John, 157
Washington, George, 37, 105
Washington Conference (1922), 70
Webster, Daniel: Aulick, 197, 198; commander, 179; Everett, 108; secretary of state, 109-110; Tyler and Pacific Coast, 153, 154; Tyler Doctrine, 176, 177, 179
West Indies: cargoes, 75; colonial trade, 2; Ledyard, 32; Monroe Doctrine, 12, 13; Salem trade, 73; trade closed, 72
Whaling industry, 208: American, 188-90; British regulation, 4; deserters, 174; grievances of whalers, 196-99; Hawaiian Islands, 166; missionaries, 170; navy, exploration by, 191-93; Japan, 208
Whampoa, 77
Wilcocks brothers, 87
Wilcocks, Benjamin, 15
Wilkes, Charles: expedition, 192; Porter's cruise contrasted, 187;

Index

Pacific Ocean hypothesis, 36; Ringgold, 203; Wilkes report cited, 55

Winship, Jonathan, 26, 47

Winship brothers, Jonathan and Nathan, 163, 164, 60

Whitney, Asa: Congress, appeal to, 69; Hill and Great Northern Railroad, 70; Jefferson's theory, 36; *National Intelligencer*, 65; publicity campaign, 67; railroad to Pacific, 64

Woodbury, Levy, 96, 192

Wyeth, Nathaniel: Cushing report, 51; Jefferson's theory, 36; Kelley's agent, 46; Pendleton report, 53

Wyllie, Robert Crichton, 172

Yankee merchant skipper, 72

Young, Brigham, 142